Helping a Neighbor in Crisis

$\mathcal{H}$ELPING
A $\mathcal{N}$EIGHBOR
IN $\mathcal{C}$RISIS

COMPLETE WITH STUDY GUIDE

FOREWORD BY
CHARLES COLSON

EDITED BY LISA BARNES LAMPMAN

TYNDALE HOUSE PUBLISHERS, INC.
WHEATON, ILLINOIS

CONTENTS

Foreword   *Charles W. Colson* *1*

To the Reader   *Lisa Barnes Lampman* *5*

Crisis Intervention   *Jayne G. Crisp* *9*

The Grief Process   *Rev. Victor M. Parachin* *17*

The Tool of Forgiveness   *Lisa Barnes Lampman* *23*

A RELATIONSHIP IN DANGER

Divorce   *Thomas Whiteman, Ph.D.* *35*

Unfaithful Spouse   *Les Parrott III, Ph.D. & Leslie Parrott, Ed.D.* . . *43*

Domestic Violence   *Rebecca Beane* *49*

CRISIS IN THE COMMUNITY

Natural Disasters   *Timothy W. Thompson, D.Min.* *57*

Community Tragedy Caused by Crime
  Melissa Slagle & Lisa Barnes Lampman *63*

WHEN THEY'RE HURTING THEMSELVES

Substance Abuse   *Thomas Gill, L.P.C.* *73*

A Rebellious Teenager   *John R. Cheydleur, Ph.D.* *79*

Eating Disorders *Anne Kellstedt Ramirez, M.S., L.C.P.C. &*
Kelleen Williamsen, M.A., L.C.P.C. *85*

Teen Pregnancy *Celine Wood Meador* *93*

WHEN JOB AND FINANCES ARE LOST

Financial Loss *Thomas Gill, L.P.C.* *101*

Employment Crisis *Diane Eble* *107*

Victims of Fraud *Mario Thomas Gaboury, J.D., Ph.D.* *113*

LIVING WITH PHYSICAL PROBLEMS

Serious Injury *Rev. Victor M. Parachin* *123*

Child with Special Needs *Dr. Rosemarie Scotti Hughes* *129*

Life-Threatening Illness *Jacqueline Gatewood, Psy.D.* *135*

HIV/AIDS *Kathi Mills* *143*

WHEN NEIGHBORS ARE IMPACTED BY CRIME

Burglary and Theft *Dr. Bill Barton* *151*

Hate and Bias Crime *Rev. Lee A. Earl* *157*

Victims and the Juvenile Justice System
Mario Thomas Gaboury, J.D., Ph.D. *163*

Imprisonment of a Family Member *Terry White* *169*

WHEN PEOPLE ARE VICTIMIZED

Child Victimization *Rev. David W. and Anne Delaplane* *179*

Eldery Victimization *Dr. Robert Denton* *187*

Drunk Driving Crash Victims *Laura Slade Hudson &*
Shirley W. Ruple *195*

Kidnapping *Kathryn M. Turman* *201*

SUPPORTING VICTIMS OF SEXUAL CRIMES

Incest *Rev. Steve and Lynn Eargle* *209*

Adult Survivors of Sexual Abuse *Dr. Jeanette Vought* *217*

Rape and Sexual Assault *Anita Armstrong Drummond, L.P.C.* . . . *225*

WHEN A LOVED ONE DIES

Death of a Loved One *Rev. Victor M. Parachin* *235*

Suicide *Janice Harris Lord* *241*

Miscarriage *Rev. Louise Upchurch Lawson* *247*

Death of a Child *Janice Harris Lord* *259*

WHEN A LOVED ONE IS MURDERED

Homicide *Mary A. White* *267*

Homicide of a Child *Cheryl Guidry Tyiska* *275*

Line-of-Duty Death *Andrew H. Ryan Jr., Ph.D.* *283*

Study Guide *Michelle Shattuck* *291*

FOREWORD

CHARLES W. COLSON

When others are happy, be happy with them. If they are sad,
share their sorrow. . . . Don't let evil get the best of you,
but conquer evil by doing good.
ROMANS 12:15, 21, NLT

There have been numerous crises in my life—times that were
decision or turning points for me. The most wonderful and joyful one was the moment, under deep conviction of the Holy
Spirit, I accepted Christ as my Lord and Savior. But there were
others—not so wonderful—such as the day I walked through the
prison gates at Maxwell Federal Prison, where I was sentenced to
spend one to three years of my life for a Watergate-related crime.
Although I had accepted Christ a year before, I went through a
time of great pain and self-examination. In those first few days in
the prison, I was at a turning point, trying to decide whether to
continue to trust God and keep turning to him *or* to believe that
he might have forgotten me.

By God's grace and through the support of my family and
my new friends in Christ, I continued to follow God. I don't
know if I could have made that decision without the support
of my brothers and sisters in Christ. Men like Doug Coe, who
discipled me; a former political enemy, Senator Harold
Hughes; Al Quie, a senior congressman; and Graham Purcell,
a former Democratic congressman. An unlikely group, but
they loved this Watergate scoundrel unconditionally. And they
made all the difference. They were constantly there for me
and Patty—to listen, love, care, provide for, and comfort. They

were the arms and the hands of Christ, reaching out to me and my family—to remind us that we were not forgotten but deeply loved by God in the midst of this crisis and pain.

Crises are a part of the tapestry of life for all of us; no one gets through life without them. Some of our crises are difficult, painful, disruptive of life, even life threatening and life destroying. And some are joyful—but crises nonetheless. Think of a new marriage, the birth of a baby, buying that first home, accepting Christ into your life.

We get our English word crisis from the Greek word *krisis* which means "a decision point." In a crisis, our normal coping skills may not work as well as we thought. We can crumble under the weight of the crisis or we can learn to develop new skills to meet it head-on.

But often we can't get through the crisis alone. We need an understanding and caring friend to come alongside us. Someone to listen, to encourage, to support us as we walk, or crawl, through the crisis.

That is the role of the body of Christ—to *be there* for one another in those times of crisis, both the joyful times and the ones that are so very difficult. It is our calling, as members of the fellowship of Christ, to be present to remind our loved ones, our friends, our fellow church members, and our neighbors that God has neither forgotten nor abandoned them. It is one of the most powerful witnesses we can make.

This book can assist you in reaching out to others in crisis. It is a practical reference guide for pastors, church counselors, lay leaders, friends, family members, and neighbors to provide assistance and support to people experiencing crises related to crime, traumatic life events, or the loss of loved ones through death. It compiles the wisdom, insight, experience, and expertise of more than thirty professional counselors, crime victim-assistance advocates, pastors, and a few "regular folks" who have effectively walked through a crisis in their lives.

Over half of the book is dedicated to helping those who have experienced a crisis related to crime. Sadly, more than 43 million of our fellow Americans become victims of crime each year! How important it is for the church to respond in a loving and compassionate way to those whose lives have been impacted by burglary, assault, rape, drunk-driving crashes, or homicide. If we don't, who will? And if we do, those affected will know, as I did in prison, the reality of the God who loves them.

For more than twenty years, Prison Fellowship Ministries, the organization I founded, has mobilized over fifty thousand church volunteers to minister to prisoners, ex-prisoners, and their families across the U.S. and around the world. But now the church must reach out to victims of crime as well. That is why Prison Fellowship started a sister organization to help crime victims: Neighbors Who Care. I am pleased that Neighbors Who Care and Tyndale House Publishers have joined together to write this practical book to help churches and individual Christians minister to crime victims and others in crisis.

A crisis is a decision point—often a point where people determine whether they will turn to God or turn away from him. My hope and prayer is that you will use this book to reach those in crisis and to wisely, appropriately, and lovingly point them to the source of love, hope, and life—Jesus Christ.

Charles W. Colson
Washington, D.C.
April 1997

To the Reader

LISA BARNES LAMPMAN
PRESIDENT OF
NEIGHBORS WHO CARE

The man wanted to justify his actions, so he asked Jesus,
"And who is my neighbor?"
Jesus replied with an illustration: "A Jewish man was traveling on
a trip from Jerusalem to Jericho, and he was attacked by bandits.
They stripped him of his clothes and money, beat him up, and
left him half dead beside the road.
"By chance a Jewish priest came along; but when he saw the man lying
there, he crossed to the other side of the road and passed him by.
A Temple assistant walked over and looked at him lying there,
but he also passed by on the other side.
"Then a despised Samaritan came along, and when he saw the man,
he felt deep pity. Kneeling beside him, the Samaritan soothed his
wounds with medicine and bandaged them.
Then he put the man on his own donkey and took him to an inn,
where he took care of him. The next day he handed
the innkeeper two pieces of silver and told him to take care
of the man. 'If his bill runs higher than that,' he said,
'I'll pay the difference the next time I am here.'
"Now which of these three would you say was a neighbor to the man
who was attacked by bandits?" Jesus asked.
The man replied, "The one who showed him mercy."
Then Jesus said, "Yes, now go and do the same."

LUKE 10:29-37, NLT

When most of us think of the Good Samaritan, we often conjure up an image of a kindly person stopping along the highway to assist a stranded driver or helping a tottering elderly woman carry a bag of groceries to her home. The actions are kind and caring, perhaps a bit inconvenient, but seldom sacrificial.

Yet when Jesus was asked to define a *neighbor,* his image of the Good Samaritan went far beyond performing niceties for those in need of a little aid. Jesus focused on helping a person *in crisis—a crime victim.* The man who was robbed and left "half dead" was a wounded, helpless stranger, who had been shamelessly ignored by people of "his own kind." Jesus' Good Samaritan was a person who personally had suffered great oppression and cruelty himself because of his race and religion. Yet he reached out—sacrificing time, money, and his own busy schedule—to help the needy stranger.

This is the mirror Jesus continues to hold before us—both individually as Christians and corporately as local churches. We are to offer the cool water of compassion and aid to those who are experiencing a crisis in their lives, even a crisis resulting from a crime.

In many cases, we, as individuals and as members of the body of Christ, are willing to help but are not aware of people in crisis who need our assistance. In other situations, we may know someone who is experiencing a crisis, but we're not sure *how* to help—or we feel we have little to offer.

The Good Samaritan didn't have to go out of his way to meet someone in crisis. In fact, the man was lying in his path. The Samaritan just opened his eyes—and his heart. Unlike the priest and the Temple assistant who ignored the man's moans and cries, the Samaritan stopped and offered help and hope to the dying man.

Most of us don't have to go beyond family, friends, neighbors, and fellow church members to find people experiencing a crisis and crying out for help. If that is the case, Jesus calls us to "go and do likewise"—to reach out and respond to our neighbors in need with concern, care, and compassion.

Helping a Neighbor in Crisis is written from a Christian perspective, providing information and practical suggestions to help you assist people in crisis—whether that crisis is crime related or not. This book is designed to be a reference guide for all those who care about family, friends, and neighbors experiencing crises. It has been written to provide a basic introduction to helping those in crisis. A more indepth understanding of each crisis may be reached by taking advantage of the resources listed at the end of each chapter, through the study guide at the end of the book, and through exploring your own community's resources.

There are thirty-four crises listed in this book—seventeen of them are crime related. Each crisis section provides important information on the crisis with specific and practical suggestions on how to help. Each section contains a true-life story about or a quote from a person who experienced the crisis. Also included are encouraging Scripture verses to share, suggested prayers to pray with or for a person in crisis, and a list of recommended books and information to further assist you in helping others.

In addition, there are a few "overview" sections that provide information and a general understanding of key issues and concepts related to crisis. These include: crisis intervention, grief, and forgiveness.

This book is the work of over thirty contributors. Some are professionals in the areas of trauma counseling and victim assistance, and some have lived through a crisis themselves and desire to share their experience and knowledge with others. I am profoundly grateful to each of them for giving of their time and talents to produce this work. I especially want to thank Jayne Crisp, a staff member of Neighbors Who Care who helped develop and organize the crime crisis sections, and Bonnie Knapton, another member of the Neighbors Who

Care team, who expertly handled the word processing and the arrangements for the book.

Many thanks go to Tyndale House Publishers and those who significantly contributed to the idea for this book as well as its writing, design, editing, and publication. I appreciate Tammy Faxel's willingness to take on this project and the good work of Sarah Peterson in coordinating the development of the book.

It is my hope that you will find the information in this book helpful and useful as you offer support to those whose lives have been touched by crisis. It also is my hope that this book would encourage you and your church to develop a ministry to victims of crime and their families in your community.

If you would like further information specifically about how to help crime victims through your local church, contact us at Neighbors Who Care. Neighbors Who Care, a subsidiary of Prison Fellowship Ministries, is a national Christian ministry to crime victims and their families. Our mission is to exhort, assist, and equip local churches and Christians in their ministry to victims of crime and their families. We have ideas, materials, and people ready to help you and your church start or enhance a ministry to victims of crime in your community.

Almost every day, you and I are given opportunities to help someone in crisis. We certainly can start by praying for those individuals and their situations. But we can also reach out to them with meaningful help and hope. My prayer is that *Helping a Neighbor in Crisis* will be mightily used by God to inform and equip his people to be Good Samaritans—to go and do likewise—for those in crisis and in need.

Lisa Barnes Lampman
Washington, D.C.
May 1997

CRISIS INTERVENTION

Have mercy on me, O God, have mercy! I look to you for protection.
I will hide beneath the shadow of your wings
until this violent storm is past.

PSALM 57:1, NLT

What is a crisis? *Webster's New World Dictionary* defines crisis as "a turning point in the course of anything, a decisive or crucial time, stage or event." We know crisis by the way we feel during a critical event. University of South Carolina professor Arlene Andrews (1990) describes people in a crisis state as "having uncontrolled emotional expressions, disorganized thoughts, anxiety, and fatigue."[1] By definition, people in crisis are beyond their normal ability to cope with the situation at hand. At this point, they may be looking for new coping methods, new ways to address the crisis, and oftentimes someone to help.

Crisis intervention is a process used to interrupt and/or positively impact a person's immediate crisis reactions. Sometimes called "emotional first aid," crisis intervention involves the use of verbal and nonverbal communication to encourage, empower, and build confidence in those who experience a crisis.[2] Crisis intervention is a technique most frequently used with victims of crime who experience one or several traumatic events. Since a significant number of people experience crime-related crises (according to Bureau of Justice statistics, over 43 million victimizations annually), it is important for all of us—

---

[1] Edwards, Seymour, Burnley. Crisis Intervention. National Victim Assistance Academy, 11-2. [2] Edwards, Seymour, Burnley. Crisis Intervention. National Victim Assistance Academy.

especially those in the church—to understand the basics of crisis intervention. However, the same principles may be applied to those who experience any type of crisis.

The goals of crisis intervention are (1) to provide immediate relief from pain, (2) to provide time for problem solving, (3) to help the individual regain old coping skills and/or develop new ones, and (4) to help the individual return to a healthy level of functioning and regain feelings of self-worth and confidence. Pastors, priests, church members, and caring family, friends, and neighbors can become Good Samaritans by providing valuable and compassionate assistance to individuals experiencing a crisis event in their lives. According to Morton Bard and Dawn Sangrey, authors of *The Crime Victim's Book,* "Minutes of skillful support by any sensitive person immediately after the crime can be worth more than hours of professional counseling later."[3] In other words, individuals who utilize crisis intervention skills can help people reconstruct their lives and reduce the need for longer-term psychological intervention later.

THE STAGES OF CRISIS

Morton Bard and Dawn Sangrey[4] identify three stages of crisis: the *impact, recoil,* and *reorganization* stages. During the *impact* stage, the safety and security of the victim is critical. The *recoil* stage provides individuals an opportunity to ventilate and have their feelings validated by caring helpers. And the *reorganization* stage gives them a time to predict and prepare for the future. Individuals recovering from trauma frequently find themselves shifting back and forth between the stages, especially during the recoil stage of crisis.

THE FIRST STAGE: Impact

How to help: Achieve contact. The first element of a crisis is that it strikes without warning and threatens our safety, security, and self-confidence. The *impact* or initial stage of the crisis often leaves people feeling numb, shocked, dazed, out of control, and in a state of disbelief and vulnerability. A day may

---

[3] Morton Bard and Dawn Sangrey, *The Crime Victim's Book,* Basic Books, 1979.   [4] Ibid.

start out like any other day, and suddenly be interrupted by tragic news, an accident, a freak storm, or an act of violence that changes lives forever. Feelings of disbelief and the thought *This can't be happening to me* are common.

The impact stage begins immediately and lasts anywhere from minutes to days to weeks after the crisis event. During this stage, it is important to *achieve contact* or "be there" for the individual in crisis. Most people think they have to say something special with profound meaning, but often the less we say to a person in crisis the better. Sometimes just "being there" and being available is a precious gift and a real comfort. A simple word, a listening ear, or a gentle touch can have the most significant and positive impact on an individual in crisis.

During the impact stage, the caregiver should be very attentive and physically and emotionally responsive to the *safety* and *security* needs of the person in crisis if there is reason to believe that he or she could be in danger. This may entail providing a temporary place to stay or changing the lock on a door, or it may only require the affirmation, "You are safe now"—if that is true.

People in the impact stage of crisis may need assistance with practical matters: transportation, food, clothing, shelter, finances, contacting family or friends. You can provide much needed and appreciated support by offering to help them in those areas. Be careful not to make decisions for them. It is important that the person in crisis feel as though he or she is regaining control over life. Questions such as "Where would you like to sit?" "Would you like a drink of water?" or "You must feel terrible" are good beginning phrases that give an individual choices and control once again. However, be careful not to become a "rescuer" by forcing the individual to depend on you. Provide gentle help assisting the person in making those first decisions.

THE SECOND STAGE: Recoil
How to help: Boil down the problem. During the *recoil* or second stage, people in crisis may experience confusion, insecur-

ity, and emotional isolation. This stage may last from days to months—and in some cases—to years after a crisis.

To provide assistance during the recoil stage, *boil down* the problem by allowing individuals to talk about the event in an effort to "normalize" the trauma and reduce the profound sense of isolation the person may experience. The individual can be encouraged to express thoughts, reactions, and emotions. A caregiver can also encourage the person to *ventilate* or express intense emotions and can *validate* those reactions and feelings by responding in nonjudgmental ways.

• Ask individuals to describe their memory of the crisis (i.e., where they were at the time of the crisis; who they were with; what they saw, smelled, heard, and felt). This helps them put order to the event and place it in the proper perspective.

• Allow individuals to tell their story (sometimes over and over). This helps them organize thoughts and provides opportunities to express and translate their intense feelings into powerful words. Validating these feelings and expressions conveys an important message that strong reactions are indeed normal reactions to abnormal events.

• Assist individuals in determining if the crisis reaction is interfering with their ability to conduct normal life activities. Many individuals appear to cope well in the aftermath of crisis, but some may develop longer-term stress reactions. These may include recurrent and intrusive distressing recollections, dreams of the event, flashbacks, and/or intense distress at exposure to events that symbolize or resemble an aspect of the crisis, including anniversaries. Individuals in crisis may experience persistent avoidance of feelings, detachment from others, loss of interest in significant activities, difficulty falling or staying asleep, difficulty concentrating, hypervigilance, and exaggerated startle responses. If a number of these symptoms persist beyond ninety days, the reactions become what is known as Post-traumatic Stress Disorder (P-tSD).[5] Referring the person to well-trained trauma counselors and pastoral

---

[5] American Psychiatric Association, DSMR-IV.

counselors for longer-term professional care may be the appropriate response for those who have experienced a particularly brutal incident or significant loss, or for those experiencing intense crisis reactions over a prolonged period of time.

THE THIRD STAGE: Reorganization

How to help: Cultivate coping skills. The third element of a crisis is that it presents challenges and dilemmas that may cause people in crisis to reassess and/or reaffirm their lives, values, and beliefs. This is the *reorganization* stage.

During the reorganization stage, the caregivers can assist individuals in identifying and *cultivating positive coping skills* and new activities that may enhance personal, physical, and spiritual growth. Individuals in crisis can take three basic steps to help themselves after a traumatic event:

1. *Seek emotional and spiritual help.* Participate in support groups. Talk with trained trauma counselors or members of the clergy.
2. *Practice positive attitudes.* Learn to accept things that cannot be changed, develop and reward a sense of humor, and surround yourself with positive and well-adjusted individuals.
3. *Practice positive actions.* Spend time in prayer and Bible study. Ask questions, set goals, say "no" once in a while, get involved in church activities and missions, listen to good music. If you can't solve a problem, manage it.

According to the National Organization for Victim Assistance, people who have experienced a crime (or another type of crisis) are best aided at this stage through opportunities to *predict* reactions and *prepare* for their future. Caregivers can help prepare individuals by helping victims anticipate predictable reactions from significant others as well as long-term physical and emotional consequences. They also can help identify effective resources and successful coping skills.

One way for a person to regain control in the aftermath of a crisis is to acknowledge what has happened and come to terms with what may happen in the future. Environmental conditions, physical health barriers, emotional distress, economic and financial challenges, and spiritual questioning may all impact the person's ability to rebuild his or her life. Asking the individual to describe what has happened since the event helps reveal whether the person has experienced additional emotional and spiritual challenges. Keeping in contact especially during anniversaries, birthdays, and holidays is very helpful.

During times of extreme stress, individuals may question their faith, seek solace in their faith, use their faith as a foundation for growth, and/or look for a "message" in the traumatic event. This is a significant time for the church family to continue to provide support and encouragement to an individual or a family in crisis. Sensitive and consistent care and the offer of assistance from the church can significantly aid in the recovery of an individual or family. Bible studies or support groups (led by trained counselors and designed to meet the needs and experiences of these individuals) can be very effective in providing ongoing assistance. Helpers should allow individuals in crisis to ask questions about faith and God and may assist victims by praying for and with them if asked. Sharing specific verses of Scripture also can bring comfort and peace to troubled hearts and minds.

Well-meaning helpers can cause what is known as "secondary victimization" or secondary trauma by offering platitudes and superficial comments such as:

- "It will take some time, but you'll get over it."
- "You can always have another child."
- "Try to be strong for your children."
- "You are lucky that it wasn't any worse."
- "It was God's will."
- "You should hear what happened to me. . . ."

- "If you had had a burglar alarm in your house, this never would have happened."
- "You should have . . ."

Comments such as these may be perceived by the person in crisis as inappropriate and insensitive to his or her need for reassurance and support. In fact, some statements can actually cause increased trauma for a person in crisis.

In my twenty-three years of experience in crime-victim assistance and counseling, I have found that those victims who have demonstrated their ability to *transcend* trauma and reconstruct their life in a healthy way after a crisis, use eight basic "survival strategies" to help them move from victim to survivor. These eight steps can be used for anyone experiencing a traumatic crisis:

1. Identify and articulate the powerful emotions and reactions related to the event.
2. Get appropriate and responsible help when needed.
3. Learn as much as possible about the event, confront the reality of the crisis, and deal confidently with the effects of the crisis.
4. Reaffirm or develop personal and spiritual values, beliefs, and faith.
5. Release the anger and rage from controlling thoughts, feelings, and reactions.
6. Reduce isolation from friends, family, and helpers.
7. Stay physically fit by eating right and exercising regularly.
8. When emotionally ready, take action by helping others who have suffered similar crises.

As someone concerned about friends or loved ones in crisis, you can provide much-needed practical help, emotional assistance, and spiritual support as you help them regain control, build trust, and reaffirm or establish new hope and faith.

ADDITIONAL RESOURCES

Forgiving the Unforgivable: Overcoming the Bitter Legacy of Intimate Wounds by Beverly Flannigan (Macmillan Publishing Company, Inc., 1992). An outgrowth of a study conducted on how people transcend terrible hurts inflicted by those they love.

When Living Hurts by Sol Gordon (Dell Publishing Company, Inc., 1985). A "what to do" book for yourself, for teens, and for young adults.

Aftermath: Survive and Overcome Trauma by Mariann Hybels-Steer (Simon & Schuster Trade, 1995).

Winning Life's Toughest Battles: Roots of Human Resilience by Julius Segal (Ivy Books, 1986). Five "keys" to help anyone emerge from victim to victor.

A Gift of Hope: How We Survive Our Tragedies by Robert Veninga (Ballantine Books, Inc., 1986). How people survive through acceptance, forgiveness, and hope.

When a Bad Thing Happens to Faith-Ful People: Crime Victims and God by A. Robert Denton, Ph.D. (Write or call the Victim Assistance Program, P.O. Box 444, Akron, OH 44309-0444; telephone (330) 376-0040.) This booklet helps people to cope with a loss and not lose faith.

Your Particular Grief by Wayne E. Oates (Westminster John Knox Press, 1981).

A Legacy of Hatred by David A. Rausch (Moody, 1986). This book discusses the Jewish holocaust.

JAYNE G. CRISP

Jayne G. Crisp is a certified trauma specialist who has been working in the field of crime victim assistance for twenty-three years. She is a recipient of the National Crime Victims Rights Week Presidential Award and is the state director of Neighbors Who Care in South Carolina.

THE GRIEF PROCESS

The Lord hears his people when they call to him for help. He rescues them from all their troubles. The Lord is close to the brokenhearted; he rescues those who are crushed in spirit.

PSALM 34:17-18, NLT

After her husband of fifteen years succumbed to cancer, Susan, forty-one, confided in a friend: "When David died I knew that I would grieve, but I just didn't know what to expect. I was both amazed and frightened by the powerful and sometimes conflicting emotions that I experienced in the months following David's death."

Feelings of grief are a natural outcome when a loved one has died. Simply defined, grief is emotional suffering caused by loss. Grief is a healthy, human response to situations such as

- the death of a family member or friend
- separation or divorce
- miscarriage
- giving birth to a child with a physical or mental disability
- loss of health
- a crime victimization against property or person
- disability or injury
- loss of a job, property, pet
- children leaving home

- giving up of a personal or professional dream
- any personal loss

Like Susan, many do not know what to expect. The following are common symptoms that may be experienced as a part of grief. Those who want to understand and help those who are grieving should keep these two factors in mind: First, some people experience all the symptoms of grief, while others experience only a few. Second, these common symptoms do not progress in any particular order for the one who grieves because every loss is unique and touches people in individual ways. Grieving takes time—sometimes many years. The individual experiencing grief needs to go through the grief process on his or her own timetable and way.

SHOCK AND DENIAL

"I can't believe this has happened!" The initial information that a loss has occurred is often shocking and numbing. The impact of the tragedy may take some time to be realized. This is God's way of protecting the individual from the immediate and full impact of the loss. Shock and numbness allow the bereaved person to gradually absorb the magnitude of the loss.

LONELINESS AND VULNERABILITY

"Without [my loved one, my job, my money, my house] I might as well be dead!" Powerful feelings of emptiness often take place after the loss, especially as family and friends return to their own daily activities. This results in feelings of loneliness, isolation, and depression becoming more intense. After her eighteen-year-old daughter was raped and murdered, Mary Louise Williams wrote: "This is the loneliest of all the experiences I have had. Dear ones and friends have helped me and continue to help, but they cannot share completely. I think joy can be

shared much more completely, for everyone longs to be joyous. No one longs to be sorrowful."[1]

TEARS AND WEEPING

"I can't stop crying." Tears are a normal, healthy response to death. They cleanse the body of toxins while providing an important release of tensions and feelings. Those who seek to help the bereaved can be guided by this statement from British author Albert Smith: "Tears are the safety valves of the heart when too much pressure is laid on it."[2]

PAIN AND HURT

"I just can't take any more." Loneliness and anxiety conspire together to create deep emotional pain. In her memoirs, Barbara Bush includes a chapter on her daughter Robin who died from leukemia at three years of age. Mrs. Bush writes that the funeral started "the most painful period of adjusting to life after Robin. We [she and her husband George] wakened night after night in great physical pain—it hurt that much."[3] Although it may seem unbearable, the pain lessens in intensity over time.

PANIC AND ANXIETY

"What am I going to do?" A loss makes it difficult to concentrate because of the constant memories of life before the loss. Grace Shafir of Englewood Cliffs, New Jersey, was thirty-five when her husband died unexpectedly, leaving her with four young daughters and a struggling family business. "After grief came a wave of terror," she recalls. "How could I keep the business going and put food in my children's mouths. I worried until I realized I was wasting energy."[4] In order to reduce the panic, Shafir began living one day at a time. Her strategy was to meet the demands and challenges of

[1] Mary Louise Williams, *Sorrow Speaks: A Month's Meditations for the Bereaved* (St. Louis, MO: Chalice Press, 1968), 17.   [2] Albert Smith cited in *New Dictionary of Thoughts*, ed. Tryon Edwards (New York: Standard Book Co., 1954).   [3] Barbara Bush, *Barbara Bush: A Memoir* (New York: Charles Scribner's Sons, 1994), 46.   [4] William Thomas Buckley, "How to Cope with a Crisis," *Reader's Digest*, July 1990, 94.

each day rather than allow herself to be overwhelmed by anticipating future problems.

Victims of natural disasters such as floods, tornadoes, and hurricanes often feel this symptom, as their houses and possessions may
have become damaged beyond use.

GUILT AND REGRET

"I should have done more." Frequently survivors recall things they
wish they had said or done. Often these feelings leave them feeling guilty. However, a closer examination usually reveals that survivors did their best under the circumstances.

ANGER AND FRUSTRATION

"How could he/she do this to me!" After Neil's wife left him and
their twenty-year marriage, he told a friend: "For me this
divorce is worse than a death. I don't understand how she
could do this to me and our children." For nearly a year,
anger was Neil's constant emotion. "I was angry that she had
left; I was angry that I was now a single parent; I was angry
when her lawyer contacted me; I was angry whenever someone mentioned her name. Finally, I realized the anger was
only making things worse and I had to find a way to let go of
the anger and hurt." Neil sought counseling, which was effective in helping him come to terms with the reality of his
divorce.

Victims of crime may understandably deal with this aspect
of grief for a long time.

DEPRESSION AND SADNESS

"Will life ever be worth living again?" Frustration over the loss
quickly gives way to deep sadness in the form of depression.
Grief therapists state that depression is natural following a
loss and has protective qualities. In his book *Death and Grief:
A Guide for Clergy*, Alan D. Wolfelt, Ph.D. notes: "Depression is
nature's way of allowing for a time-out while one works to heal
the wounds of grief. Depression shuts down the physiological sys-

20

tem and prevents major organ systems from being damaged."[5] Friends can help relieve some depressive states by helping those who are hurt resist the temptation to isolate themselves and completely withdraw from others. Depressed feelings are eased when grievers force themselves to remain engaged with life.

HOPE AND FULFILLMENT

"My life is richer because of the heart attack!" At first, Rodney felt helpless when a heart attack nearly took his life at the age of thirty-four. Physicians told him he had to make major lifestyle changes. The doctors told Rodney that if he did not, he might not be able to walk up a flight of stairs, play with his children, or even hold a job. "The idea that my life was basically over at thirty-four prompted me to respond positively to their advice," he says. Rodney went on a low-fat diet and lost 125 pounds. With the backing of his cardiologist, he began taking brisk walks and later took up jogging. Rodney regained good health and now runs two marathons a year.

Other losses, especially those involving serious crime, may not have the positive outcome the above illustration portrays. However, there can come a time when the individual begins to look ahead in life and adjusts to the way life has become.

RECOVERY AND READJUSTMENT

"Knowing I am adjusting to life again would please my loved one." Survivors know they are through the most difficult aspect of grief when they can recall the deceased without those memories inciting great pain. In fact, the memories become a pleasant experience. In his book *Grief Counseling and Grief Therapy,* J. William Worden, Ph.D., writes:

> One benchmark of a completed grief reaction is when the person is able to think of the deceased without pain. There is always a sense of sadness when you think of

[5] Alan Wolfelt, Ph.D., *Death and Grief: A Guide for Clergy* (Muncie, Ind.: Accelerated Development Publishers, 1988), 57.

someone that you have loved and lost, but it is a different kind of sadness—it lacks the wrenching quality it previously had. One can think of the deceased without physical manifestations such as intense crying or feeling a tightness in the chest.[6]

Finally, caregivers should understand there are some people who become "stuck" in their grieving. Such individuals are not passing through the experience, and their grieving is not coming to a conclusion. If it appears that a person is "stuck" in the process of grief, professional intervention is highly advisable. Such individuals should be encouraged to seek a therapist experienced with grief issues. Usually such professional aid will help a person identify the blocking issue, complete the grieving, and get back to living.

A D D I T I O N A L   R E S O U R C E S

Grief Counseling and Grief Therapy: A Handbook for the Mental Health Practitioner by J. William Worden, Ph.D. (New York: Springer Publishing Co., 1982). Although the book has an academic title, it is a short book that is well written and easy to read.

Death and Grief: A Guide for the Clergy by Alan Wolfelt, Ph.D. (Muncie, Ind.: Accelerated Development Publishers, 1988). This book is written in a clear, concise way and is useful for both clergy and laity.

V I C T O R   M .   P A R A C H I N

Reverend Victor M. Parachin is an ordained minister and counselor, serving churches in Washington, D.C., and Chicago. He is the writer of *Hope,* a monthly newsletter written for those who are grieving.

---

[6] J. William Worden, *Grief Counseling and Grief Therapy: A Handbook for the Mental Health Practitioner* (New York: Springer Publishing Co., 1982), 16.

The Tool of Forgiveness

Once when Jesus had been out praying, one of his disciples came to him as he finished and said, "Lord, teach us to pray, just as John taught his disciples." He said, "This is how you should pray: Father, may your name be honored. May your Kingdom come soon. Give us our food day by day. And forgive us our sins—just as we forgive those who have sinned against us. And don't let us yield to temptation."

LUKE 11:1-4, NLT

A number of the crises mentioned in this book describe situations of deep and intense human pain and conflict. Whether it is the dissolution of a marriage, a fraud committed by a trusted employee, the disappointment of being fired from a job, or the devastating news of the sexual assault of a child, there are often deep hurts and wounds that last for many years.

Crises can cause wounds. They are the wounds of the soul and spirit—not easily touched and not easily healed. How can we help others in crisis to get through the crisis and then begin to heal those wounds?

In this book the authors give you specific tools to help others experiencing a variety of crises. But there is another tool, a God-given tool, that can greatly assist in the healing and restoration process. It is the tool of forgiveness.

Forgiveness is a highly volatile subject, especially with crime victims and the pain and wrong they have suffered. Many crime victims have shared stories with me about being "revictimized" by a well-meaning church friend or even a pastor who insisted that they *must* forgive the one who perpetrated the crime. In some cases, those words have felt like a weapon used against them, which has built up barriers and solidified their commitment to *never* forgive.

In some cases, forgiveness itself seems unfair and unnatural. Why should a woman forgive a robber who killed her husband as he was trying to protect their home? Why should a father forgive the man who raped his twelve-year-old daughter? The hurt and pain are too much. Lives are radically and tragically altered—even destroyed. Why should we forgive?

Lewis Smedes, a professor at Fuller Seminary and a nationally recognized Christian author on the subject of forgiveness, writes in his book *Forgive and Forget:*

> The honest heart is outraged by cheap nostrums for unfair hurts; it does not want to forgive at all, if forgiving leaves the victim exposed and encourages the wrongdoer to hurt again.
>
> So we shall ask: Why forgive?
>
> And we shall answer: Because forgiving is the only way we have to a better fairness in our unfair world; it is love's unexpected revolution against unfair pain and it alone offers strong hope for healing the hurts we so unfairly feel.[1]

But more can be added. God beckons us to use the tool of forgiveness with those who have wronged us and hurt us. He does this not because he wants to push us into corners and demand that we suffer even more. No, he provides the tool of forgiveness because he first loved us and forgave us.

For Christians, the concept of forgiveness is inextricably linked to divine forgiveness. It is God's forgiveness of men's and women's sins through the death of Christ on the cross that puts human forgiveness in perspective and gives us the strength and power to forgive. God through Christ walked that path of forgiveness before us. We can forgive others because Christ forgave us and enables us to extend forgiveness to those who have hurt or wronged us. As Lewis Smedes again writes:

[1] Lewis B. Smedes, *Forgive and Forget* (HarperSanFrancisco, 1984), 160.

Forgiveness is God's invention for coming to terms with a world in which . . . people are unfair to each other and hurt each other deeply. He began by forgiving us. And he invites us all to forgive each other.

Forgiving is love's toughest work and love's biggest risk. If you twist it into something it was never meant to be, it can make you a doormat or an insufferable manipulator.

Forgiving seems almost unnatural. Our sense of fairness tells us that people should pay for the wrong they do. But forgiving is love's power to break nature's rule.[2]

Despite the difficulties of the issue of forgiveness and the many nuances and gray areas that each crisis situation contains, it is true that in forgiveness there is healing. Forgiveness may be heartbreaking—it may seem impossible to do; but nonetheless, the truth remains that forgiveness can bring healing, freedom, and blessing from God for one who is able to forgive.

A COSTLY TOOL

Forgiveness is often an intensely painful struggle, but forgiveness was not made to come easily. No matter who or what is involved, true forgiveness is a costly tool and often involves sacrifice. It is costly because to pick it up and use it, you often must sacrifice what you are holding. Sometimes it is a sacrifice of pride; sometimes a letting go of a hurtful memory; sometimes it is more intense, such as releasing anger, malice, or hate. Sometimes the sacrifice seems like a kind of death.

HOW THE TOOL WORKS:
STAGES OF FORGIVENESS

Dr. Smedes outlines the stages of forgiveness. He describes the first stage in forgiveness as *feeling the pain*. "But in its essence, the miracle of healing happens when one *person* feels the pain and forgives the *person* who opened the wound."[3] It is not easy

[2] Ibid., 12. [3] Ibid., 47.

to experience pain, and most of us readily shy away from it, deny it, bury it, or project it on someone or something else. However, for the wound to heal, we must recognize that pain is there—accept it and even embrace it.

The second stage is *facing the hate*. In some situations, people cannot shake off the depth of the pain and hurt. They hold tightly to it and make the transition from anger to hate. Hate nourishes the desire for the one who hurt you to suffer as much or more than you are suffering.

The third stage is *forgiving the one who offended*. Lewis Smedes tells us that forgiving is an honest release of emotions and pain. It is honest because it occurs with

> honest judgment, honest pain, and honest hate. True forgivers do not pretend they don't suffer. They do not pretend the wrong does not matter much. True forgivers desire true justice which can hold someone accountable for wrong acts. You will know that forgiveness has begun when you recall those who hurt you and feel the power to wish them well.[4]

The fourth stage is *freeing for reconciliation*. Reconciliation should not be pushed on anyone as an obligation. Not all situations will allow or should allow for reconciliation between the one offended and the offender. This is especially the case with crime victims and their offenders. However, in some cases, reconciliation is not only possible but desirable between the two parties. In that situation, both parties freely and voluntarily need to desire reconciliation and be willing to work toward it.

Churches can play a major role in offering opportunities for victim-offender reconciliation and for mediation between Christians in dispute. Information on both church-based reconciliation and mediation is listed at the end of this section.

[4]Ibid., 47.

These four stages may be repeated over time and not necessarily in a particular order. Forgiveness may not be limited to a one-time occurrence—for some it may be necessary to go back and begin the process again.

OFFERING THE TOOL

If we can see forgiveness as a tool that we as helpers can *offer* to others and not force upon them, we will assist people in their healing process. There are four characteristics of forgiveness to highlight:

- Forgiveness cannot be forced on or demanded of another. No one can be forced to forgive. It must happen in a person's own time and own way. Forgiveness is a personal choice one makes that can become a turning point in reconstructing life after a crisis.
- Forgiveness takes time to understand, learn, and use. Forgiveness can take a lot of time—years, decades, even scores of years. It is a process that requires patience, diligence, and prayer. It allows individuals opportunities to break free of the painful bonds that may control their lives.
- Forgiveness has no time or distance barriers. Anyone can extend forgiveness to another who is across the miles, whom they haven't seen or talked to for years, and even someone who is no longer alive.
- Forgiveness cannot be used by another. If you were not the one who was wronged or injured, you cannot extend forgiveness. You may be outraged by the actions of another. However, you cannot forgive another on behalf of a person in crisis. Attempting to do so may discount the responsibility and authority of the person in crisis as well as undermine efforts to restore his or her life.

WHAT FORGIVENESS IS NOT

As you seek to help those in crisis, it is important not only to understand how to use the tool of forgiveness but also to understand what forgiveness is *not*.

Dr. Reverend Richard Lord, a pastor from Ft. Worth, Texas, who has worked extensively with crime victims and issues of forgiveness and recovery, writes: "As crime victims share their resistance to forgiveness, they seem to focus on two elements: forgiveness as forgetting and forgiveness as excusing."[5]

- *Forgiveness is not forgetting.* People don't have to forget after they forgive. Oftentimes, individuals interpret forgiveness as acting as if the harm had never occurred. They may remember the crisis or the harm done, but in forgiveness the debilitating pain is not so acute. In situations where loved ones have been killed through a criminal act, survivors are clear they do not want their loved one forgotten.

As Dick Lord discovered through his work with crime victims,

> many victims speak of getting to the stage of "letting go." That is, with time and support, they can let go of much of their hate, anger, rage, despair. . . . They are no longer willing to allow the perpetrator to be the center of their lives. They focus on the present and future. Sometimes this "letting go" is what people mean when they say, "You must forgive." . . . It does seem necessary for a person's health for this to happen eventually.[6]

- *Forgiveness is not excusing.* The second perception of forgiveness that bothers victims is that it may imply *excusing* or trivializing the wrong. Forgiveness doesn't excuse or forget actions or words that have caused great harm and wrong. But forgiveness has the ability to free the one who was wronged from the pain, anger, and hate that results from the wrong. In forgiving, one does not excuse but actually holds individuals accountable for their actions

[5] Richard P. Lord from an unpublished work entitled *Out of the Depths,* 1997.   [6] Ibid.

and then chooses, with God's help, to move beyond the wrong and pain.

- Forgiveness is not tolerating what others have done. Forgiveness doesn't "put up" with wrong. It sees it clearly, calls "wrong" what it is, and then extends the grace of forgiveness in spite of the wrong.
- Forgiveness is not blindly trusting the offender. Trust has to be rebuilt and proven once again. And yet trust may or may not be rebuilt. Forgiveness is a new responsibility. It can cause one to become a more vulnerable, trusting, and open individual.

In summary, forgiveness doesn't excuse or forget actions or words that have caused great harm and wrong. But forgiveness has the ability to free the one who was wronged from the pain, anger, and hate that understandably result from the wrong.

PREREQUISITES FOR FORGIVENESS

So far, we have looked at forgiveness from the point of view of the one who has been wronged. What about the one who *committed* the wrong? What are his or her responsibilities, if any? Dietrich Bonhoeffer (a German theologian who was imprisoned in a Nazi death camp for his opposition to Hitler's regime) gave us the phrase "cheap grace." "Cheap grace is the preaching of forgiveness without requiring repentance."[7] Repentance, as Dr. Lord also describes, involves four aspects which guard against cheap grace: remorse, repentance, restitution, and regeneration.[8]

- *Remorse*—acknowledges that harm has been done: "I'm sorry."
- *Repentance*—goes beyond remorse and moves to making a fundamental change in how the offender lives and operates: "I won't do that again."
- *Restitution*—represents an effort to restore what was hurt,

[7] Dietrich Bonhoeffer, *The Cost of Discipleship*, (New York: Macmillan Publishing Co., Inc., 1963). [8] Lord, *Out of the Depths.* 3.

wounded, or broken and assumes responsibility for the harm that was done: "I will make up for the harm that I caused."

- *Regeneration*—seeks renewal of his or her life and shows the "fruits of repentance" that the harm will not be repeated.

But what about the offender who has no interest in remorse, repentance, restitution, or regeneration? When this happens, Marie Fortune (founder of the Seattle-based Center for Prevention of Sexual and Domestic Violence) suggests that the four aspects of seeking forgiveness become the responsibility of the wider community—church, family, and friends. These people can step in and be the ones who acknowledge the wrong done and say, "We're sorry you were hurt and want to help do something about it."[9] This is *not taking the responsibility for the offender* or the offense, but rather serves as a means of *acknowledging the wrong* when the offender is unwilling or unable.

A QUESTION OF HEALING

The ultimate question that is posed to those who have experienced deep pain and hurt as a result of a crime or a wrong committed against them is, *Do I want to be healed?*

Lewis Smedes writes of his own experience with forgiveness. "My hurt brought me into the first stage of forgiving—the critical stage at which I had to make a simple decision: **Did I want to be healed, or did I want to go on suffering from an unfair hurt lodged in my memory?**" He goes on, "We are always, all of us, pushed into this crucial stage when we feel that somebody has hurt us deeply. **Will we let our pain hang on to our hearts where it will eat away our joy? Or will we use the miracle of forgiving to heal the hurt we didn't deserve?**[10]

[9] From an article entitled "Forgiveness: The Last Step" by Marie Fortune, in *Abuse and Religion,* ed. Anne L. Horton and Judith A. Williamson (Lexington, Mass.: D. C. Heath and Company, 1988), 215–220. [10] Smedes, *Forgive and Forget,* 21, bold added.

ADDITIONAL RESOURCES

Forgive and Forget by Lewis B. Smedes (HarperSanFrancisco, 1984). A good basic overview on forgiveness.

Embodying Forgiveness by L. Gregory Jones (Grand Rapids: William B. Eerdmans Publishing Co., 1995). A theological analysis of forgiveness.

Forgiving the Unforgivable: Overcoming the Bitter Legacy of Intimate Wounds by Beverly Flanigan (New York: Macmillan Publishing Co., 1992).

For information on church-based victim offender reconciliation, contact:
Mr. Ron Claassen
Restorative Justice Ministries
Fresno-Pacific University
1717 S. Chestnut Avenue
Fresno, CA 43702
(209) 453-2064

For information on Christian mediation and reconciliation, contact:
Institute for Christian Conciliation
1537 Avenue D
Suite 352
Billings, MT 59102
406-256-1583

LISA BARNES LAMPMAN

Lisa Barnes Lampman serves as the president and CEO of Neighbors Who Care (NWC), a nonprofit organization committed to mobilizing and equipping local churches to provide practical and spiritual assistance to victims of crime. NWC is the crime victim assistance ministry of Prison Fellowship Ministries.

A
RELATIONSHIP
IN
DANGER

DIVORCE

Peace has been stripped away, and I have forgotten what prosperity is.
I cry out, "My splendor is gone! Everything I had hoped for
from the Lord is lost!"
The thought of my suffering and homelessness is bitter beyond words.
I will never forget this awful time, as I grieve over my loss.
Yet I still dare to hope when I remember this:
The unfailing love of the Lord never ends! By his mercies
we have been kept from complete destruction. Great is his faithfulness;
his mercies begin afresh each day."

LAMENTATIONS 3:17-23, NLT

When my husband first told me that he was
leaving, I thought that I would die. He was the
most important thing in my life, and now he was
leaving me for someone else. I didn't know where to turn.
All I could do was cry out to God!"

❏ *Woman whose husband left her*

EFFECTS OF THE CRISIS

Divorce is very much like a death. One grieves the death of
a relationship, the death of a dream. But in death there is
usually a clean break—a near-surgical severing. In divorce
there is not a clean cut but a ripping apart of the one-flesh
relationship. And an ex-spouse can move in and out of one's

life, reopening the old wounds over and over, making the healing process much more difficult.

HOW YOU CAN HELP AND ENCOURAGE

A person going through a divorce feels a tremendous sense of loss. And it's not just the loss of a spouse, though that is considerable. Most experience devastating financial losses and broken relationships with their children, as well as shame and isolation from family, friends, and sometimes even the church. The fact is, many family and friends don't want to take sides or don't know what to say. So they say nothing.

Having already experienced rejection from their "life partners," divorced people tend to be very sensitive. When others are silent, or when the church does not provide concrete help, most divorced people can't help but feel rejected again.

Therefore, it is most important that you communicate support and understanding. A listening ear and an open heart will go a long way toward healing. If you've ever suffered a significant loss or betrayal, then you can probably relate to what the person is going through. If not, that's OK. You can still listen.

The divorced person will go through the typical grieving process (see chapter on grief, p.17), with anger and depression being especially prevalent. This recovery process often takes two to five years—depending on how intense the conflict and how much emotional support the person gets.

In the early stages, the person can be expected to blame the ex-spouse or others or to have distorted perceptions about the divorce. While there are always two sides to the story, you should not try to point out the person's own fault in the breakup, at least not right away. At some point the divorced person may need to take a more critical look at his or her actions, but the immediate need is for support and comfort in the grieving process.

A person usually plunges into self-blame once he or she reaches the depression phase. At this point, a person may look inward, perhaps for the first time since the divorce, and may uncover a lot of guilt, hopelessness, and self-pity.

Depression feels awful, but it's actually the healthiest phase of the process—it's closest to acceptance. Once a person comes to the end of the proverbial rope, he or she can begin to reach outward and upward. As a loyal friend or counselor, you can gently help your friend rebuild his or her life.

At this point, you can begin to put the divorce issues into perspective, helping the person to acknowledge an appropriate amount of responsibility for the split—but always with an underlying sense of forgiveness and future improvement. These issues can be delicate, so proceed gently, without condemnation, and always with love.

Although every situation is different, I usually recommend that a divorced person stay out of new romantic relationships for at least two years after the breakup. During recovery, such people are extremely vulnerable. They need to focus on full recovery and emotional wholeness. When hurried by a new love, healing doesn't happen properly. It's like a broken bone that is set improperly: It may have to be broken again in order to heal right. Rebound relationships usually just cause more pain.

When I went through my own divorce almost twenty years ago, I felt abandoned by friends, the church, and even by God. However, I had one longtime friend, who continually reached out to me. He invited me over to talk . . . or not to talk if I didn't feel like talking. He gave me a key to his house and encouraged me to stop over anytime—to eat his food, to crash on his sofa, or to sit up most of the night complaining about how unfair life was. I took him up on his offer.

For a while I was not much of a friend to him. The relationship was very one-sided. He gave and I took. But at that time, he gave me exactly what I needed. As I began to heal, I was able to recognize how lopsided our relationship was. I determined that, as I was able, I would try to be the same type of person for others. I will always be thankful for his friendship. In time he was able to challenge me, push me in healthy directions, and give me a stable friendship from which I could take new risks as I sought to rebuild my life. Eventually I joined a church singles group, which was instrumental in my spiritual and emotional growth.

Divorced people need the support of people with listening ears and compassionate hearts. As they begin to rebuild their lives, they need a new social support system—one that can provide a safe environment for healing a broken heart and learning how to trust and commit again. The process takes a long time, usually years, so be patient as you nurture them toward emotional wholeness. Yet they will be forever grateful that you stood with them during one of the most difficult times in their lives.

HELPFUL THINGS TO SAY AND DO

- "You can talk with me whenever you need to."
- "Divorce is not the unforgivable sin. God understands."
- "Go slow. Give yourself time to grieve, time to heal."
- "Can I help you with the kids?"
- Encourage them to avoid a new relationship until they are ready.
- Offer to get together regularly to support and pray with them.
- Provide financial counseling and support to adjust to a new lifestyle.

HURTFUL RESPONSES TO TRY TO AVOID

- "What did you do to make your spouse leave you like this?" (Eventually they will begin to take a share of responsibility, but you don't need to hurry this.)
- "Do you realize what this is going to do to your kids?" (They probably know and are worried about it.)
- "You need to get out into circulation again. Your children

need two parents." (Rebound relationships will only cause more pain to the person and the family.)

- "God hates divorce." (It's true, but divorced people can easily conclude that God hates them, which is very false.)

RELATED SCRIPTURE

Don't be afraid, for I am with you. Do not be dismayed, for I am your God. I will strengthen you. I will help you. I will uphold you with my victorious right hand. ISAIAH 41:10, NLT

The unfailing love of the Lord never ends! By his mercies we have been kept from complete destruction. Great is his faithfulness; his mercies begin afresh each day. I say to myself, "The Lord is my inheritance; therefore, I will hope in him!" LAMENTATIONS 3:22-23, NLT

"Should a man be allowed to divorce his wife for any reason?"

"Haven't you read the Scriptures?" Jesus replied. "They record that from the beginning 'God made them male and female.' And he said, 'This explains why a man leaves his father and mother and is joined to his wife, and the two are united into one.' Since they are no longer two but one, let no one separate them, for God has joined them together."

"Then why did Moses say a man could merely write an official letter of divorce and send her away?" they asked.

Jesus replied, "Moses permitted divorce as a concession to your hardhearted wickedness, but it was not what God had originally intended. And I tell you this, a man who divorces his wife and marries another commits adultery—unless his wife has been unfaithful."
MATTHEW 19:3-9, NLT

Now, for those who are married I have a command that comes not from me, but from the Lord. A wife must not leave her husband. But if she does leave him, let her remain single or else go back to him. And the husband must not leave his wife.

Now, I will speak to the rest of you, though I do not have a direct command from the Lord. If a Christian man has a wife who is an unbeliever and she is willing to continue living with him, he must not

leave her. And if a Christian woman has a husband who is an unbeliever, and he is willing to continue living with her, she must not leave him. For the Christian wife brings holiness to her marriage, and the Christian husband brings holiness to his marriage. Otherwise, your children would not have a godly influence, but now they are set apart for him. (But if the husband or wife who isn't a Christian insists on leaving, let them go. In such cases the Christian husband or wife is not required to stay with them, for God wants his children to live in peace.) You wives must remember that your husbands might be converted because of you. And you husbands must remember that your wives might be converted because of you.

1 CORINTHIANS 7:10-16, NLT

PRAYER

A prayer to share with your friend:

Lord, I feel so alone and abandoned. I know you are still beside me, but help me to be more aware of your presence and what you might be trying to teach me through this crisis.

Protect me, and protect my children. Help us to forgive and to learn to be content—even in the times of trial and tribulation.

I know that you desire good for us. Please guide and direct my paths. Amen.

ADDITIONAL RESOURCES

The Fresh Start Divorce Recovery Workbook by Bob Burns and Thomas Whiteman (Thomas Nelson Publishers, 1992). How to recover from separation and divorce, with workbook interactions included.

Innocent Victims: Understanding the Needs and Fears of Your Children by Thomas Whiteman, Ph.D. (Thomas Nelson Publishers, 1993). How to help children recover from the trauma of divorce.

Sex and Love When You're Single Again by Thomas Jones (Thomas Nelson Publishers, 1990). How to move forward in your life following a divorce.

The Fresh Start Single Parenting Workbook by Thomas Whiteman, with Randy Petersen (Thomas Nelson Publishers, 1993). How to raise healthy children when you're doing it all alone.

Helping Children Cope with Divorce by Edward Teyber (D. C. Heath & Company, 1994). A secular resource for parents that explains children's major problems resulting from divorce. Includes chapters on child rearing after divorce, including problems of stepfamilies.

Marriage and Divorce: God's Call, God's Compassion by M. G. McLuhan (Tyndale House Publishers, 1991). An experienced counselor gives a scriptural view of marriage and divorce, compassionately considering the situations of those who are divorced.

THOMAS A. WHITEMAN

Thomas A. Whiteman, Ph.D., is the president of Life Counseling Services, a large Christian counseling program in the Philadelphia area. He is also president of Fresh Start Seminars, which conducts relationship seminars throughout the United States.

Unfaithful Spouse

Yet I am confident that I will see the Lord's goodness. . . . Wait patiently for the Lord. Be brave and courageous. Yes, wait patiently for the Lord.

PSALM 27:13-14, NLT

W e had such a strong marriage, for the most part. I simply never imagined that Bill would even be interested in another woman."

❏ *Woman whose husband was unfaithful after eighteen years of marriage*

Effects of the Crisis

It is difficult for someone who has not experienced a partner's affair to understand the shock, sadness, and pain that comes when someone who had pledged to "forsake all others," betrays that sacred promise. Infidelity shakes its victims to the very core.

How You Can Help and Encourage

In 1974 Dr. Bernard Greene, drawing on 750 case histories of married men, stated that 60 percent of his subjects had been unfaithful.[1] In 1981 Shere Hite reported in her study of over 7,000 males that 72 percent of men married more than two

[1]Bernard Greene, Ronald Lee, and Noel Lustic, "Conscious and Unconscious Factors in Marital Infidelity," *Medical Aspects of Human Sexuality,* September 1974, 87–111.

years had cheated on their wives.[2] More than 15 percent of men report having a series of affairs.[3] The same disturbing trend is found in studies examining women who are unfaithful. In 1987 Shere Hite reported that her survey of several thousand women indicated that 75 percent of women married five years or longer were having or had had an affair.[4]

These startling statistics reveal the pervasiveness of this serious sin and sound the alarm for those who would like to help a friend whose partner has been unfaithful. The following are some of the most effective methods for helping those who hurt.

To begin with, make sure the individual knows they are not to blame for their spouse's choice. Some individuals will not need much convincing of this and will need to be allowed to vent their anger. Others, however, will need you to comfort them and remind them that they are loved as a child of God and should not punish themselves for their spouse's fault.

Next, you can help this hurting person realize that the affair doesn't have to be the end of the marriage. While the couple will certainly be left with a permanent scar on their relationship, God's grace can bring healing and restoration to those who rely on him and seek to learn from the experience and the subsequent counseling.

After plenty of time has been devoted to allowing your friend to vent his or her anger and pain, help the person process whether it is possible to work on the marriage. The majority of evangelical Bible scholars believe that Scripture teaches that adultery is one of the biblical grounds for divorce and remarriage, if one so chooses to exercise that option. If this is the spouse's first affair, and there is a willingness to repent, it is probably best to facilitate a process of forgiveness. If a spouse has had a series of affairs with little or no change in lifestyle or

[2] Shere Hite, *The Hite Report on Male Sexuality* (Garden City, N.Y.: Alfred A. Knopf, 1981). [3] Laurel Richardson, *The New Other Woman: Contemporary Single Women in Affairs with Married Men* (New York: The Free Press, 1985), 1. [4] Shere Hite, *Women and Love: A Cultural Revolution in Progress* (New York: Alfred A. Knopf, 1987).

evidence of genuine remorse, however, it is probably best to facilitate an assertive confrontation of his or her lifestyle.

Recognize that a period of separation may be needed. Before a decision can be made to terminate the affair, the unfaithful spouse may need the extra motivation of experiencing how much he or she would lose by leaving the family. The individual may need a separation to make it clear that the unfaithful spouse will not be allowed to have both a marriage spouse and a lover. During the separation, encourage the unoffending spouse to use humor, dress his or her best, interact with his or her social support group, and stay active in usual routines.

For those individuals willing to continue their marriage, guide them toward disclosing the information they have to their spouse about the affair. They may be tempted to play games and manipulate or trap their spouse. This has too much potential for backfiring. Instead, they should tell their spouse what they know and how they came to know it. In an honest and nonvindictive way, they should let their spouse know that they are deeply hurt. A vindictive expression of anger is likely to create destructive barriers.

In time, help the individual explore how his or her spouse's choice of an affair partner can identify unmet needs in the marriage. Obviously, the unfaithful spouse has made a sinful choice that may have little to do with the spouse who was hurt (such as an addiction to pornography), but in a crisis like this there is much to be learned (regardless of the cause) by both to rebuild as strong a marriage as possible. A common assumption is that the problem is sexual; most likely it is not. The unfaithful spouse can be included in this exploration if it seems appropriate, but remember that an angry betrayer will try to blame his or her spouse for deterioration in the relationship. In other words, even if the unfaithful person feels guilty about the unfaithfulness, he or she may deal with the guilt by finding fault with the spouse to justify the affair. For this reason, be very cautious about a premature joint session. You may be wise to focus on having the individual look at his or her own possible contribution to the affair and ways to improve the marriage over time. As you do this, however, be sure to stay clear of guilt. You do not want to negatively impact them in the process. The goal is to help them build a stronger, healthier relationship upon reunion.

Having an unfaithful spouse is not an injury that one recovers from quickly. It takes years of healing to overcome such a painful tragedy. And participating in long-term counseling with a specialist can be one of the most important things this person (and this couple) can do.

HELPFUL THINGS TO SAY AND DO

- Allow plenty of time for grief, sadness, and anger.
- Keep them from apologizing for not being good enough partners.
- Help them send healthy messages by setting boundaries.
- Help them learn more about how they can improve the marriage upon reunion.
- Guard against unhealthy hostility.
- Explore the meaning and practice of forgiveness.
- Encourage them to rely on God for their worth.
- Pray that God will bring healing to their spirit and rejuvenate their soul.
- Let them know that God loves them and wants the best for them.

HURTFUL RESPONSES TO TRY TO AVOID

- Don't rail at and denounce the unfaithful partner.
- Do not insinuate blame on the part of the one who was betrayed.
- Don't make decisions for the individual concerning working on the marriage. Help them see the options and support them as they consider their next steps.

RELATED SCRIPTURE

God wants you to be holy, so you should keep clear of all sexual sin.
Then each of you will control your body and live in holiness and honor.
1 THESSALONIANS 4:3-4, NLT

But when the Holy Spirit controls our lives, he will produce this kind
of fruit in us: love, joy, peace, patience, kindness, goodness, faithful-
ness, gentleness, and self-control. Here there is no conflict with the law.
   Those who belong to Christ Jesus have nailed the passions and
desires of their sinful nature to his cross and crucified them there.
GALATIANS 5:22-24, NLT

Give honor to marriage, and remain faithful to one another in
marriage. God will surely judge people who are immoral and those
who commit adultery. HEBREWS 13:4, NLT

Stop loving this evil world and all that it offers you, for when you love
the world, you show that you do not have the love of the Father in you.
For the world offers only the lust for physical pleasure, the lust for
everything we see, and pride in our possessions. These are not from the
Father. They are from this evil world. And this world is fading away,
along with everything it craves. But if you do the will of God, you will
live forever. 1 JOHN 2:15-17, NLT

PRAYER

A prayer to share with your friend:
Lord God, my heart is breaking. I have been wronged by the one per-
son I thought would never look at another.
   Give me your wisdom and strength as I face the coming days and
years. Give me a heart that is open to your guidance in all things. Amen.

ADDITIONAL RESOURCES

Broken Promises: Understanding, Healing, and Preventing Affairs in Christian
Marriages by Henry A. Virkler (Word, Inc., 1992). This book explains how Christians

become involved in affairs, how to help Christians after an affair, and how to prevent affairs in Christian couples.

Men Who Can't Be Faithful by Carol Botwin (Warner Books, 1989). While the author takes a nonjudgmental stance on sex outside of marriage, she has many excellent insights into why men are unfaithful and how to respond when there has been infidelity.

Sex, Guilt & Forgiveness by Josh McDowell (Tyndale House Publishers, 1990). This book offers practical counsel on learning to forgive oneself and others following sexual experiences outside of marriage.

L E S   A N D   L E S L I E   P A R R O T T

Les Parrott III, Ph.D. and Leslie Parrott, Ed.D. are codirectors of the Center for Relationship Development at Seattle Pacific University. Their books include *Saving Your Marriage before It Starts, Becoming Soul Mates,* and *Questions Couples Ask.* Les Parrott's most recent book is *High-Maintenance Relationships.*

DOMESTIC VIOLENCE

It is not an enemy who taunts me—I could bear that.
It is not my foes who so arrogantly insult me—
I could have hidden from them.
Instead, it is you—my equal, my companion and close friend.
What good fellowship we enjoyed as we
walked together to the house of God.

PSALM 55:12-14, NLT

Ginny[1] married Andrew after only six months of dating. "I loved him, and he was a Christian," she explains, "and that made me happy."

But Ginny's happy illusions exploded when Andrew began using violence to control her. Just months into their marriage, he started yanking her hair and smashing her head against the wall for such "disobedience" as talking with a friend too long, frying an egg incorrectly, or failing to serve dinner precisely at 4:30 p.m.

"I felt like a nonperson," Ginny remembers. "I couldn't even think for myself."

One wintry day, after twenty-two years of marriage, Andrew stabbed Ginny repeatedly with a knife, then tried to smother her with a pillow. Fortunately, she got away and fled to a neigh-

[1]The victim's name has been changed to protect her privacy.

bor's house, screaming for help. One year later a jury convicted Andrew of attempted murder and aggravated assault.

Ginny still carries an overwhelming feeling of betrayal. "I was attacked in my home, which should have been a safe place for me. I was attacked by my husband, who was supposed to love me."

UNDERSTANDING THE CRISIS

According to the U.S. Department of Justice, domestic violence refers primarily to the sexual assault, rape, aggravated assault, or simple assault of a married, divorced, or separated woman by a relative or other person well known to the victim. Men may also be victims of domestic violence, but the overwhelming majority of victims are women. For this section, the victim will be referred to as a woman. Verbal abuse invariably accompanies physical abuse.

EFFECTS OF THE CRISIS

Victims of repeated abuse commonly suffer significant physical injuries and many debilitating effects: low self-esteem; fear; isolation from family, friends, and other supportive relationships; inability to make their own decisions; self-blame—holding themselves responsible for their partners or spouse's abusive behavior; severe mood swings; and feelings of helplessness, guilt, and shame. Many victims experience acute physical reactions—headaches, rashes, insomnia—as well as severe psychological effects, such as depression and eating disorders. Some domestic violence situations may even end in the death of the victim.

HOW YOU CAN HELP AND ENCOURAGE

Sadly, and far too frequently, the tragedy of domestic abuse in Christian homes has been augmented by the church's inadequacy in caring for the victims. Church teachings on men's and women's roles commonly focus much more on the wife's submission to the husband than on the husband's responsibility to love and cherish his wife. This imbalance, along with extreme interpretations of male "headship" in the family, has often reinforced violence in Christian homes.

Ginny's husband, even after being convicted of attempted murder, refused to relinquish his claims to control. In one letter from prison, he wrote to Ginny: "Throughout all of this I've let my headship slide, but I *am* head of the family, I have certain spiritual responsibilities, and I *will* now exercise that authority. . . ."

The most effective helpers for a victim of domestic violence are those who encourage the woman to make choices that will *protect* her and her children and who *hold her abuser* accountable for his violent—and sinful—behavior. A woman's actions do not govern her husband's violence; he deliberately *chooses* to act violently.

Therefore, the primary concern should be the woman's safety. *Do not* make her decisions for her but provide possible alternatives. If she considers leaving her abuser, suggest options for a "safe place"—a women's shelter or the home of a friend or family member. Get to know the domestic violence shelters in your community and the criteria for using them. Give possible safety steps to take in leaving (such as financial arrangements).

Separating from an abusive husband does not necessarily lead to divorce, and it is beyond the scope of this essay to discuss the biblical teachings on when divorce is justified. However, confronting the abuser with his sin and subsequent attempts at reconciliation cannot effectively take place *until the woman is separated from danger.*

While abhorring the abuse, many women hesitate to leave their violent husbands out of fear of enraging their husbands, losing their financial security, having their shame exposed, or failing to "make it" on their own. Many of these are realistic fears. A woman making the courageous decision to leave her abuser needs the church to come alongside to assist and support her in confronting the abuser in wise and safe ways. In addition, the church can provide needed practical help—such as temporarily providing funds for relocating, paying bills, getting professional counseling, etc.

Be willing to *enter into* the victim's pain, looking for specific ways to help bear the burden, rather than advising from the sidelines. Because of their low self-esteem and feelings of helplessness, victims of abuse often have trouble making and acting upon wise decisions in their own behalf.

Perhaps the hardest concerns to address are related to faith: "Where is God in all of this? Why doesn't he stop the suffering?" Understandably, victims may express intense anger toward God—or fear of him—or envy that he gives good gifts to others while apparently tossing them only spoiled crumbs. Such feelings reveal what counselors Dan Allender and Tremper Longman call the "cry of the soul," and such emotions—which often add to the *helper's* discomfort—should not be minimized or dismissed with platitudes.

Do not, for example, idealize abuse as "a privilege of sharing in the sufferings of Jesus." There is a vast difference between voluntary and involuntary suffering. Some Christians may *choose* to suffer for a greater benefit—as Jesus chose to suffer in payment for our sins, or as missionaries have chosen to face hostile circumstances for the sake of spreading the gospel. But most abused wives *involuntarily* suffer from another's egregious sin. Even when women "choose" to stay in the situation, it is because they can't see any other workable choice. Rather than focusing on the "benefit" of suffering, focus instead on how Jesus, *because* of his own sufferings, knows and understands the victim's pain and anguish.

HELPFUL THINGS TO SAY AND DO

- "It takes a lot of courage to talk about something so painful. Thank you for trusting me enough to share this with me."

- "I imagine this is very difficult to talk about. Just take your time."
- "It's not your fault. You are not responsible for your husband's abusive behavior."
- "I'm sorry this happened to you. Abuse is not a part of God's design for marriage (and the church does not condone it)."
- "Your safety is important to me. What will help you feel safe?" (If necessary, help her find a safe location.)
- Provide financial counseling or assistance as appropriate. But be sure not to encourage dependence.

HURTFUL RESPONSES TO TRY TO AVOID

- "If you just pray and continue to love him, things will get better."
- "The most important goal is keeping your family together." (This places the preservation of the marriage structure above the safety and sanctity of her *life*.)
- "You need to submit more to your husband (be a better wife, be more patient, be more forgiving, etc.)"

RELATED SCRIPTURE

You hear, O Lord, the desire of the afflicted; you encourage them, and you listen to their cry, defending the fatherless and the oppressed, in order that man, who is of the earth, may terrify no more.
PSALM 10:17-18, NIV

In you, O Lord, I have taken refuge; let me never be put to shame; deliver me in your righteousness. Turn your ear to me, come quickly to my rescue; be my rock of refuge, a strong fortress to save me.
PSALM 31:1-2, NIV

For he will deliver the needy who cry out, the afflicted who have no one to help. He will take pity on the weak and the needy and save the needy from death. He will rescue them from oppression and violence, for precious is their blood in his sight. PSALM 72:12-14, NIV

PRAYER

A prayer to share with your friend:

Lord Jesus, help me to trust you in all things, especially in the despairing times of my life. Help me when I am tempted to act out of fear rather than out of faith in you. Thank you that you understand my pain because you suffered, too. You know what it is like to be betrayed by someone you love, to be unjustly beaten, to feel alone and abandoned. Thank you for promising that you will never abandon me and that I can always come to you to find love and compassion. It is not your will that a man beat his wife, though men may twist your Word to justify their violence. Give me the strength, courage, and wisdom to respond effectively to my husband's abuse—in a way that will honor and uphold your righteousness. Amen.

ADDITIONAL RESOURCES

Abuse and Religion: When Praying Isn't Enough by Anne L. Horton & Judith A. Williamson, eds. (Free Press, 1988). A compilation of articles on various aspects of domestic abuse and the church's influence (both positive and negative) in seeking to resolve the problem.

Battered into Submission: The Tragedy of Wife Abuse in the Christian Home by James Alsdurf & Phyllis Alsdurf (InterVarsity Press, 1989). Details the emotional, spiritual, and relational impact of wife beating and calls the church to take its responsibility in addressing the issue.

Cry of the Soul by Dr. Dan Allender & Dr. Tremper Longman (NavPress Publishing Group, 1994). Drawing from the book of Psalms, shows how the expression of our "dark" emotions—fear, anger, despair, etc.—can drive us *to* or *away from* the heart of God.

Women, Abuse, and the Bible: How Scripture Can Be Used to Hurt or Heal by Catherine C. Kroeger & James R. Beck, eds. (Baker Books, 1996). Speaks frankly of how the Bible can be used either as a reinforcement of abusive behavior or as a balm for victims' emotional and spiritual recovery.

REBECCA BEANE

Rebecca Beane is a senior editor and writer with Prison Fellowship Ministries. She has researched and written on a number of issues related to prisoners, ex-prisoners, crime victims, and their families.

CRISIS

IN THE

COMMUNITY

NATURAL
DISASTERS

"Your sons and daughters were feasting in their oldest brother's home.
Suddenly, a powerful wind swept in from the desert and hit the house on all
sides. The house collapsed, and all your children are dead.
I am the only one who escaped to tell you."
Job stood up and tore his robe in grief. Then he shaved his head
and fell to the ground before God. He said, "I came naked from my mother's
womb, and I will be stripped of everything when I die.
The Lord gave me everything I had, and the Lord has taken it away.
Praise the name of the LORD!"

JOB 1:18-21, NLT

Once you have seen this, something changes inside. Once you have absorbed what nature and the forest can do; once you have seen the majestic glorious redwoods turned into bludgeons and the good earth stirred into soup; once you have seen all this you will never walk the same way in the forest again."[1]

❏ *Charles Kurault's impression of the mud slides and the resulting*
deaths that occurred in the Love Creek flood in Santa Cruz, California,
in 1982.

[1] Life Net, *fall 1996.*

UNDERSTANDING THE CRISIS

The very nature of a natural disaster is its forcefulness, sudden-ness, and unpredictability. We respond with a sense of helpless-ness and disbelief, often accompanied by tears, confusion, and great emotion. Natural disasters are sometimes referred to as "acts of God." However, it is the fallen nature of all creation that creates disasters from natural phenomena. God isn't causing a flood or fire or earthquake to get even with us or to punish our sinfulness. The same winter storm that can cause flooding and hazardous driving conditions resulting in death on our highways will later water our crops and help provide food for thousands.

HOW YOU CAN HELP AND ENCOURAGE

People are often surprised how long it takes to recover after a natural disaster. In our culture we are used to watching dra-matic disasters happen in a sixty-minute television program. In that brief time actors can go through a disaster, stagger through the aftermath, work through the issues, recover, and go on with life—all in sixty minutes! In real life, recovery does not work so cleanly or quickly as television portrays. The truth is, recovery from a natural disaster can take months and even years! The first rule might be: *Have realistic expectations and be patient.*

The chances are extremely good that if you are helping a neighbor in recovery from a natural disaster, you, too, are a victim and in need of support. So, the second rule is: *Be sure you have a support system in place for yourself.* Without this you can become a casualty and be unable to care for your own family's needs.

PRAY

This may sound trite; in fact, it has become almost a cliché in Christian circles to say to a person, "I'll pray for you." The truth is that prayer is a very powerful healing tool. Studies have been conducted in hospitals, where one group of patients was prayed for (without their knowledge) and other patients were not. The patients receiving prayer were discharged from the hospital days earlier than those not receiving prayer!

"As for me, far be it from me that I should sin against the LORD by failing to pray for you. And I will teach you the way that is good and right" (1 Samuel 12:23, NIV).

NORMALIZE REACTIONS

There are many different reactions people may have to natural disaster, such as sleeplessness, recurring intrusive images, startle response, nightmares, agitation, irritability, or debilitating fear. It helps to realize that these are normal reactions. Some people try to fight them through self-determination or willpower and say they will not have a nightmare; or they will be less irritable or stop being so hypervigilant. It does *not* help to fight symptoms. In fact, it may create new levels of tension and defensiveness that impede recovery. It *does* help, however, to turn these responses over to God and to talk about them with other survivors. For the nonbelievers we help, this may be a brief window of opportunity for us to share Christ in a meaningful way. In order to do so, we must not give pat answers but rather demonstrate our faith through our patience with their feelings and gently lead them to go on with life in all of its uncertainty. We, as believers, do not know what tomorrow holds but we do know who holds tomorrow. As we pray, God will make us equal to the task and bring other people who can support and encourage us!

IDENTIFY LOSSES

In a natural disaster your entire community can be affected: homes, schools, businesses. You may have lost your church building, members of your church may have died, or you may have even lost your pastor. Other members may have to relocate because of the damage done to their homes. You may have some survivors living with you in your home. After some disasters, such as tornadoes, earthquakes, floods, fires, or landslides, the topography of the land may have changed so much that it may be unrealistic to rebuild a neighborhood, church, or a person's home. Some homes may be condemned, and new streets may have to be built or rerouted, changing the configuration of the entire community. Therefore, it is helpful to sit down and make a list of the losses that you or your "neighbor" have experienced. This list may then be a benchmark for recovery in seeing emotions subside over time as you review the list. It may also provide a reminder for replacement of items that will be needed in order to get back to a normal life.

LISTEN

The essential form of communication that works in most crisis situations is "active listening," in which the listener "tunes in" to the feelings of the speaker and paraphrases what he or she is saying. We all have a natural tendency to give advice, especially when we believe our advice is scripturally and spiritually sound! We will help more by allowing others to express *their feelings*. This may be a very difficult thing to do for some of us, especially if we too have suffered losses.

Here are a few questions that may reflect some of the inner struggles people go through following a significant loss from a natural disaster. This list should help you to better understand what you should listen for.

- Do you feel guilty that you were not hit as hard as others were?
- Do you feel angry (with perhaps even God) because you experienced more loss than others?
- Was your faith weakened or shaken by this disaster?
- Did you find comfort in any Scripture passages or draw a blank?
- Were you tempted to abandon your faith because of losses?

HELPFUL THINGS TO SAY AND DO

- Be patient, recovery may be slow.
- Listen, listen, listen, and be slow to speak.

- Be practical. When food, shelter, clothing, medical care, or psychological care are needed, provide these first.
- Pray *for* others always; pray *with* others when appropriate, asking first for their permission.
- Provide for your rest and recovery, too.

HURTFUL RESPONSES TO TRY TO AVOID

- Don't give advice when a victim is expressing hopelessness or other negative feelings.
- Don't try to provide everything that another may need by yourself. Know and use community services.
- Don't overspiritualize the circumstances of another person's life and losses.
- Don't criticize or blame anyone or any agency, regardless of the situation.

RELATED SCRIPTURE

Peace I leave with you; my peace I give you. I do not give to you as the world gives. Do not let your hearts be troubled and do not be afraid. I have told you these things, so that in me you may have peace. In this world you will have trouble. But take heart! I have overcome the world.
JOHN 14:27; 16:33, NIV

No, despite all these things, overwhelming victory is ours through Christ, who loved us. And I am convinced that nothing can ever separate us from his love. Death can't, and life can't. The angels can't, and the demons can't. Our fears for today, our worries about tomorrow, and even the powers of hell can't keep God's love away. Whether we are high above the sky or in the deepest ocean, nothing in all creation will ever be able to separate us from the love of God that is revealed in Christ Jesus our Lord. ROMANS 8:37-39, NLT

Stay away from the love of money; be satisfied with what you have. For God has said, "I will never fail you. I will never forsake you." That is why we can say with confidence, "The Lord is my helper, so I will not be afraid. What can mere mortals do to me?"
HEBREWS 13:5-6, NLT

I command you—be strong and courageous! Do not be afraid or discouraged. For the Lord your God is with you wherever you go.
JOSHUA 1:9, NLT

PRAYER

A prayer to share with your friend:
O God, Maker of all that is and all that shall be, Ruler of the universe, to you I commit my life and trust in you for all my needs.

I do not understand the reason for the disasters that befall humankind, nor do I need to. My intent is to fully trust and fully accept the gifts you give as necessary and beneficial for my eternal good. Teach me to be thankful even when my immediate reaction is fear and distrust. Help me to be strong in my faith, to ever seek your face, and in every circumstance to give thanks, as this is your holy will for my life.

Finally, Father God, bring me at last into your presence, where all will be known to me as it has been known to you from before the beginning of time. Amen.

A D D I T I O N A L   R E S O U R C E S

I Can't Get Over It by Aphrodite Matsakis (New Harbinger Publications, 1992). A good secular resource for trauma survivors.

When God Doesn't Make Sense by Dr. James Dobson (Tyndale House Publishers, 1993). A practical approach to those struggling with suffering.

In addition, most insurance companies and the American Red Cross publish a number of pamphlets that deal with the preparation for disasters and care of their victims. I strongly recommend these for much practical advice.

T I M O T H Y   W .   T H O M P S O N

Timothy W. Thompson, D.Min., has a dramatic ministry responding to emergency situations involving the dying, critically/terminally ill, victims of crime, and victims of natural disaster. He serves as a chaplain to the law enforcement community, local hospital, hospice, and California Army National Guard, where he was mobilized for the 1996 floods in California.

COMMUNITY
TRAGEDY
CAUSED BY CRIME

God is our refuge and strength, always ready to help
in times of trouble. So we will not fear, even if earthquakes come
and the mountains crumble into the sea.
Let the oceans roar and foam.
Let the mountains tremble as the waters surge!

PSALM 46:1-3, NLT

Have mercy on me, O God, have mercy!
I look to you for protection.
I will hide beneath the shadow of your wings
until this violent storm is past.

PSALM 57:1, NLT

There was a sound. Terry[1] was not sure whether she heard the sound or felt it. The clock hands pointed to 9:02 A.M. on this beautiful April morning in Oklahoma City in 1995. She was used to hearing the muffled boom from jets, but somehow this sound was different . . . a deafening blast . . . then silence. One hundred and sixty-eight friends, neighbors, and family members were killed in the Oklahoma City bombing. Life would never be the same again.

[1]Name has been changed to protect her privacy.

UNDERSTANDING THE CRISIS

Disasters and critical incidents occur on a random, arbitrary but continuing basis affecting communities throughout the United States. They come in the form of natural disasters, such as tornadoes, hurricanes, earthquakes, floods, fire, etc. Catastrophes also can be caused *directly* by individuals with criminal or purposefully cruel intent (terrorism, hostage taking, crime) or *indirectly* by accidents (plane crashes, road and train accidents, etc.). In addition, acts of violence against a few individuals in a community may cause the entire community to be in crisis, such as the case when a child is brutally murdered or a schoolteacher is gunned down by a student. For the purpose of this section, we will focus on community tragedies as caused by criminal acts.

EFFECTS OF THE CRISIS

In a community disaster, individuals may experience physical reactions of shock, disorientation, and numbness. Among all those impacted there can also be an emotional response of shock, disbelief, and denial. Shock is often accompanied by an overwhelming cataclysm of emotions, including anger or rage, fear or terror, frustration, confusion, guilt or self-blame, grief, or sorrow.[2] In addition to victims who personally are affected by the crisis, family members, neighbors, friends, rescue workers, and others may also experience physical and emotional reactions as well.

HOW YOU CAN HELP AND ENCOURAGE

In a disaster, the community experiences *shared* loss, devastation, destruction of property, place, and culture, as well as a questioning of values and faith. Some of the physical structures can be rebuilt and restored within a few months; however, the psychological and spiritual impact on the community may take years to fully address. Many find that life is

[2]"Responding to Communities in Crisis," copyright, 1994, National Organization for Victim Assistance, Washington, D.C., 1994, 2–7.

never again the same. In one shattering moment, people, places, community services—everything familiar—is gone without warning. It is at these critical moments that the church and caring individuals can provide needed assistance to help victims and communities recover after the crisis.

In assisting in a community tragedy, the primary goal is to provide safety and assistance to individuals and families. You may want to offer not only your services but those of your church to assist agencies and organizations, rescue workers, or family members. One major area in which the church can assist is to provide homes or church buildings as safe places for victims and their families. There are numerous other practical ways that you and your church can be of assistance: providing emergency food, clothing, child-care services, transportation, or property repair or replacement.

Those associated with the church may be called upon by victims, family members, and rescue workers to not only help with practical and emotional needs but to also address spiritual needs of the survivors. The following are suggestions on how to discuss spiritual issues with those who have experienced a disaster:

- Allow the victims to express their questions, concerns, and even anger at God. Survivors often look for "permission" to confront spiritual questions openly.
- Listen without judgment. In the days, weeks, and months after a crisis, the survivors need to turn to people of faith, who will listen carefully and without judgment.
- Affirm the wrongness or evil of what has happened. This is particularly important when the trauma has been caused by human cruelty or brutality.
- As appropriate, encourage the victims to talk about how their faith and belief may help them cope with what has happened.

In addition to addressing spiritual concerns and issues, you and your church can help in the recovery and healing after a community tragedy. Some specific suggestions include:

- Pray for the victims, their families, the rescue and support workers, and all those impacted by the disaster. You and your church can be of vital importance through intercessory prayer. You may want to encourage your church, Bible study, or prayer group to hold a special time of prayer for all those impacted by the disaster. (Be careful not to publicly announce any tragic news of which a family has not yet been informed.)
- Organize a special church service. It could be a service that provides support and encouragement for the survivors and their families or a memorial service for those whose lives were lost in the disaster. Such services bring the community together and allow for corporate prayer, expressions of shared loss and grief, and remembrance, which can help significantly in the healing process.
- Offer ongoing support groups for survivors and their families in the weeks, months, and even years after the crisis. These groups should be overseen by a professional counselor with experience in trauma and crisis counseling.

THE NEED TO PREPARE

The very nature of community tragedies implies that a community is taken by surprise. However, you and your church can take important steps to prepare to respond to a crisis if one occurs. In developing an effective response *before* a crisis, it is important to meet with representatives from surrounding communities' governments and social service relief organizations to establish a predisaster plan and to identify strong, well-organized leadership.

The following is a suggested outline for establishing your own church or community crisis response team and plan:

1. *Identify existing resources.* Research agencies and organizations that provide assistance in response to a community disaster. Determine if a community crisis-response plan is already in place. If it is, you may want

to learn about the plan and offer your services if needed. If there is no plan or crisis-response team, try to arrange to meet with established service organizations to determine what crisis-response assistance is available and what additional services need to be provided for a variety of possible disasters.

2. *Establish your team.* After identifying resources, establish a cohesive team that will oversee and carry out the plan and is representative of, and sensitive to, the economic, cultural, social, faith, and political groups and issues in your community.

3. *Develop your plan.* Once you've done your homework and your team is in place, develop your crisis-response plan for a variety of possible disasters, including designing services and identifying those responsible for providing the services.

4. *Train and prepare leaders and key volunteers.* After preparing the plan, designate and train leaders and key volunteers to carry out parts of the plan. You may want to stage a mock disaster situation to test the skills and readiness of the crisis-response team.

HELPFUL THINGS TO SAY AND DO

- "I am very sorry that this happened to you and to our community." Offer your condolences and express your concern for their well-being.
- "May I assist you by _____?" Provide specific suggestions on how you might be able to assist individuals.
- "May I pray with you or for you at this time?" Offer to pray with them or for them, if they are comfortable. Most people deeply appreciate the offer of prayer.

HURTFUL RESPONSES TO TRY TO AVOID

- "You should be glad that it wasn't worse."
- "This must be God's will." Rather, let them know that

God is present with them in their suffering and that he is the great Comforter and Provider in the midst of pain and tragedy.

RELATED SCRIPTURE

Who shall separate us from the love of Christ? Shall trouble or hardship or persecution or famine or nakedness or danger or sword? . . . No, in all these things we are more than conquerors through him who loved us. For I am convinced that neither death nor life, neither angels nor demons, neither the present nor the future, nor any powers, neither height nor depth, nor anything else in all creation, will be able to separate us from the love of God that is in Christ Jesus our Lord.
ROMANS 8:35-39, NIV

Have no fear of sudden disaster or of the ruin that overtakes the wicked, for the Lord will be your confidence and will keep your foot from being snared. PROVERBS 3:25-26, NIV

The days of the blameless are known to the Lord, and their inheritance will endure forever. In times of disaster they will not wither; in days of famine they will enjoy plenty.
PSALM 37:18-19, NIV

PRAYER

O Lord, we have experienced a great tragedy and wrong. We as a community are suffering and grieving over our pain and loss. Please help us. Please come and comfort us in our heartache and grief. Give us wisdom to know how to help one another through this crisis. Give us strength to do the practical things that are necessary. Give us discernment to help each other in our personal and corporate suffering. Give us renewed faith to trust in you. And give us hope that we may be vessels of your goodness and mercy as we wait upon you. Amen.

ADDITIONAL RESOURCES

Critical Incident Stress and Trauma in the Workplace: Recognition, Response, Recovery by Gerald W. Lewis., Ph.D. (Accelerated Development, Inc., 1994). This book provides a comprehensive understanding of physiological and psychological reactions to stress; how to provide assistance to families and organizations.

Critical Incident Stress Debriefing (CISD): An Operations Manual for the Prevention of Traumatic Stress among Emergency Services and Disaster Workers by J. T. Mitchell and G. S. Everly (Chevron Publishing Corporation, 1993).

Note: Many thanks to the National Organization for Victim Assistance (NOVA) for their excellent materials and training on community crisis-response teams, from which material for this section was taken. For more information on setting up your own community crisis-response team, contact NOVA at (202) 232-6682 or write:

NOVA
1757 Park Road, NW
Washington, DC 20010

MELISSA SLAGLE

Melissa Slagle, MSSW, is the founder and CEO of Living Solution Christian Counseling in Tulsa, Oklahoma. She is a licensed clinical social worker, marriage and family therapist, and a certified trauma specialist.

LISA BARNES LAMPMAN

Lisa Barnes Lampman serves as the president and CEO of Neighbors Who Care (NWC), a nonprofit organization committed to mobilizing and equipping local churches to provide practical and spiritual assistance to victims of crime. NWC is the crime victim assistance ministry of Prison Fellowship Ministries.

WHEN THEY'RE HURTING THEMSELVES

Substance
Abuse

Save me, O God, for the floodwaters are up to my neck.
Deeper and deeper I sink into the mire;
I can't find a foothold to stand on.
I am in deep water, and the floods overwhelm me.
I am suffering and in pain.
Rescue me, O God, by your saving power.

PSALM 69:1-2, 29, NLT

I'm in despair. . . . I've been through this so many times
. . . depressed . . . spent a lot of time in prayer. I feel so
ashamed, I know I shouldn't be doing this, but I've tried
everything I know. I spend a lot of time in prayer."
❑ *A substance abuser*

Effects of the Crisis

An individual who is actively abusing drugs or alcohol is often
not aware of the problem or denies the problem. These individuals are highly given to denying any problems resulting
from their use. The pleasure and/or relief felt when a person
is intoxicated becomes a powerful motivator to use chemicals
repeatedly or habitually. It is important to recognize that most
serious abusers are filled with guilt and shame following the
return to a sober condition and are afraid and very defensive

that others will pressure them to give up their "best friend." Significant abusers have developed a personal relationship with their chemicals; they have become best friends.

UNDERSTANDING THE CRISIS

Substance abuse is a term normally used to refer to a condition in which chemical agents, either legal or illicit, have been consumed to such a degree that the individual's life has been negatively affected, in some significant way, by the use of the chemicals.

HOW YOU CAN HELP AND ENCOURAGE

Substance abuse is so destructive and yet so subtle in its progression that it is often only the family members or significant others who first recognize and feel the pain of the losses they have incurred.

As crises happen in the abuser's life, friends and family members are provided with an opportunity to demonstrate "tough love." An alcoholic and addict, however, has ultrasensitive antennae for detecting unloving and condemning actions directed toward him or her. If you are a family or close friend, it is important to evaluate your motivation. Discuss your hurt and anger toward this person by talking to another close and mature friend. Ensure that your interaction is not based on retaliation, bitterness, or selfish purposes alone.

While you need to be absolutely clear, both in your own mind and in your communication with the abuser, concerning his or her need to stop using the drug(s) or alcohol, you also need to communicate your love and concern for the person's well-being. If you cannot come to this position, you will not be able to successfully intervene and give your support.

The substance abuser may believe that he or she cannot expect to be treated with respect by others. In order to be as tough as we need to be, we must first be clear in our love and concern for the abuser.

A scriptural principle that is well-recognized but difficult to apply is that of being direct and honest about your feelings and observations (Ephesians 4:15). Relate these clearly, describing how this person's alcohol/drug use has negatively affected you. Share your fears, worries, anger, and how it affects your ability to relate positively to him or her. In the case of an adolescent abuser, it is always helpful, if not necessary, to have specific evidence that objectifies your fears concerning his or her use. Be firm and clear in explaining what specific behavioral response you expect from the adolescent in changing his or her use. If he or she does not begin to make changes, you may need to further clarify how you must change your behavior with the abuser in order to protect yourself emotionally and/or physically.

Confronting the substance abuse of a family member can be a very difficult process for the members of the family. If you are assisting or counseling with the family, remember that these loved ones need a great deal of encouragement and support since they may tend to fear they are exacerbating the problem by talking openly about it. Praying with them, listening to them process their feelings, and keeping them focused will help them stick with what needs to be done.

HELPFUL THINGS TO SAY AND DO

- Encourage the substance abuser to talk honestly with family members and close friends about the reality of the situation and to seek help from a pastor or counselor.
- Validate the feelings and experiences of family members. Have them write down how the abuser has hurt, embarrassed, or disappointed them because of his or her alcohol/drug use.
- Encourage family and friends not to overreact with punishing demands out of anger, but rather with firm limits out of love.
- "I know something of what you're experiencing; my _____ has a substance abuse problem too" (if applicable).

HURTFUL RESPONSES TO TRY TO AVOID

- Your own alcohol/drug use as you deal with the abusing loved one.
- Blaming yourself for the problem.
- Believing that keeping quiet is the best approach (or at least will not make things worse).
- Believing that, "I must have failed [as a spouse, parent, child, friend]."

RELATED SCRIPTURE

Therefore each of you must put off falsehood and speak truthfully to his neighbor, for we are all members of one body. "In your anger do not sin." EPHESIANS 4:25-26, NIV

Don't be drunk with wine, because that will ruin your life. Instead, let the Holy Spirit fill and control you. EPHESIANS 5:18, NLT

So I say, live by the Spirit, and you will not gratify the desires of the sinful nature. GALATIANS 5:16, NIV

A new command I give you: Love one another. As I have loved you, so you must love one another. JOHN 13:34, NIV

You may say, "I am allowed to do anything." But I reply, "Not everything is good for you." And even though "I am allowed to do anything," I must not become a slave to anything.
1 CORINTHIANS 6:12, NLT

Or don't you know that your body is the temple of the Holy Spirit, who lives in you and was given to you by God? You do not belong to yourself, for God bought you with a high price. So you must honor God with your body. 1 CORINTHIANS 6:19-20, NLT

PRAYER

Dear Father, we pray that you will deliver _____ from the clutches of substance abuse. Lord, help _____ to realize that you will provide

him/her with the strength needed to defeat this habit. _____ has been created in your image; make him/her realize this high calling.

We also pray for those who love and care for _____. Give them patience, love, and wisdom as they decide how to encourage _____ and love him/her as you would have them love. Father, they have been hurt. Wrap your loving arms around them and give them peace.

Help us all through the power of the Holy Spirit. Amen.

ADDITIONAL RESOURCES

Good News for the Chemically Dependent and Those Who Love Them by J. VanVonderen (Bethany House Publishers, 1991). More complete presentation of chemical dependence and how families and loved ones can deal with that effectively.

Codependent No More: How to Stop Controlling Others & Start Caring for Yourself by Melody Beattie (Hazelden Foundation, 1987). Explains and encourages the setting of appropriate limits and boundaries with alcohol abusers.

Caring Enough to Confront by David Augsburger (Regal Books, 1981). Encourages effective and caring confrontation in relationships.

Forgive and Forget by Lewis Smedes (HarperSanFrancisco, 1984). Helps the reader understand what true forgiveness is and what it is not. Explains how to deal with the wounds of the past.

Life Recovery Bible edited by David Stoop and Stephen Arterburn (Tyndale House Publishers, 1992). This Bible has help notes and commentary for persons in, or seeking to be in, recovery.

Many people find support groups to be especially helpful when dealing with a substance abuse problem. The following organizations offer support groups around the country:

- Alcoholics Anonymous (look in your local directory)
- Narcotics Anonymous 1-800-333-1235
- Cocaine Anonymous 1-800-333-1518
- Al-Alon for families of alcoholics (look in your local directory)

THOMAS GILL

Thomas Gill, his wife, Denise, and two daughters live in Wheaton, Illinois, where he maintains a private counseling practice as a licensed professional counselor working with substance abusers and individuals facing other problems, specializing in ministry to churches, denominations, and mission boards through counseling, seminars, and consultation. Tom is a graduate of Moody Bible Institute and Wheaton College Graduate School. He and Denise have served in Nigeria with Sudan Interior Mission.

A REBELLIOUS
TEENAGER

*A rebellious son is a grief to his father and
a bitter blow to his mother."*

PROVERBS 17:25, TLB

When my son was arrested and jailed for possession of drugs, I was angry at him and also at the police for not letting me talk to him. I swore and cried and prayed to God. Finally, we got him out of jail. When he came home, I hugged him and told him I loved him but I also said that he would have to get a part-time job to pay off the fine. It took him almost a year."

❑ *Father of teenage boy arrested for drug possession*

EFFECTS OF THE CRISIS

One of the most difficult and frustrating experiences for parents is to feel that a teenage son or daughter is rebelling against them and what they know is best. Whether this is an incident of rebellion, an extended period of rebellion, or participation in a rebellious lifestyle that rejects the parents' cherished values, they may feel either anger or despair or even like a failure as parents, asking themselves, "What have we done wrong?" In a two-parent family, the parents may blame each other for the teenager's rebellious attitude or behavior.

UNDERSTANDING THE CRISIS

Teenage conflict with parents and other authority figures is not uncommon and, by itself, does not indicate mental illness. In some complex cases, psychological review may diagnose such related problems as attention deficit disorder, opposition disorder, conduct disorder, or identity disorder.

HOW YOU CAN HELP AND ENCOURAGE

The various forms of teenage rebellion may trigger different reactions on the part of parents. They may blame themselves, blame each other, or blame their teenager and deny any parental responsibility.

If you are in a helping/counseling situation with the parents, it is important at first to neither agree nor disagree with the way the parents present the situation to you. Just listen and allow them to feel whatever they are feeling at the moment. As you listen to the causes of their anguish, the story will unfold, and you will begin to understand what they are concerned about.

Some frightened or rigid parents may be very emotional over a one-time incident of childish irresponsibility. They will need your friendship, care, and some contact with other parents to put this in perspective so that they can react rationally to the needs their child has for love and guidance and the careful setting of limits for future behavior.

Other parents may be dealing with a teen with an extended period of rebellious attitudes, emotions, or behaviors following a forced adjustment, such as a move to a new home or school, adaptation to a divorce or to a new stepparent, change in a parent's job or income, etc. As you listen, you may find that the parents' own sense of "guilt" or "responsibility" makes it difficult for them to hear their teen's feelings and establish clear rules about acceptable and unacceptable ways to express negative emotions. Your recommendation of a good family counselor may help the various members of a family in transi-

tion to contract with each other for the positive rewards for
behaviors that are expected and the agreed-upon negative
consequences for those actions and attitudes that are hurting
the teenager and the family.

Certain parents dealing with a teenager engaged in an
ongoing lifestyle of rebellion, such as sexual promiscuity,
repeated theft, ongoing alcohol or drug abuse, violence,
repeated truancy from school, or criminal activity leading
to arrest, may find themselves experiencing episodes of irrational anger, desperate despair, or uncontrollable emotional
anguish due to their inability to control their teen. One support
you can provide for the parents is to encourage them to participate in parent support groups, where they can discuss these
issues with other parents experiencing similar difficulties and
struggling with the necessity for parental "tough love."

Some teens caught up in severely rebellious lifestyles will
benefit from placement in specific Christian residential programs, such as those operated by Teen Challenge, the Institute of Basic Youth Conflicts, Victory Outreach, The Salvation
Army, New Hope Treatment Centers, and others. Often, such
a placement can be made in cooperation with the court, as an
alternative to incarceration. Parents should not be made to
feel guilty or inadequate when such a residential placement is
appropriate, but they should be helped to understand that
they are doing what they believe is best for their child.

You can be of specific help to these parents by making it
your business to get acquainted with the Christian residential
facilities available to teenagers in your area.

If you are able to have a number of meetings with the
parent(s) and the teenager involved, you may want to observe
whether the teenager seems to have *no personal control* over his
or her behavior, *limited personal control,* or *intact personal control.*
This will affect the counsel you provide to the parent(s).

The teen with *no personal control* has little or no sense of
cause and effect. He or she claims or appears to be controlled by drugs, alcohol, sex, demons, or voices, etc. If not

already arrested and placed in a detention facility, this child will probably require some form of residential rehabilitation as described above. Parents usually cannot solve the problems of this type of child on an "at home" basis.

Give the parents permission to remove themselves from the "fight" between this teen and their various authority figures, such as school, police, etc., but encourage them to continue to provide love at times when the teen will accept it.

The teen with *limited personal control* is able to respond appropriately to short-term rewards and punishments. He or she complies with positive authority figures (parents, teachers) when present but also responds to negative authority figures (peer influence, gang leaders) in other settings. This child's parents need help to develop a home environment with clear communication, consistent love and discipline, strong spiritual values, short time lines for duties and chores (which are then inspected), and regular (weekly or even daily) written communications between parents, teachers, and other adult leaders (youth pastors, etc.). Unsupervised free time for this child should be limited, except at home with a responsible adult in the house or apartment.

The teen with *intact personal control* will exhibit good internalized values, a healthy sense of shame and guilt, and a basically positive sense of self-esteem but with one or more wrong life choices or rebellious behaviors—possibly including rude speech toward parents. You will want to encourage the parent(s) of this teen to participate with the child in personal Scripture study, have the child become involved on a regular basis with a Christian youth group, set up a regular schedule of positive parent-child activities, create clear family guidelines about positive behaviors that are privileges (auto use, allowance) and points toward valued items, and negative behaviors, which are punished by specific restrictions (curfew, adult supervision requirements).

Physical punishment (spanking, hitting, etc.) of teenagers by parents is never appropriate.

Remember that the rules and procedures that will work for this family may be different from those that work for you and your family. Encourage them when they succeed, and lift them up when they fail.

HELPFUL THINGS TO SAY AND DO

- "I accept your feelings."
- "My teen also has experienced some rebellion" (if true).
- "He [or she] will always be your son [or daughter]."
- "Let's pray together for wisdom."
- "There is always hope."

HURTFUL RESPONSES TO TRY TO AVOID

- "You're right and your spouse is wrong."
- "If only you had done _____ differently!"
- "What your teenager has done cannot be forgiven."
- "Don't tell anyone else about this."
- "Don't feel that way."

RELATED SCRIPTURE

Children, obey your parents because you belong to the Lord, for this is the right thing to do. EPHESIANS 6:1, NLT

And this is the promise: If you honor your father and mother, "you will live a long life, full of blessing." EPHESIANS 6:3, NLT

And now a word to you fathers. Don't make your children angry by the way you treat them. Rather, bring them up with the discipline and instruction approved by the Lord. EPHESIANS 6:4, NLT

Patience can persuade a prince, and soft speech can crush strong opposition. PROVERBS 25:15, NLT

For I can do everything with the help of Christ who gives me the strength I need. PHILIPPIANS 4:13, NLT

Give all your worries and cares to God, for he cares about what happens to you. 1 PETER 5:7, NLT

PRAYER

A prayer to share with your friend:
Lord, we want so much for our children to grow up healthy and holy and doing the right thing. Our hearts are torn apart by pain when our children are in rebellion or in trouble of any kind. We feel so inadequate to the task of parenting, O Lord, but we know we can do all the things that are necessary, because you strengthen us and give us fresh wisdom every day, through Jesus Christ our Lord. Amen

---

ADDITIONAL RESOURCES

Helping Teens in Crisis by Miriam Neff (Tyndale House Publishers, 1993). An experienced high school counselor explores serious issues that teens face daily. Parents anticipating or facing a crisis in their teen's life will learn how to prevent problems and how to intervene if they occur.

The New Dare to Discipline by James Dobson (Tyndale House Publishers, 1992). A classic Christian book on child rearing and discipline, recently updated.

High-Maintenance Relationships by Les Parrott, Ph.D. (Tyndale House Publishers, 1996). A new book about the differences in personalities that teaches how to set boundaries, avoid power struggles, and say no without feeling guilty.

Becoming Your Own Best Friend by Thomas A. Whiteman, Ph.D., and Randy Peterson (Thomas Nelson Publishers, 1994). An excellent book on Christian self-development; helpful for both parents and teens.

Parents in Pain by John White (InterVarsity, 1979). This book offers comfort for parents of children with severe problems, such as alcoholism or homosexuality. It includes practical suggestions for coping, and helps parents deal with guilt, anger, frustration, and inadequacy.

JOHN R. CHEYDLEUR

John R. Cheydleur, Ph.D., is a psychologist who is also a Salvation Army captain. He is the author of *How to Find and Be Yourself* and *Every Sober Day Is a Miracle!*

EATING
DISORDERS

O my people, trust in him at all times.
Pour out your heart to him, for God is our refuge.

PSALM 62:8, NLT

W hat I do is so disgusting! People would be repulsed
by me if they knew what I did."
❑ *Young woman struggling with bulimia*

"In the grips of anorexia I withdrew from meaningful relationships with people, and my focus became controlling my food
intake. It was the one thing I could do better than almost
anyone. It gave me a sense of identity."
❑ *Recovered anorexic*

UNDERSTANDING THE CRISIS

There are two types of eating disorders:

1) Anorexia nervosa: Intense fear of weight and fat; distorted view of one's own body, "feeling fat" even when underweight; absence of at least three consecutive menstrual cycles;
at least 15 percent below normal body weight; preoccupied
with food and weight many hours each day.

2) Bulimia nervosa: Recurring episodes of eating a large
amount of food within a discrete period of time; feeling out of

control of the binging; use of vomiting, laxative, or diuretic abuse; excessive dieting or vigorous exercise to prevent weight gain; overconcern with body shape and weight.

EFFECTS OF THE CRISIS

Those who struggle with anorexia or bulimia are generally unable to truly pour out their hearts to God or to others, despite the intense underlying pain they may be experiencing. In the midst of the anorexic or bulimic struggle, these individuals often have extreme difficulty talking about how they are feeling, even when asked. Some common feelings that are often experienced, but remain unspoken, include fear of being imperfect, fear of feelings that seem unacceptable (anger or disappointment), fear of disappointing others (family and/or God), and fear they will not be truly accepted as they are.

In the moment of crisis the eating-disordered individual is eager to find someone who will hear her,[1] without attempting to control the eating behavior or to change her. Despite how illogical it may seem to an outsider, these individuals are often attempting to create a sense of identity or personal competence by controlling their weight. Eating disorders are a symptom of significant underlying difficulties of emotion and self-esteem.

HOW YOU CAN HELP AND ENCOURAGE

When any caring person becomes aware that someone he or she knows may have an eating disorder, a natural response is to try to get involved—helping the individual eat more or attempting to monitor or control binging and purging. Ironically, getting involved in monitoring another person's food consumption often leads to unhelpful power struggles. These interventions don't address the underlying problems that cause the disorder and, in fact, can sometimes make the symptoms worse.

[1]The feminine pronoun is chosen because most eating disorders are found in girls and women. Please note, however, that up to 10 percent of the eating disorder population may be men.

Interestingly, the most helpful way to approach someone with an eating disorder is to first recognize your own limitations in fixing this problem. Remember that eating disorders represent serious psychological problems. Anorexia and bulimia are, in fact, two of the most life-threatening of all psychiatric illnesses. Studies indicate that the fatality rate for anorexia is between 5 and 20 percent. While there are fewer studies of bulimia, it is generally acknowledged that the risk of suicide is greater, due to overwhelming feelings of despair. The longer eating disorders go on, the more chronic they become and the more the fatality rate increases. In most cases, the intervention of professionals is required to make a significant difference in recovery. Professional help will also ease the burden that friends and family typically feel as they confront the disorder. If you have time to plan your conversation, you can prepare in the following ways.

Decide who is the best person to confront the behavior. Initial confrontations are best done by someone the individual feels is caring, concerned, and on her side. Sometimes further confrontation is required if the individual refuses to get a special evaluation or if she refuses treatment when the evaluation indicates that treatment is necessary. In that case, it can be helpful to enlist the person with the most leverage. This may be a parent, school counselor, spouse, or minister. If the individual is teen- or college-age, leverage is gained by telling the individual that she will have to choose between treatment and a desired privilege (participation in track, ballet, outings with friends). Always use whatever leverage you have with the same goal in mind— getting the person to agree to receive a professional evaluation and/or treatment with an eating disorder specialist.

Review the following checklist of behaviors which can be symptoms of eating disorders, and write down observed behaviors if necessary. Talk with the individual about the specific behaviors you have observed or that others have told you about. Keep coming back to your deep concern about these behavioral observations. Eating-disordered individuals will work hard to get you to join them in their fantasy that they are fine and that the situation is under control.

For anorexia:
- Preoccupation with food and weight
- Perfectionistic and/or excessive exercise
- Low food intake or only eats "healthy," very low fat foods
- Menstruation has ceased to be regular
- Complains of "feeling fat" even when underweight; distorted view of body
- Complains of always feeling cold
- Uncomfortable around food and restaurants
- Dizziness, fainting, or irregular breathing
- Occasional hair loss and the growth of fine new hair on the body
- Increased isolation; prefers being alone

For bulimia:
- Eating large amounts of food in a short time
- Using bathrooms after meals to vomit
- Use of laxatives or diuretics
- Intense episodes of dieting and exercise to prevent weight gain
- Self-worth and mood determined by weight
- Frequent weight fluctuations
- Puffy cheeks and/or sore throat
- Finger calluses from purging
- Bloodshot or dark-circled eyes
- Other observable impulsive behaviors—e.g. substance use, excessive spending
- Menstrual irregularities

In some situations, where there is concern about death or other serious medical complications, consider taking the individual to a specialist or hospital immediately. An eating-disordered individual's personal judgment can be seriously impaired by the side effects of the disorder.

HELPFUL THINGS TO SAY AND DO

- Choose a time to talk with the individual in crisis when you are calm and rational, not angry.
- Remember that your primary crisis intervention is connecting the person with specialized medical and psychological help.
- "I've been worried about you lately and I haven't known whether to approach you, but I'm too concerned not to say anything."
- "I really respect your courage in talking about this. I know many people like to keep their eating-disorder behavior a secret."
- Close the conversation with a statement about what you will do next; i.e., "I'll check back with you in a week to see what you are thinking about treatment" or "I'm going to see what professional resources are available."

HURTFUL RESPONSES TO TRY TO AVOID

- Don't make blaming statements, such as, "Don't you see how much this is hurting others?" or "You could eat differently if you put your mind to it . . . you just don't want to."
- Don't say, "If you will be accountable to me, I can help you get through your problem by monitoring your eating." Do not agree to monitor someone's eating behavior or weight, even if invited.
- Don't make promises to keep the eating disorder a secret. Outside intervention and family involvement are generally necessary for recovery.
- Don't try to talk the person out of her feelings by making a case for why she "shouldn't" feel that way, such as, "You

say you feel lonely . . . but you shouldn't feel that way because you're not alone."

RELATED SCRIPTURE

Then Jesus said, "Come to me, all of you who are weary and carry heavy burdens, and I will give you rest. Take my yoke upon you. Let me teach you, because I am humble and gentle, and you will find rest for your souls. For my yoke fits perfectly, and the burden I give you is light." MATTHEW 11:28-30, NLT

You may say, "I am allowed to do anything." But I reply, "Not everything is good for you." And even though "I am allowed to do anything," I must not become a slave to anything.
1 CORINTHIANS 6:12, NLT

Or don't you know that your body is the temple of the Holy Spirit, who lives in you and was given to you by God? You do not belong to yourself, for God bought you with a high price. So you must honor God with your body. 1 CORINTHIANS 6:19-20, NLT

But remember that the temptations that come into your life are no different from what others experience. And God is faithful. He will keep the temptation from becoming so strong that you can't stand up against it. When you are tempted, he will show you a way out so that you will not give in to it. 1 CORINTHIANS 10:13, NLT

They promise freedom, but they themselves are slaves to sin and corruption. For you are a slave to whatever controls you.
2 PETER 2:19, NLT

PRAYER

Lord, I place in your hands this person I care about who may have an eating disorder. For myself I ask you for wisdom in interacting with her and that you lead us to appropriate help and resources, if needed. Help me to be patient as I watch her heal one step at a time.

I ask that you help my friend/daughter/sister to face the problem squarely and without shame. Give her as many people as she needs for

support as she begins to risk pouring out the pain of her heart. Give her hope when change seems impossible. Let her know that others care and that you abide with her always. Amen.

ADDITIONAL RESOURCES

Surviving an Eating Disorder: Strategies for Family and Friends by M. Siegel, J. Brisman, and M. Weinshel (Harper Perennial, 1988). To family and friends: If you only read one book, we recommend this one! Clear, concise suggestions for all phases of anorexia and bulimia.

The Best Little Girl in the World by S. Levenkron (Warner Books, 1981). Very readable, fictional account of a young woman's struggle with anorexia and the beginning of recovery.

Looking Good, Feeling Bad by M. Mayo (Servant Press, 1992). A Christian author addresses the range of eating disorders in women—from issues of negative body image to serious anorexia and bulimia nervosa.

National Association of Anorexia Nervosa and Associated Disorders (ANAD). P.O. Box 7, Highland Park, IL 60035; (847) 831-3438. National information and referral organization. Able to assist with referrals to eating disorder groups and treatment providers.

ANNE KELLSTEDT RAMIREZ

Anne Kellstedt Ramirez received her master's degree in counseling psychology from Illinois Benedictine University. Currently she works as a counselor at the Wheaton College Counseling Center and in private practice. She enjoys working with eating disorders, self-esteem problems, and improving intimacy and relational skills.

KELLEEN WILLIAMSEN

Kelleen Williamsen graduated from the Wheaton College Graduate School in 1988 with an M.A. in clinical psychology. Her work experience includes nine years at Wheaton College, where she is currently the associate director of counseling as well as counseling in private practice. As a therapist she specializes in eating disorders, sexual identity, and women's issues.

TEEN PREGNANCY

And we know that God causes everything to work together
for the good of those who love God and are called
according to his purpose for them. . . .
And I am convinced that nothing can ever separate us
from his love. Death can't, and life can't.
The angels can't, and the demons can't.
Our fears for today, our worries about tomorrow,
and even the powers of hell can't keep God's love away.

ROMANS 8:28, 38, NLT

I couldn't believe it when I found out that I was pregnant—I only had sex twice, and I just never really thought about that happening. I went to a ladies' clinic for a free test, and the woman wanted me to have an abortion. She said I shouldn't even tell my parents—that I shouldn't worry them with my problem. When I told my boyfriend, he said I had to have an abortion—that I could ruin his life if I didn't. I thought he loved me, that he'd always be there for me, but I never heard from him again. I knew that I would never kill my baby, though, no matter who said I should. I am so glad I made that decision. Things are not easy, being a single mom, but we *are* going to make it."

❏ *Eighteen-year-old single mother*

EFFECTS OF THE CRISIS

When a young, unmarried woman learns she is pregnant, the emotional overload is enormous. She must confront the baby's father: If he turns his back on her (or the pregnancy), she is likely to be devastated. She must face her parents: If they are not supportive, her self-esteem is further damaged, and she is even more alone. So, then, she must face the church and society. This is where we may have an opportunity to help her not only survive but triumph in her situation. This is an opportunity to give her love and affirmation and support—and the good news that God is willing and more than able to redeem any situation that we bring to him.

HOW YOU CAN HELP AND ENCOURAGE

Today, when a young woman seeks counseling because she has chosen to give birth to an inconvenient, unplanned child rather than to opt for the supposedly "sensible" alternative of abortion, there is a great deal to be thankful for. First, praise her—for her character and for her courage. It is a mature choice to make this decision in a society that often scorns godly behavior in favor of "political correctness." So, let the young woman know in no uncertain terms that you admire her for choosing to let her baby live.

Second, if she communicates any feelings of guilt, assure her that God wants nothing more than to forgive the mistakes in our life—sexual or otherwise. All we need to do is ask. Remind her that we all make mistakes and wander away from God's laws. Read Romans 8:28 and 8:38, and suggest that she might want to write down some Scriptures that deal with God's presence and his power.

Third, while you applaud her decision to have the baby, keep in mind that she may be undecided as yet about whether to accept a mother's role. She may be thinking of giving her baby up for adoption. Try to be as open-minded as possible while pointing out the pros and cons of each choice. Be very careful not to use guilt or to manipulate her to give up her baby solely because of youth and inexperience. Youth is a great source of strength, and we are all inexperienced as parents when we begin. This ultimately must be her decision because she will live with it for the rest of her life. There are times when either of these decisions could be the right one for both mother and baby.

Help her find whatever support that may be available from family and friends. Guide her toward a church family that will be loving and supportive (and to appropriate government help if she needs it). Remember, pregnancy is a frightening time to be alone. Also, be aware that she may be considering whether or not to involve the child's father from this point forward. Again, this must ultimately be her call. He may have been abusive and/or a forceful proponent of abortion (which is often the case). Or, he may be married to someone else. Sometimes the only real choice is to sever all ties. Be sensitive that it may be extremely painful for her to admit negative things about him— she may still have deep feelings—healthy or not.

Try to end each time you have together on a positive note, *if possible,* with one or more of the following topics. Again, commend her choice—for life. Remind her that many of life's greatest rewards come from overcoming difficulties and meeting challenges head-on. Assure her that God will honor her because she has honored him with her decision. Finally, ask her if she would like you to pray with her for God's help and his blessing on her life.

HELPFUL THINGS TO SAY AND DO

- Encourage immediate appropiate medical attention for an expectant mother. Suggest appropiate government programs, such as WIC (Aid to Women and Infant Children) or MPW (Medicaid for Pregnant Women).
- Ask if she needs help facing her parents or the child's father.
- Look for a possible friend/mentor who has been in the same situation and who would have positive input. (This can be more helpful than almost anything else.)

- Tell her that you are proud of her, that you believe in her, and that you know she has what it takes to make it through this.
- Provide financial counseling, assistance in completing her education or developing job skills as appropriate.

HURTFUL RESPONSES TO TRY TO AVOID

- Being judgmental, overly religious, or disapproving—she doesn't need that.
- "Talking down"—she probably won't respond well to being treated like a child.
- Asking questions such as, "Weren't you aware that you could get pregnant?"
- Pushing her toward the father at all costs—remaining single is better than a bad marriage, or
- Putting down the father—it could drive her back to him.
- Pushing for or against adoption.

RELATED SCRIPTURE

I prayed to the Lord, and he answered me, freeing me from all my fears. Those who look to him for help will be radiant with joy; no shadow of shame will darken their faces. I cried out to the Lord in my suffering, and he heard me. He set me free from all my fears.
PSALM 34:4-6, NLT

He has not punished us for all our sins, nor does he deal with us as we deserve. For his unfailing love toward those who fear him is as great as the height of the heavens above the earth. He has removed our rebellious acts as far away from us as the east is from the west.
PSALM 103:10-12, NLT

Don't be afraid, for I am with you. Do not be dismayed, for I am your God. I will strengthen you. I will help you. I will uphold you with my victorious right hand. ISAIAH 41:10, NLT

I—yes, I alone—am the one who blots out your sins for my own sake and will never think of them again. ISAIAH 43:25, NLT

Jesus said to the people, "I am the light of the world. If you follow me, you won't be stumbling through the darkness, because you will have the light that leads to life." J O H N 8 : 1 2 , N L T

PRAYER

A prayer to share with your friend:

Lord, your Word assures me that you will never leave me or forsake me and that you will give me strength and joy in the midst of my trials. Teach me to trust you, Lord, for myself and for my child. Let me stay close to you now, and show me your power. Thank you for providing for my needs and for sending people into my life with wisdom, godly love, and emotional support. Remove from me all fear, bitterness, and self-pity, giving me instead peace, forgiveness, and joy.

Finally, Lord, thank you for using me as a light and an encouragement to others in this earthly journey and for taking me home with you when this journey ends. Amen.

ADDITIONAL RESOURCES

Mayo Clinic Book of Pregnancy & Baby's First Year by The Mayo Foundation for Medical Education and Research (William Morrow and Company, Inc., 1994). This secular resource is an excellent clinical guide to a well-informed pregnancy and to early childhood development.

Daddy, I'm Pregnant by Bill Putnam (Questar Publishers, Inc., 1988). A Christian father reflects on his teenage daughter's pregnancy.

Pregnant and Alone: How You Can Help an Unwed Friend by Henrietta VanDerMolen (Harold Shaw Publishers, 1989). A Scripture-based guide to helping a woman who is pregnant and unwed.

CELINE WOOD MEADOR

Author and speaker Celine Wood Meador has been involved in various aspects of lay counseling for fifteen years. She resides in Charlotte, North Carolina, with her husband, Aubrey, and daughter, Reed. Interestingly, Celine became a Christian in 1976 while living in the Cayman Islands—primarily through the influence of Chuck Colson's book *Born Again.*

WHEN JOB AND FINANCES ARE LOST

FINANCIAL LOSS

"So I tell you, don't worry about everyday life—
whether you have enough food, drink, and clothes.
Doesn't life consist of more than food and clothing?
Look at the birds. They don't need to plant or harvest
or put food in barns because your heavenly Father feeds them.
And you are far more valuable to him than they are."

MATTHEW 6:25-26, NLT

When I lost my business and my new home, several of my friends, even at church, accused me of being worldly in wanting too much, desiring the biggest and the best. They seemed to be questioning my sensitivity and obedience to the Lord. I felt people were talking behind my back. No one knew what to say so no one said anything."

❑ *Man who experienced a major financial loss*

EFFECTS OF THE CRISIS

Financial losses have significant impact on the emotional and spiritual life of an individual or family in addition to the economic hardship. Financial loss can result in feelings of anger or fear as well as loss of self-esteem and self-confidence. Perhaps the most common emotional reaction may be that of second-guessing or questioning yourself and your actions.

Often people begin asking, "What if I had only . . . ?" Frequently the immediate response is fear based on the anticipated repercussions or consequences of the loss of finances. Many people begin to ask and fear, "What will I [we] do now?"

UNDERSTANDING THE CRISIS

Financial loss, whether the result of investments/market changes, business/employment changes, poor decisions, illnesses, or illegal actions taken against you (robbery, fraud, embezzlement, etc.) is only significant if the finances were considered and thought to be essential or critical to the individual's present or future well-being.

HOW YOU CAN HELP AND ENCOURAGE

Financial loss, surprisingly, is oftentimes something that is not immediately obvious to others. Many people may at least initially believe they must keep their loss quiet and to themselves. As a result, the person with a heart and mind to support their friends and loved ones in this type of situation must exhibit great sensitivity to his or her friends. We must be actively looking for areas of need and emotional, spiritual, and material changes in those significant people God has placed in our "sphere of influence." This mind-set is essential in effectively meeting the needs existing in financial loss.

Many of us may need to deal with the covert belief that if someone has lost money through investments gone bad or something other than being robbed, the individual is "responsible" for the loss and perhaps "should have known better." While this is sometimes an accurate belief, it is more often irrational and a barrier to any meaningful support that could be offered.

When financial loss is precipitated by robbery or other traumatic, felonious, or hostile action, the victim is often left feeling vulnerable and at risk. It is quite normal for people to experience intense levels of shock, anxiety, denial, guilt, anger, shame, and grief during the phase of recovery from the loss. Comparison to others is usually not helpful during the process and may even result in establishing unrealistic expectations that lead to the victim feeling more discouragement and despair. As soon as possible after a traumatic event leading to loss, it is imperative the victim be able to talk about the trauma in detail and in a supportive context. This talking can be encouraged by the simple question "How are you doing with this?"

There may be a common reaction by victims of questioning themselves as to what they had done wrong. At these times, it is often best to initially allow individuals to express themselves and support them in their sense of guilt or shame. It is not helpful to dispute their feelings of causing the loss, especially since in some cases that may be true. Rather, support them by reassuring them of your concern and understanding.

As time goes on, being able to more objectively evaluate the loss and its causes and implications can be very helpful in assisting individuals in regaining a sense of stability, safety, and hope for the future.

Financial loss is not something that should be kept secret and hidden from a spouse. Sharing the burden of loss is important and allows the individual to share the hope of re-establishing stability in the future. Learning to grieve the loss together enables a couple to learn the joy of resting in the peace of acceptance.

When financial loss is experienced as a trauma, it is usually the result of the belief that those funds were necessary and essential to an individual's or family's well-being in the future (near or distant). As friends, then, we have an opportunity to encourage individuals to refocus their dependence upon the eternal and all-powerful God. This overwhelming loss can be reframed in our conversation and thinking and be reexperienced by the individuals as a gift, since it is now God, not the individuals or their own financial ability, who will provide "everything we need for life and godliness." God often provides the needs of his people through the caring acts of others. As friends of individuals who through financial loss may be questioning that, we have the opportunity to remind them of that truth by word and deed.

A group of friends, a Sunday school class, or the church body can help answer financial needs temporarily by giving financial and/or material gifts. Remember to maintain your interest and active concern over the longer term and not simply during the initial week or month after the loss. Continue to inquire after six months or twelve months have passed.

HELPFUL THINGS TO SAY AND DO

- "How are you doing with this?"
- "I know it's traumatic for you."
- Inquire specifically regarding their financial/material needs (if you or your church are willing and ready to assist in this way).

HURTFUL RESPONSES TO TRY TO AVOID

- "Didn't you investigate the history of that investment/company?"
- "Surely you have other investments/savings to cover you through this period."
- "Who is your financial advisor?"
- "Were you carrying cash?"
- "At least you weren't killed or raped."
- "It could be worse."

RELATED SCRIPTURE

Out of the depths I cry to you, O Lord; O Lord, hear my voice. Let your ears be attentive to my cry for mercy. PSALM 130:1-2, NIV

So do not fear, for I am with you; do not be dismayed, for I am your God. I will strengthen you and help you; I will uphold you with my righteous right hand. ISAIAH 41:10, NIV

Because of the Lord's great love we are not consumed, for his compassions never fail. They are new every morning; great is your faithful-

ness. I say to myself, "The Lord is my portion; therefore I will wait for him." LAMENTATIONS 3:22-24, NIV

He will give you all you need from day to day if you live for him and make the Kingdom of God your primary concern.
MATTHEW 6:33, NLT

At the moment I have all I need—more than I need! I am generously supplied with the gifts you sent me with Epaphroditus. They are a sweet-smelling sacrifice that is acceptable to God and pleases him. And this same God who takes care of me will supply all your needs from his glorious riches, which have been given to us in Christ Jesus.
PHILIPPIANS 4:18-19, NLT

PRAYER

A prayer to share with your friend:
Lord, you know the motivation in my heart, you know my comings and goings, my heart through and through. Reveal any improper intentions, forgive me for any sin, and help me to see this situation through your eyes. Help me to trust you to provide for me and my family, to meet all our needs. Help me, Lord, to trust you for my safety and well-being and to trust others again. Amen.

ADDITIONAL RESOURCES

Does God Care If I Can't Pay My Bills? by Linda K. Taylor (Tyndale House Publishers, 1995). This book provides strong encouragement based on God's Word as well as tools to overcome any financial crisis.

Getting Out of Debt by Howard L. Dayton Jr. (Tyndale House Publishers, 1986). A financial expert provides the practical steps the reader needs to get out of debt and create a solid financial base.

When God Doesn't Make Sense by Dr. James Dobson (Tyndale House Publishers, 1993). Assists the reader to be open about asking hard questions of God and being open to receiving lessons from the hurts of life.

Meeting God at a Dead End by R. Mehl (Multnomah Press, 1996). Assisting the reader in thinking through how God can use the dead ends in life.

Where Is God When It Hurts? by Philip Yancey (Zondervan Publishing Corp., 1977).

Christian Financial Concepts
601 Broad Street, SE
Gainesville, GA 30501

T H O M A S   G I L L

Thomas Gill, his wife, Denise, and two daughters live in Wheaton, Illinois, where he maintains a private counseling practice as a licensed professional counselor, specializing in ministry to churches, denominations, and mission boards through counseling, seminars, and consultation. Tom is a graduate of Moody Bible Institute and Wheaton College Graduate School. He and Denise have served in Nigeria with Sudan Interior Mission.

EMPLOYMENT CRISIS

Turn to me and have mercy on me, for I am alone and in deep distress.
My problems go from bad to worse. Oh, save me from them all!
Feel my pain and see my trouble. Forgive all my sins.
See how many enemies I have, and how viciously they hate me!
Protect me! Rescue my life from them!
Do not let me be disgraced, for I trust in you.
May integrity and honesty protect me, for I put my hope in you.

PSALM 25:16-21, NLT

For eight years, my husband, Gene, and I dreaded the question: "So, Gene, what do you do for a living?"

Gene was working odd jobs while trying to break into a new field. None of those jobs added up to "a career," something respectable that would give him status in the eyes of others. So he tried to make our situation more palatable to those around us, all of whom seemed to be charging toward the American Dream while we trailed behind in the dust.

❑ *Author Diane Eble*

EFFECTS OF THE CRISIS

Whether the cause is downsizing, reorganization, difficulty finding one's career niche, or a mismatch with one's employer, unemployment or underemployment is not just an economic crisis. It is a crisis involving one's identity, marriage, family life, social life, and even one's relationship with God. Indeed, few areas of life are untouched when an employment crisis strikes—especially for a man. Men in our culture are often defined by others—and themselves—in terms of the work they do. When that work is taken away, so is a large chunk of their identity.

HOW YOU CAN HELP AND ENCOURAGE

When an employment crisis strikes, most people hide the truth. They struggle alone with issues of self-esteem and respect. They try to deal with the disappointment that comes when dreams die, the anger that strikes both spouses at unplanned moments. They may struggle financially, selling most of what they own before they'll ask for help.

Because of the denial and shame that are often present, it can be difficult to reach out to someone in an employment crisis. Yet it is during such times that the support of others is so crucial. If you want to reach out to someone in an employment crisis, first work through your own attitude. How do you really feel about the person or couple who is having career struggles? Do you feel he or she is lazy or incompetent? Do you pity or feel superior?

Here there may be a gender difference. Men are especially quick to sniff out pity on the part of another man. "If you're hurting and a male friend talks to you, he may look at you like you're handicapped," says Bob. "He may pity you or act superior, and that will change the relationship. Either you start acting and feeling inferior, or the relationship ends. Rarely will a man simply recognize you're hurting and have the ability to relate to that." Women, on the other hand, may have that ability, and a woman in crisis may be more likely to welcome sympathy.

At any rate, it takes humility and empathy to realize that a friend's career struggles could be your own someday, given a certain set of unfavorable circumstances. That's one reason an individual or a couple's denial is unconsciously encouraged by those around them.

Be on the lookout for hints that a couple is in crisis. Often a person in denial will test the waters gingerly, hoping someone will be sensitive enough to pick up on a hint. The hint might come through a prayer request at church or a brief mention that a spouse is still looking for work. Remembering and asking a few weeks later how they are can show a couple you've heard and you care.

Well-meaning friends are often quick to offer advice, but the best thing to do is listen. A person or couple often feels alone in their struggle. They need an empathetic listener who can say, "Sounds like you're feeling pretty angry—and I would be, too." Often a listener can help put perspective back in the life of a couple facing persistent unemployment.

Be persistent in your caring. You may be rebuffed the first time you reach out. The couple or person may still be denying the fact that there's a problem. The first time two friends tried to reach out to Gene and me, we told them everything was fine—even though it wasn't. But later, when they asked, "How's it going?" we were ready to tell the truth. If they hadn't asked again, we would have missed out on their support.

Give practical help. Formerly unemployed couples told me with deep-felt appreciation about resumés passed on to potential employers, odd jobs offered, even money sent anonymously through the mail. One woman who baby-sits in her home found people in her church asking her to care for their children. One church, aware of a couple's deep financial and marital problems, paid for them to see a marriage counselor.

But even more important than financial needs are emotional and social needs, so offer moral support. Realize that your friends may not invite you over for dinner because they're too embarrassed to feed you the fare they've been eating, or maybe they're embarrassed by needed repairs on their house.

One couple demonstrated sensitivity to Gene and me by

passing on tickets to a play they couldn't attend. Other couples reported the moral support they received when someone invited them over for dinner or out to a movie. Husbands told me how meaningful it was when another man asked them out to lunch. Even if the subject of the job search is not brought up directly, the moral support is felt.

Most important of all, pray. Knowing that others truly care and are praying specifically for an upcoming job interview or the money to buy a pair of shoes bolsters a couple like nothing else. But don't pray only for the material needs. Pray for spiritual needs, such as the faith to believe God's promises, or the perspective that a person's worth doesn't depend on his or her career.

HELPFUL THINGS TO SAY AND DO

- Allow the person to grieve the loss of the job.
- Help defuse the shame—communicate that the person is worthy apart from a job.
- Treat the person and family normally.
- Reach out according to the level of relationship already established.
- Share your own experiences if applicable.
- Get your church involved.

HURTFUL RESPONSES TO TRY TO AVOID

- Offering platitudes.
- Talking too much about your own job.
- Taking sides (i.e., wife against husband or vice versa).
- Offering advice.
- Judging the person in crisis.

RELATED SCRIPTURE

"I know the plans I have for you," declares the Lord, "plans to prosper you and not to harm you, plans to give you hope and a future. Then you will call upon me and come and pray to me, and I will listen to

you. You will seek me and find me when you seek me with all your heart." JEREMIAH 29:11-13, NIV

I will repay you for the years the locusts have eaten. . . . You will have plenty to eat, until you are full, and you will praise the name of the Lord your God, who has worked wonders for you; never again will my people be shamed. JOEL 2:25-26, NIV

Therefore, since we have been justified through faith, we have peace with God through our Lord Jesus Christ, through whom we have gained access by faith into this grace in which we now stand. And we rejoice in the hope of the glory of God. Not only so, but we also rejoice in our sufferings, because we know that suffering produces persever- ance; perseverance, character; and character, hope. And hope does not disappoint us, because God has poured out his love into our hearts by the Holy Spirit, whom he has given us.
ROMANS 5:1-5, NIV

Praise be to the God and Father of our Lord Jesus Christ, the Father of compassion and the God of all comfort, who comforts us in all our troubles, so that we can comfort those in any trouble with the comfort we ourselves have received from God.
2 CORINTHIANS 1:3-4, NIV

Consider it pure joy, my brothers, whenever you face trials of many kinds, because you know that the testing of your faith develops persever- ance. Perseverance must finish its work so that you may be mature and complete, not lacking anything. JAMES 1:2-4, NIV

PRAYER

Dear God, help me to find my worth in my relationship with you, not in my employment. I want to use the gifts you have given me in the workplace. I pray that you will lead me to a job where I can most effec- tively serve you. Please give me patience as I wait, and courage to continue my pursuits. Amen.

ADDITIONAL RESOURCES

Men in Search of Work and the Women Who Love Them by Diane Eble (Zondervan Publishing Corp., 1994). Coping strategies for men, their wives, and anyone who loves those in an employment crisis.

Finding Work without Losing Heart by William Byron (Adams Publishing, 1995). Written especially for executives who have been downsized; deals with psychological and spiritual dimensions.

Healing the Wounds: Overcoming the Trauma of Layoffs and Revitalizing Downsized Organizations by David Noer (Jossey-Bass, Inc., Publishers, 1993). Looks at those who have surived the layoff.

When God Doesn't Make Sense by Dr. James Dobson (Tyndale House Publishers, 1993). Assists the reader in being open to asking hard questions of God and being open to receiving lessons from the hurts of life.

Meeting God at a Dead End by R. Mehl (Multnomah Press, 1996). Assists the reader in thinking through how God can use the dead ends in life.

Where Is God When It Hurts? by Philip Yancey (Zondervan Publishing Corp., 1977).

DIANE EBLE

Diane Eble is the author of *Men in Search of Work and the Women Who Love Them, Knowing the Voice of God,* and several other books and articles.

VICTIMS
OF FRAUD

Don't worry about the wicked. Don't envy those who do
wrong. For like grass, they soon fade away. Like springtime
flowers, they soon wither. Trust in the Lord and do good.
Then you will live safely in the land and prosper. Take
delight in the Lord, and he will give you your heart's
desires. Commit everything you do to the Lord. Trust him,
and he will help you. He will make your innocence
as clear as the dawn, and the justice of your cause
will shine like the noonday sun.

PSALM 37:1-6, NLT

A successful businessman, John had built a very prosper-
ous retail store over the last thirty years. Well-respected
in the community, John now is experiencing
tremendous embarrassment by his current state of affairs. A few
years ago, John had entrusted his bookkeeper with responsibility
for the finances of his company. He later found out that the
bookkeeper had bilked him and the company out of nearly two
hundred thousand dollars in the course of only fifteen months.
Facing financial ruin and the loss of his business, John sadly
states, "We would still be in business today if not for this. It
continues to leave me in a state of shock."

UNDERSTANDING THE CRISIS

Although fraud crimes involve certain basic criminal activities (such as theft or larceny), they also typically involve certain types of offenders and specific types of activities. Generally speaking, fraud is committed by a person who is in a position of trust or authority, gains the victims' confidence, or otherwise is (or appears to be) in a position of respectability. Fraudulent activities are characterized by dishonesty, deceit, trickery, and misuse of trust and authority to obtain money, property, or other gain. Examples of fraud include embezzlement, telemarketing schemes, credit card theft, and investment scams.

EFFECTS OF THE CRISIS

Victims of fraud crimes can experience a great sense of loss, not only economically but also emotionally and even spiritually. Often, those victims describe the tremendous violation of their personal integrity by using such phrases as "It was like being physically assaulted," or "I've lost all of my sense of trust." Because these psychological "wounds" are not seen in the same way as wounds to the body, the impact on victims of fraud is often, and inappropriately, minimized. Although not a "physical" violation of a person's body, the crime of fraud is a violation nonetheless.

Fraud victims also can experience intense guilt and shame, disbelief, anger, depression, betrayal, loss of trust, and related emotional anguish. They may be at a heightened risk of suicide, as suicide is frequently an outcome of the depression involved in these cases. There is also the possibility that the victims' anger will be expressed through physical violence. Other issues that may need to be addressed in helping victims of fraud include the need for professional counseling and the potential for the development or exacerbation of substance abuse problems.

How You Can Help and Encourage

Fraud victims can share many of the devastating outcomes experienced by those who were physically victimized. In certain fraud crimes, victims may suffer just as much, if not more, emotional distress. These emotional repercussions are often misunderstood by law enforcement, criminal justice, and victim service providers, as well as family, friends, and fellow church members. The victim often is doubly victimized by this lack of understanding. The church community is in a unique position to offer the kind of understanding that will provide great assistance to these victims.

It is important to understand the high level of embarrassment these victims feel. Unfortunately, they are often viewed with great skepticism by the criminal justice system. They can be treated like "dupes" due to their "lack of good judgment" by family, friends, and neighbors. Those who may not know the victims well may convey a sense that they must be "awfully greedy" to have such an obvious scam succeed with them. These types of reactions, in addition to the knowledge that life savings have been lost, can be unbearable to these victims.

Victims of crimes of fraud also experience high levels of self-blame that may be debilitating for the individual. This self-blame is increased by the often insensitive responses from friends, family and church members, and criminal justice professionals. In addition, the perpetrators of fraud crimes typically use methods that gain the confidence and trust of the victims, and then employ manipulation and trickery to achieve the goal of bilking the victims of their various assets. As a result, not only is their money gone, but the victims' ability to trust is shattered as well.

The first step in helping a victim of fraud is to listen. Allow him or her to discuss the crime and its impact without judging. Ask if there is anything you can do to be helpful at this time. Offer to pray with or for the victim. To help you prepare, you may want to review the information on crisis intervention provided at the beginning of this book.

As you assist a person who has been the victim of fraud, it is important to carefully and sincerely maintain or build a trusting relationship. Be sure to keep your word with the victim and do not promise to do things that you cannot fulfill. Offer to help the victim in concrete and practical ways, such as offering to drive him or her to appointments with creditors, running errands, etc.

Fraud crime victims justifiably feel that a tremendous violation has occurred. The net result can be a life in financial and emotional ruin—seemingly out of control with no recovery in sight. Because these schemes often appear obvious in retrospect, victims are typically not viewed as "legitimate" crime victims. This is compounded by the fact that many of these fraud crime schemes involve investments and other financial arrangements that may lead some to feel that it was the victims' greed that caused them to be blinded to the realities of the situation. Therefore, many family members and friends do not often exhibit that sense of outrage about the crime that may accompany a response to victims of violent crime. As a concerned friend, family member, or pastor, you can and should express outrage at the acts of the wrongdoer here!

Similar to victims of violent crime, victims of fraud crime may never meet or see the perpetrator of their crime (for example, as in a telemarketing scheme). In a number of cases, the perpetrator is never identified or apprehended. If the offender *is* identified and apprehended, it is very possible that he or she may escape all accountability or punishment. Often the fraud scheme has been adequately layered with buffers, which keep the offender from prosecution. Even if the offender is prosecuted, he or she can use methods such as bankruptcy to avoid any restitution or compensation for losses. Even when these cases are successfully prosecuted and restitution is awarded, the victims may endure months—even years—of struggle and turmoil, only to see a small amount of their losses returned. Finally, it is not uncommon for victims to be swindled on several occasions, sometimes repeatedly by the same offender and other times by additional swindlers who have acquired their name as potential targets.

In helping a victim of fraud, you can provide nonjudgmental support and unconditional understanding of the victim's plight. It is extremely important not to inadvertently blame the victim for being trapped in a fraud scheme. The blame is appropriately placed on the offender, not the victim.

Also, the church community can provide tangible assistance required for victims to overcome the personal and financial devastation wrought by many fraud schemes. This may be a time to take the victim's need to the church for consideration of financial support during the crisis (see Matthew 25:31-46; James 2:14-17).

HELPFUL THINGS TO SAY AND DO

- Learn to truly *listen* to victims of fraud. The act of truly listening will confirm your acceptance and validation.
- Help reestablish the victims' sense of trust. Suspend any interactions that are overly upsetting to the victims, and focus on being there for them until they are able to talk more about it.
- "Can I/we help provide a meal or some other assistance to your family?" Attempt to carefully and sensitively discern specific concerns or anxieties the victims may be experiencing. Ask about their material needs (food, shelter, clothing). These basic needs are of the utmost importance.
- "May I/we be of assistance with your boss or any of your creditors?" Offer to intervene and assist with specific, difficult tasks that victims must handle. Often pastors and church leaders are viewed as acceptable intervenors in these circumstances.
- "Is there any outside assistance I/we may provide or assist you in obtaining?" This line of questioning is very sensitive and should be pursued carefully. It may be that the victims would prefer to receive counseling from a source

other than the church for a variety of very legitimate reasons.

- Pray with them and for them: "Would you like me/us to pray with you or for you?" Be sure to offer *but* don't insist on prayer. You can always pray on your own for the victims and their recovery.

HURTFUL RESPONSES TO TRY TO AVOID

- "You shouldn't have trusted someone with your money like that." Do not imply that the victims contributed to their own victimization.
- "This must have been the Lord's will." Be careful not to place the responsibility for this evil on God.
- "Why would you trust somebody like that?" Be careful not to ask *why* questions as they infer guilt and wrongdoing on the part of the victims.
- "Thank God it was only money that you lost." The loss of one's life savings is a very violent and emotionally taxing event. To some individuals, the loss of even small amounts of money is the difference between eating or not eating, and affording medications.
- "In order to get on with your life you should forgive the offender." Allow the victims to consider forgiveness at their own pace. Also, forgiveness should not and cannot be forced on the victims. This part of their spiritual healing will come at the appropriate time and in the appropriate way for them.

RELATED SCRIPTURE

I will bless the Lord who guides me; even at night my heart instructs me. I know the Lord is always with me. I will not be shaken, for he is right beside me. No wonder my heart is filled with joy, and my mouth shouts his praises! My body rests in safety. For you will not leave my soul among the dead or allow your godly one to rot in the grave. You will show me the way of life, granting me the joy of your presence and the pleasures of living with you forever. PSALM 16:7-11, NLT

The unfailing love of the Lord never ends! By his mercies we have been kept from complete destruction. Great is his faithfulness; his mercies begin afresh each day. I say to myself, "The Lord is my inheritance; therefore, I will hope in him!" LAMENTATIONS 3:22-24, NLT

The wicked put up a bold front, but the upright proceed with care. PROVERBS 21:29, NLT

PRAYER

A prayer to share with your friend:
Dear Lord, help me to remember that you, too, were betrayed, and on that night you proclaimed a new covenant with your people. Help me to remember my covenant with you, and assist me in being faithful to you. Please give me the grace and strength to face this terrible difficulty that has befallen me. I know that with your help anything is possible. Amen.

ADDITIONAL RESOURCES

White Collar Crime: The Uncut Version by E. H. Sutherland (Greenwood Publishing Group, Inc., 1983).

"White-Collar Crime: Prevalence, Trends, and Costs" by C. F. Wellford and B. L. Ingraham, in *Critical Issues in Crime and Justice,* ed. A. R. Roberts (Thousand Oaks, Calif: Sage, 1994).

Also, please note that the National Citizens Crime Prevention Counsel has numerous brochures and pamphlets regarding the issues of fraud victimization that may be obtained by calling them at 1-800-WE-PREVENT.

MARIO GABOURY

Mario Thomas Gaboury, J.D., Ph.D. is associate professor of criminal justice at the University of New Haven where he also directs UNH's crime victim study center. He has worked in the area of crime victims rights and services for almost two decades and is formerly deputy director of the U.S. Justice Department's Office for Victims of Crime and formerly Legislative Specialist at the National Organization for Victim Assistance.

LIVING WITH PHYSICAL PROBLEMS

SERIOUS
INJURY

*Why am I discouraged? Why so sad? I will put my hope in
God! I will praise him again—my Savior and my God!*

PSALM 42:11, NLT

I t was overwhelming for me to be so busy at one minute
and the next minute be completely down, depending on
others for everything. But it was very encouraging to
receive so many cards and letters from people all over the
world. It's amazing to know how many people care."
□ *Woman who survived a crash with a semitrailer*

HOW YOU CAN HELP AND ENCOURAGE

When suffering is shared by others, its impact can be downsized and reduced to a manageable level. That is why the Bible
consistently calls on Christians to help bear the burdens of
other people. In the New Testament, Paul urges: "Carry each
other's burdens" (Galatians 6:2, NIV). And in the Old Testament the prophet Isaiah declared that it was a divine require-
ment for God's people "to share your food with the hungry
and to provide the poor wanderer with shelter—when you see
the naked, to clothe him, and not to turn away from your own
flesh and blood" (Isaiah 58:7, NIV). Here are some simple but

123

important ways you can support someone who has experienced a serious accident or physical injury.

Pray.   Before you visit, pray for guidance. In order to avoid doing or saying the wrong things, pray and seek God's guidance before you visit. These prayers can be brief and to the point and even be offered in a car while driving to visit the person: "O God, help me; help me to say and do the right things." "Dear God, give me wisdom and insight as I visit. Empower me to be a source of blessing." Then make your visit with the security that God will indeed guide you to speak and act wisely.

Be there.   Recently I conducted a funeral for a forty-seven-year-old man named Gary. Two years earlier he had been seriously injured in an automobile accident. Because his spinal cord had been severed, he suffered paralysis from the waist down and could only move via a wheelchair. Gary had spent most of the previous two years recovering from his injuries and battling with various ailments. His death was the result of heart failure, which physicians felt was related to the accident. When I met with his wife to discuss the funeral service, she commented sadly, "Although Gary was a highly regarded executive in the community, after his accident most friends fell away. He had spent most of the last two years feeling isolated. Only his family remained faithful to him, and one or two friends. It was an additional burden for him to realize that his friends seemed to have forgotten about him."

Unfortunately, Gary's experience is not an unusual one. The lesson: Give as much love and support as possible to the recently injured person. Be there as soon as you hear of the injury or accident. Continue to visit, phone, and send encouraging notes. Your presence and support will contribute greatly to the individual's physical, emotional, and spiritual survival.

Practice unconditional love and acceptance.   When you visit, suspend all judgment about how the person should feel, what he/she should say, think, act, etc. Be there as a healing presence to comfort, support, and listen. Listen with your heart, and be as accepting as possible.

Here is good advice from counselor Amy Hillyard Jensen. Although her advice is offered to those who seek to comfort the grieving, her words apply equally to those suffering from an accident or injury: "If the mourner doesn't feel like talking, don't force conversation. Silence is better than aimless chatter. The mourner should be allowed to lead. . . . Is he emotional? Accept that. Does he cry? Accept that too. Is he angry at God? God will manage without your defending him. Accept whatever feelings are expressed. Do not rebuke. Do not change the subject. Be as understanding as you can be."[1]

Don't make God responsible for the accident or injury. Avoid any statement or hint that the accident was God's will for some reason. This will only frustrate and anger the individual. Rather affirm whatever level of faith the hurt person may have. Gently remind him or her that God is constantly present to help all of us through whatever life may bring. When it seems appropriate, share comforting passages of Scripture.

Recommend a support group or an individual who has been through a similar crisis. Often those most effective in helping someone who has been seriously injured or hurt are those individuals who have been through a similar experience. People who have been in the same situation can offer valuable support and insight and be a reminder that the person is not alone in his or her injury.

Help your friend by locating two or three support groups in your community if available. Write down the pertinent information about the groups: where they meet, times of the meetings, phone number of a contact person from whom more information can be gathered. Give that written information to your friend. Don't place any pressure on the person to attend

---

[1] Quote from Amy Hillyard Jensen from Nancy O'Connor, Ph.D., *Letting Go with Love: The Grieving Process,* (Apache Junction, Ariz.: La Mariposa Press, 1985), 183.

but simply remind him or her that a support group that meets locally is another resource to consider.

Finally, remain in touch. With the passing of time many other friends, neighbors, and colleagues will drop off as they resume their daily responsibilities. As others become less available, your faithful and continuous visits or phone calls or letters will be most welcome and cherished.

RELATED SCRIPTURE

God is our refuge and strength, an ever-present help in trouble. Therefore we will not fear. PSALM 46:1-2, NIV

"My thoughts are completely different from yours," says the Lord. "And my ways are far beyond anything you could imagine. For just as the heavens are higher than the earth, so are my ways higher than your ways and my thoughts higher than your thoughts."
ISAIAH 55:8-9, NLT

Don't be troubled. You trust God, now trust in me. There are many rooms in my Father's home, and I am going to prepare a place for you. If this were not so, I would tell you plainly. When everything is ready, I will come and get you, so that you will always be with me where I am. And you know where I am going and how to get there.
JOHN 14:1-4, NLT

Can anything ever separate us from Christ's love? Does it mean he no longer loves us if we have trouble or calamity, or are persecuted, or are hungry or cold or in danger or threatened with death? (Even the Scriptures say, "For your sake we are killed every day; we are being slaughtered like sheep.") No, despite all these things, overwhelming victory is ours through Christ, who loved us.
ROMANS 8:35-37, NLT

Now we see things imperfectly as in a poor mirror, but then we will see everything with perfect clarity. All that I know now is partial and incomplete, but then I will know everything completely, just as God knows me now. 1 CORINTHIANS 13:12, NLT

PRAYER

A prayer to share with your friend:
Lord God, give me the inner strength to follow you as I am laid up with this injury. I pray for quick, thorough healing and an attitude of love for all those around me. Amen.

ADDITIONAL RESOURCES

Finding the Right Words by Wilfred Bockelman (Augsburg Fortress Publishers, 1989). Guidelines for offering care and comfort when you don't know what to say.

Head Injury Guide for Survivors, Families, and Caregivers, ed. by Delores M. John (Diane Publishing Co., 1993). Practical advice on living with someone who has experienced head trauma.

When God Doesn't Make Sense by Dr. James Dobson (Tyndale House Publishers, 1993). A practical approach to those struggling with suffering.

VICTOR M. PARACHIN

Reverend Victor M. Parachin is an ordained minister and counselor, serving churches in Washington, D.C., and Chicago. He is the writer of *Hope,* a monthly newsletter geared for those who are grieving.

CHILD WITH
SPECIAL NEEDS

All praise to the God and Father of our Lord Jesus Christ.
He is the source of every mercy and the God who comforts
us. He comforts us in all our troubles so that we can
comfort others. When others are troubled, we will be able to
give them the same comfort God has given us. You can be
sure that the more we suffer for Christ, the more God will
shower us with his comfort through Christ.

2 CORINTHIANS 1:3-5, NLT

I prayed a lot. . . . I have a best friend who has a son that's a month older. . . . We talk a lot, and I think that's helped, too. . . . I've counseled new parents, and I think that's helped me because I've had the opportunity to tell them of the good times and the bad times."[1]

❑ *Parent of a child with a disability*

EFFECTS OF THE CRISIS

When parents learn that their child has a disability, it becomes a moment frozen in time. All parents can tell you how they felt when they heard the news of their child's disability. From that day their lives are changed. Nothing will ever be

[1] *Parenting a Child with Special Needs* by Rosemarie S. Cook (Grand Rapids, Mich.: Zondervan, 1992), 219.

the same. The mind is flooded with questions: Why? How? What do I do now? The parent experiences a wide range of emotions, from fear to anger to relief at getting a diagnosis. A lifetime of riding an emotional roller coaster has just begun.

UNDERSTANDING THE CRISIS

A developmental disability is a condition that originated before age eighteen that is considered to be permanent or of indefinite length and is a substantial impediment to the person's ability to function independently and normally in society.[2]

HOW YOU CAN HELP AND ENCOURAGE

As a parent of an adult with a disability, I have always appreciated acceptance and understanding, both for my son and for our family. When you have a child with special needs, you can feel isolated and alone. When a child looks, acts, and sounds different from other children, some people shy away from reaching out. People aren't sure how to act or what to say.

You can put aside your own fears and awkwardness and learn how to be a friend to this family. The first step in acceptance is to act toward the family as you would toward any other person in crisis. That is, be there. Visit and give physical help where needed. People tend to say, "Let me know if you need anything," but a better question that will lead to giving real help is, "What do you need right now?"

The family may need any one of a number of things, such as transportation to a medical appointment, baby-sitting for other children, housekeeping, meal preparation, or assistance with grocery shopping. They may have medical bills and subsequently need financial help with other household or personal expenses. By asking, "What do you need right now?" you allow the parents to have control over how they are assisted. Having choices is important when so much in their lives seems beyond their control.

[2]Kathleen Burch Caries and Marie Weil, "Developmentally Disabled Persons and Their Families" *Case Management in Human Services,* ed. Marie Weil, James M. Karls, and associates (San Francisco: Jossey-Bass, 1985), 234.

When a family has sufficient resources, they may turn down an offer for physical or financial help. If that is the case, then a neighbor can be a supportive, caring friend. You can show interest in the child, asking appropriate questions. Most parents are willing to discuss the child's disability. Your willingness to listen conveys to the parents that this child is important to you. Parents then will feel that you understand them and what they are going through.

You might want to perform some random acts of kindness toward this family: Bring a dessert or meal over now and then without being asked, or deliver some fresh flowers with a note that says you are thinking of them. These sound like small items for a large problem, but they ease the daily stresses. If you belong to a church and the family does not, you might invite them to come. Talk with the nursery people in advance to prepare for the child, if that is necessary. If the child is older, find the appropriate Sunday school class (if your church has Sunday school), and inform the teacher of any special needs beforehand. If your church cannot accommodate a wheelchair, special stroller, or other physical equipment, perhaps this is the time for you to address your church council about making your church building handicap accessible. Not only will you be helping this family now, but you will make your church a welcoming place for other families in the future.

Your prayers are the most powerful ministry you have to this family. Support them in prayer, and if possible, ask others to do so also. Parents with a special needs child need continuing patience and wisdom as they interact with their child and plan for the future. The crisis of a disability is not a point-in-time crisis, although, certainly the day they learned of the child's disability was crucial. When parents have a child with a disability, the crises come in series. There are new challenges daily. Your continuing prayers and neighborly help are valuable to this family.

The parents of a child with a disability face many challenges. Medical problems are often ongoing. Finding baby-sitters, school placements, physical and speech therapists, and recreational activities for the child may not be easy. Finding time for their other children and for themselves as a couple can also be difficult.

You might be able to offer baby-sitting or transportation for the other children for after-school activities, such as ball games or dance classes. You could also be a standby when emergency help is needed, such as if a child gets sick at school and needs to be picked up or Mom isn't feeling well and needs some help.

Parents appreciate friends who can remain friends through all the crises as well as the day-to-day struggles they go through with their children. They may need someone to talk to who listens without making judgments. They may need a friendly ear when they want to tell about a bad day or when they question why this ever happened to them. If you are willing to be a helpful neighbor, you will find many ways for the Lord to use you.

HELPFUL THINGS TO SAY AND DO

- "You have a precious child."
- "I am blessed when I see the love in your family."
- "This is not an easy time for you, but I am here for you."
- "I know that sometimes things just don't make sense."

HURTFUL RESPONSES TO TRY TO AVOID

- "I know just how you feel."
- "You must be very special people for God to have sent you such a child to love."
- "How did this happen?"
- "Do you have other people in your family with this problem?"

RELATED SCRIPTURE

For you created my inmost being; you knit me together in my mother's womb. I praise you because I am fearfully and wonderfully made.
PSALM 139:13-14, NIV

Fear not, for I have redeemed you; I have summoned you by name; you are mine. ISAIAH 43:1, NIV

Then Jesus said, "Come to me, all of you who are weary and carry heaven burdens, and I will give you rest. Take my yoke upon you. Let me teach you, because I am humble and gentle, and you will find rest for your souls. For my yoke fits perfectly, and the burden I give you is light." MATTHEW 11:28-30, NLT

I have come that they may have life, and have it to the full. JOHN 10:10, NIV

So be truly glad! There is wonderful joy ahead, even though it is necessary for you to endure many trials for a while. 1 PETER 1:6, NLT

Give all your worries and cares to God, for he cares about what happens to you. 1 PETER 5:7, NLT

PRAYER

Lord, you said to suffer the little children to come to you. We ask that you, who came into the world as a child, help parents whose children have special needs. Give them wisdom and patience, endurance and strength. Help us to reach out to them in your love and grace. Amen.

ADDITIONAL RESOURCES

Parenting a Child with Special Needs by Rosemarie S. Cook (Zondervan, 1992). Practical help for parents and any relatives of children with disabilities, with author's personal story.

I'll Love You Forever by H. Norman Wright (Focus on the Family Publishing, 1993). How to accept your child, from his own family's experience.

A Difference in the Family: Living with a Disabled Child by Helen Featherstone (Viking Penguin, 1981). A parent's experience with her disabled child and her examination of meaning and hope.

Counseling Families of Children with Disabilities by Rosemarie S. Cook (Word, Inc., 1990). For pastors, professionals, and parents who want to learn more about family dynamics and developmental stages of the child.

ROSEMARIE SCOTTI HUGHES

Dr. Rosemarie Scotti Hughes is the dean of the School of Counseling and Human Services at Regent University, a licensed professional counselor, and the mother of an adult son who has a disability.

LIFE-
THREATENING
ILLNESS

When you go through deep waters and great trouble,
I will be with you. When you go through rivers of difficulty,
you will not drown! When you walk through the fire of oppression,
you will not be burned up; the flames will not consume you.

ISAIAH 43:2, NLT

H ow can this be happening? I feel like I'm being controlled by this disease. It's in control—determining
my future."
❑ *A young woman who has been hospitalized more than fifty times*

EFFECTS OF THE CRISIS

When faced with a potentially fatal illness, individuals act
and react in different ways. These reactions may vary from
simple acceptance to clinical depression. Asking, "What did I
do to deserve this?" is a typical response. The reality of possibly facing the end of life brings a host of emotions: anger,
frustration, hopelessness, isolation, confusion, and despair.
These all have their roots in fear. Navigating through this
minefield of emotions can be very difficult, not only for the
patient but for those who are close to the patient.

How You Can Help and Encourage

The diagnosis of a life-threatening illness brings a tremendous challenge to the individual and his or her caregiver. The impact on the individual's life is far reaching and invades every aspect of daily existence—physical, emotional, and spiritual.

PHYSICAL

Depending on the nature of the illness and the course of treatment, there may be physical changes in the individual's appearance (hair loss, bloating, skin rashes, etc.). Medications often have unpleasant side effects (nausea, diarrhea, etc.). Be sensitive to the individual's physical circumstances. If the individual wants to talk about them, don't act as though they don't exist.

Acknowledge the reality of the changes. Often the individual is embarrassed by these changes, and they are one of the reasons some have given for not wanting to be around people. Keep the discussion light, try some humor (if it seems appropriate). Remind the patient that the essence of who he or she is resides within the individual and is not tied to physical aspects.

Keeping life as normal as possible is important for a person who is living with a life-threatening illness. Since the quality of life has probably diminished, normalcy may mean having a day without experiencing pain or nausea. However, some may be able to function fairly well and may struggle with the fact that they cannot do all the things they once were able to do. Most do not want to treated like a "sick" person.

Finding some kind of balance is important. Give the patient permission to take each day as it comes and not put unrealistic expectations on the ability to do all the things he or she once did is a key factor in adjusting to the restrictions that this illness has imposed. For example, when a patient says, "Some days all I want to do is sleep," acknowledge it and accept it.

Give honest encouragement to the patient. Focus on any small improvement. Perhaps you might notice that his eyes seem a bit brighter today, or the voice is stronger. There's a bit more color in the cheeks, or how good it is to see him sitting up and enjoying the sunshine. It's all right to talk about the problem, but balance it with talk about the rest of life. If the person isn't up to talking, then share some things from your life.

Follow the patient's lead. Be sensitive about asking for information regarding the diagnosis or treatment. Do not question the treatment plan, the medical procedures, or the doctor's capabilities. The patient has likely heard horror stories about his illness and what the future may hold. Share *positive* stories about others who have gone through similar circumstances. Reassure, comfort, and instill hope.

EMOTIONAL

The emotional aspects of a life-threatening illness can be as devastating as the physical impact. Anger and frustration often give way to a sense of helplessness, despair, and *fear.*

The patient tends to feel helpless in the face of invasive tests, surgeries, and endless medications. Something is taking over a major part of his or her existence. The days begin and end with a keen awareness of the changes that are taking place. Plans are put on hold—daily schedules are disrupted. Hospitals and doctor's waiting rooms become all too familiar. Sickness has come as an unwelcome guest and rearranged life.

How a person responds emotionally will differ greatly from one individual to another. *Be tenderly aware of the patient's emotional vulnerability.* This is not a time to be a Pollyanna or the eternal optimist. Neither is it a time for negative thinking. This is a time for empathy. Allow the patient to express feelings, fears, and the sense of isolation and confusion he or she feels. These are normal responses in such a grave situation. Listen with gentleness and compassion—a reply is not required.

Lift the individual's spirits by ministering to his needs. If the patient is able to be up and about, offer to drive him to the doctor and sit with him in the waiting room. (This also provides comfort for the ones close to him by giving them some relief from the unending demands.) Take the person shopping, out to eat, or over to a friend's house for a visit. Do the laundry, vacuum, clean out the refrigerator, or mow the lawn. Talk positively about the future—plan a future event. What would you appreciate if the roles were reversed? *When you offer to do something, be specific.*

If the individual is hospitalized or confined to home, assist in the daily routine wherever possible. The body becomes weary. Give a gentle arm/leg massage with a fragrant lotion (be sure this is approved by the doctor). Music can be a blessing—share tapes and CDs. Organize a daily delivery of meals to be brought to the home by friends and church members, or find out what special treat you can bring to the hospital. Share reading materials, but keep in mind that the attention span may be short now, so find materials that are not lengthy—a page or two with a thought or story. Find stories with successful outcomes.

SPIRITUAL

The spiritual dimension of facing a life-threatening illness is critical. What a person believes about himself, his relationship to God, and his perception of God's relationship to him is of primary concern. Current literature suggests that a positive attitude plays a vital part in a person's ability to face life's most difficult challenges. An individual's belief system is the core from which such an attitude is formed. Providing spiritual encouragement and support is essential. Be considerate of the person's spiritual background—use wisdom.

There are no simple answers for those who are suffering. They need support, encouragement, and a firm commitment that we are upholding them in prayer. A Scripture that is most comforting is found in 1 Peter 5:7: "You can throw the whole weight of your anxieties upon him, for you are his personal concern" (Phillips). When overwhelmed with sickness, pain, tests, and surgeries, it is easy to lose sight of this promise.

Supporting a person facing such a great challenge will entail a commitment that includes your time and your prayers. Assure the individual that you will pray for him or her (and also will pray for the caregivers) if you are willing to make that commitment. Pray for wisdom for the doctors and nurses who are caring for the individual. Pray for family members who are living daily with this difficult situation. Offer to ask church elders, priests, or pastors to come and pray for the individual if he or she so desires.

When visiting the patient, share a short devotional, a Scripture, and prayer. Do not impose your beliefs about healing on the patient. If you do not expect God to intervene and heal the person, don't verbalize this—it could be a real source of discouragement. On the other hand, if you do believe that God will heal the person, it may create confusion and despair when he or she is still suffering in the weeks and months to come. Give encouragement. Unless you have walked the same path, it is difficult to understand the struggle.

HELPFUL THINGS TO SAY AND DO

- "I can't imagine what you must be going through."
- "I really admire your courage."
- "Can I [clean the kitchen, pick up something at the store, go with you to the doctor] for you?" Be specific.
- Do something for the caregivers (parents, spouse, etc.). The patient often feels guilty about the demands that have been placed on the caregivers and appreciates any kindness shown to them.

HURTFUL RESPONSES TO TRY TO AVOID

- "I know exactly how you feel" (no one knows fully how another feels).

139

- "I hate to tell you, but my brother died of this same thing."
- "If you need something, you know how to reach me."
- "How much time do you have?"
- "Did you ignore the warning signs?"
- Don't drop in, stay long, or make lengthy phone calls to the patient.

RELATED SCRIPTURE

God is our refuge and strength, always ready to help in times of trouble. So we will not fear, even if earthquakes come and the mountains crumble into the sea. PSALM 46:1-2, NLT

Whom have I in heaven but you? I desire you more than anything on earth. My health may fail, and my spirit may grow weak, but God remains the strength of my heart; he is mine forever.
PSALM 73:25-26, NLT

"For I know the plans I have for you," says the Lord. "They are plans for good and not for disaster, to give you a future and a hope."
JEREMIAH 29:11, NLT

Now you are going through pain, but I shall see you again and your hearts will thrill with joy—the joy that no one can take away from you.
JOHN 16:22, PHILLIPS

I have become absolutely convinced that neither death nor life, neither messenger of Heaven nor monarch of earth, neither what happens today nor what may happen tomorrow, neither a power from on high nor a power from below, nor anything else in God's whole world has any power to separate us from the love of God in Christ Jesus our Lord!
ROMANS 8:38-39, PHILLIPS

PRAYER

Heavenly Father, it is with thanksgiving in our heart that we can come to you, who created the earth and all that dwells within, who created man in your image, who knows the beginning from the end,

Alpha and Omega. This body is weary, but the heart responds to your promise that we are your "personal concern." If we wait upon you, our strength will be renewed, and we will fly like eagles. Come now, Lord, and refresh your servant.

May we fly above the pain and struggle and find comfort in your everlasting love. Amen.

ADDITIONAL RESOURCES

Dear Lillian by Gene Edwards (Tyndale House Publishers, 1992). This book gives a beautiful view of the believer's relationship to death and the afterlife and places the Christian's life in God's eternal perspective.

Living with Cancer, ed. Mary Beth Moster (Tyndale House Publishers, 1985). This Bible-based book helps readers deal with the fears and facts of cancer, including self-esteem, treatment and side effects, emotional pain, and spiritual questioning.

My Journey into Alzheimer's Disease by Robert Davis (Tyndale House Publishers, 1989). A book of encouragement of how one man of faith faced the oncoming darkness of Alzheimer's disease.

When God Doesn't Make Sense by Dr. James Dobson (Tyndale House Publishers, 1993). A practical approach for those struggling with suffering.

Comfort and Care for the Critically Ill by June Cerza Kolf (Baker Book House, 1993). Encouragement for those who are critically ill and for their caregivers.

When Your Friend Gets Cancer: How You Can Help by Amy Harwell and Kristine Tomasik (Harold Shaw Publishers, 1987). Giving support to someone who has a serious illness.

JACQUELINE GATEWOOD

Jacqueline Gatewood, Psy.D., is an assistant professor at the School of Counseling and Human Services at Regent University. Her experience with life-threatening illness centers primarily around her daughter, who has been hospitalized over fifty times and has undergone four organ transplant surgeries.

HIV/AIDS

*I assure you, when you did it to one of the least of these
my brothers and sisters, you were doing it to me!*

MATTHEW 25:40, NLT

I know I made you promise never to preach to me. But
now that this disease is killing me, I just want to know one
thing: Do you really believe all this 'Jesus stuff' about forgiveness and heaven and hell and all that? Because if you do,
you've got five minutes to tell me why I shouldn't just kill
myself right now."

❏ *Young man in the last stages of AIDS*

UNDERSTANDING THE CRISIS

Whether or not we are aware of it, almost every one of us
knows someone who has the human immunodeficiency
virus (HIV)—and each and every person who has HIV will
eventually develop acquired immunodeficiency syndrome,
or AIDS. AIDS is fatal, and it is incurable. Some people with
AIDS live longer than others, but none will avoid death
indefinitely. And that death is usually quite painful and
often quite lonely.

In the five or ten minutes it takes you to read this short
chapter, between fifty and one hundred people worldwide will
become infected with HIV. Victims are unaware of the initial

invasion of this disease, and it usually goes undetected for months or even years. For some, it might even be a decade before the symptoms appear. In the interim, depending on each individual's lifestyle, countless others may also become infected. The long-term implications are chilling.

No one is immune to AIDS, but by avoiding certain risky behaviors, chances of contracting the disease are minimal. A small percentage of people with AIDS have been infected through contaminated blood transfusions, but the vast majority of cases have been spread through promiscuous sex and intravenous drug use.

Although there has been talk of the development of an AIDS vaccine for years, that has not yet happened. However, there have been many significant breakthroughs in treatment, allowing people to live better and much longer. While there are still no cures and treatments are not effective in all cases, many people are helped to some degree.

EFFECTS OF THE CRISIS

AIDS destroys the body's immune system. Nearly all those who have succumbed to this deadly disease have died as a result of certain types of unusual infections or cancers that would have had little or no effect on a healthy immune system.

Many people with AIDS die alone, abandoned by friends and family to suffer in solitude. Whether out of guilt, fear, pain, self-loathing, or a combination of any or all of these emotions, these lonely sufferers can lash out at those who try to come near, driving away the very comfort and help they desire and need.

People with AIDS are often treated as modern-day lepers—the "untouchables" of society. As a result, their lives are impacted not only physically but emotionally and spiritually. They can find themselves isolated from others at a time when they most need a compassionate touch, and they are angry at God when they most need his love and acceptance.

How You Can Help and Encourage

The first and most important thing you can do to help those facing the crisis of HIV/AIDS is to understand that you cannot contract the disease through casual contact. The AIDS virus is transmitted through the exchange of bodily fluids, particularly during sexual intercourse or the sharing of intravenous needles.

The reason this understanding is so important is that those who are dying of AIDS are often avoided by friends and family, even some medical personnel, because people are afraid to come near and touch them. Yet, despite their sometimes defensive or even hostile reactions to those who might try to approach them, people with AIDS are actually starved for human contact. Besides needing assistance with their everyday physical needs such as preparing meals, doing laundry, or driving to a doctor's appointment, AIDS victims need emotional support, comfort, and companionship. They need to be touched. Something as simple as a handshake when meeting for the first time, or reaching out to hold a hand—or the person—upon learning of his or her HIV status, says to them, "I don't reject you, and I'm not afraid of what you have."

In addition to their emotional and physical needs, most people with AIDS are fearful of what lies ahead. Many have never made a commitment to Christ or, if they did at one time, they have been away from God for so long that they have come to believe there is no turning back. As these desperate people find their physical condition deteriorating and their suffering increasing, some even choose suicide over a lingering, excruciating death.

This was the choice faced by the young man whose quote opened this chapter. We had developed a rapport over a period of several months as I ministered to as many of his practical needs as I was able. Although he had been unwilling to discuss spiritual matters in the earlier stages of his disease, by the grace of God, he turned to Jesus rather than to suicide just a couple of weeks before he died.

Not everyone with AIDS will make the choice that my friend made. However, whether they do or not, we still have a wonderful opportunity to model to them the unconditional love of Jesus. Undoubtedly, if he walked the earth today, Jesus would be moving among people living with AIDS, touching and healing, forgiving and loving.

HELPFUL THINGS TO SAY AND DO

- Learn the basic facts about HIV/AIDS so that unfounded fears will not hinder you in your care and service to people with AIDS; seek to teach these facts to others.
- Look for practical ways to help, such as bringing a meal, picking up a prescription, or washing some dishes.
- Find out what the person enjoys doing for relaxation or rejuvenation and then join him or her in that activity if possible.
- Learn about services available to people with AIDS and help them avail themselves of that assistance.
- Be a good listener when they need to talk, or simply sit and keep them company if they are no longer able to carry on lengthy conversations.
- Ask God to show you any areas of self-righteousness or judgment in your own life so you will be free to minister humbly, totally dependent on God's grace.

HURTFUL RESPONSES TO TRY TO AVOID

- Avoid condemning statements such as "AIDS is God's punishment for the sin of homosexuality/drug use."
- Don't make promises you can't keep, such as "I've prayed for you, and I *know* God is going to heal you," or "I'll talk to your family and get them to come and visit you."

- Don't criticize government agencies, hospitals, or medical personnel for not providing the sort of help either you or the person with AIDS feels is needed.
- Don't take it personally if your visits or words are rejected; simply remain available should he or she reconsider and reach out at some future time.

RELATED SCRIPTURE

Suppose you see a brother or sister who needs food or clothing, and you say, "Well, good-bye and God bless you; stay warm and eat well"—but then you don't give that person any food or clothing. What good does that do? So you see, it isn't enough just to have faith. Faith that doesn't show itself by good deeds is no faith at all— it is dead and useless. JAMES 2:15-17, NLT

*Large crowds followed Jesus as he came down the mountainside. Suddenly, a man with leprosy approached Jesus. He knelt before him, worshiping. "Lord," the man said, "if you want to, you can make me well again." **Jesus touched him.** "I want to," he said. "Be healed!" And instantly the leprosy disappeared.* MATTHEW 8:1-3, NLT, emphasis added

Stop judging others, and you will not be judged. MATTHEW 7:1, NLT

PRAYER

Father God, I make myself available to minister to those who have contracted this terrible disease of AIDS. Search my heart, Lord, so that I may go in your name, with pure intentions and a humble spirit. Order my steps, God, and show me the way. Put a watch on my lips that I might speak only the words that you give me. Open doors, prepare hearts, and be glorified in all I say and do, as you use me to accomplish your purposes in the lives of these precious people who are even now facing death. In Jesus' name. Amen.

ADDITIONAL RESOURCES

AIDS: A Christian Response by Howard E. Mueller (Concordia Publishing House, 1996).

An Epistle of Comfort: Scriptural Meditations & Passage for Persons Suffering from AIDS by William J. Dobbels (Sheed & Ward, 1990).

When AIDS Comes to Church by William E. Amos Jr. (Westminster/John Knox Press, 1988).

Burden of a Secret: A Story of Truth & Mercy in the Face of AIDS by Jimmy Allen (Ballantine Books, Inc., 1995).

Creating Compassion: Activities for Understanding HIV-AIDS by Phyllis Vos Wezeman (Pilgrim Press, The United Church Press, 1994).

Voices of Strength & Hope for a Friend with AIDS by Joseph Gallagher (Sheed & Ward, 1987).

When AIDS Comes Home: Answers to the Most Commonly Asked Questions: What to Say, What to Do, & How to Live with AIDS by Mignon Zylstra and David B. Beibel (Thomas Nelson, Inc., 1997).

KATHI MILLS

Kathi Mills is an author, editor, minister, and Bible teacher, who has worked with and ministered to people with AIDS, as well as to the homeless and those in prisons and rescue missions, for more than ten years. She also served for five years as a biblical counselor on the pastoral staff of South Coast Fellowship in Ventura, California.

WHEN NEIGHBORS ARE IMPACTED BY CRIME

BURGLARY
AND THEFT

*Unless the Lord builds a house, the work of the builders is
useless. Unless the Lord protects a city, guarding it with
sentries will do no good. It is useless for you to work so
hard from early morning until late at night, anxiously
working for food to eat; for God gives rest to his loved ones.*

PSALM 127:1-2, NLT

They had broken into nine houses on our side of the
street—including my family's. They also had used chloroform on every person as they slept, to assure not
being interrupted. Within six months, the same two persons
tried once again to break into the same neighborhood using the
same mode of operation. That was over 40 years ago during a
hot South Florida summer—but the memory of that time still
affects me. My childhood fears and terrors from the experience
of the burglary resurface every so often. The burglars took more
than things that hot summer night—they stole my ability to
enjoy a peaceful night's rest even now.

❏ *A burglary victim*

UNDERSTANDING THE CRISIS

Burglary is unlawful entry into a dwelling or a business that
usually, but not necessarily, includes theft. In 1995 two of every

three burglaries were residential. The entry may be by force, such as picking a lock or breaking a window, or it may be unforced, such as entry through an unlocked door or window. More than one half of all burglaries are committed by strangers.[1] According to the U.S. Department of Justice National Crime Survey, burglary occurs more often in the warmer months, and most burglaries occur between midnight and 6 A.M.

EFFECTS OF THE CRISIS

People historically consider their home to be their "castle," a place where they can feel safe and secure from the emotional distress of their day-to-day lives and certainly from physical distress and intrusion. Their physical surroundings provide a sense of safety and security.

When a home is burglarized, much more than physical possessions are stolen. The individual's sanctuary is penetrated and his or her place of safety and security is invaded. They have been personally violated. The theft also relieves the victims of the security and peace of mind that they enjoyed prior to the crime.

Every twelve seconds, a burglary occurs in the United States.[2] They leave victims feeling vulnerable, violated, and fearful. Many victims dramatically limit their mobility and activities. Elderly burglary victims frequently fear losing their independence. Burglary victims frequently grieve for those stolen articles that have irreplaceable sentimental and/or historical value.

HOW YOU CAN HELP AND ENCOURAGE

In Joshua 8:1 we read, "And the LORD said unto Joshua, Fear not, neither be thou dismayed" (KJV). The Hebrew word for "dismayed" conveys the idea of not allowing past negative experiences to control you in the present.

Victims of burglary frequently feel frightened, violated,

[1] From the Report to the Nation on Crime and Justice, second edition, 1988. Published by the U.S. Department of Justice, Bureau of Justice Statistics.   [2] Crime in the United States 1994, Uniform Crime Reports, Federal Bureau of Investigation, U.S. Department of Justice, Washington, D.C. 20535.

confused, and vulnerable. Helpers can assist by providing some structure and guidance after the event. Since safety and security will be burglary victims' primary concern, practical aid such as repairing broken doors or windows, replacing locks, assisting with cleanup, providing transportation, or offering to stay with the victims during times they feel most vulnerable can be extremely helpful. Offering to contact insurance agencies, assist with credit-card companies and document replacement can be of enormous value to burglary victims. The helper should listen to those concerns expressed by burglary victims, and provide comfort and assistance accordingly.

If you are going to encourage individuals affected to discuss their fears, have some positive suggestions as to how they can enhance their security and safety. Most law enforcement offices offer free home-security reviews which provide reasonable and cost-effective suggestions on how to secure a home. Some of the suggestions will likely include: light the outside of the house; trim the shrubs so they don't block your view or provide a shield for potential burglars; install good deadbolt locks and window grates; keep an inventory of valuables so you will know immediately whether anything is missing; lock outside doors and ground-floor windows, including those in the garage—even when a person is home; and some people find it comforting to have a dog trained to bark as a warning and deterrent. You might suggest that the person work with his or her neighbors and the local police department to develop a neighborhood watch program.

Be prepared to validate the experience and resulting anxieties of the victim. If the victim wants to retell the burglary experience, listen with empathy, not in judgment. Give reasonable guidance and practical support. Do not second-guess the victim and assume you know what he or she needs. Be careful not to make judgments about what you think the victim should have or could have done.

Help victims gain control over their anxieties, environment, and own security. As victims tell their stories, they will have an opportunity to listen to their own reactions and may hear things they have not considered as "solutions" to one or various problems. Pay specific attention to their body language and speech patterns as they retell their burglary experience. The reliving of a traumatic event can be distressing. It may be helpful for victims to talk with other individuals who have experienced a similar situation—perhaps in a support group meeting or an individual meeting. This can significantly reduce the sense of isolation and vulnerability that many experience. Allow victims to express anger, rage, and feelings regarding retribution. If you do have the opportunity to connect individuals with like experiences, make sure the burglary "survivors" have successfully coped with their burglary experience and can provide hope and encouragement to the "new" victims.

Very often children are the "forgotten victims" in a burglary. They may insist that their light be left on and the bedroom door be left ajar. In addition, a number of senior citizens live in fear of the night as a result of a burglary. They may change their sleeping habits and stay up late at night and sleep more during the daylight hours. The elderly particularly can be traumatized by a burglary, especially if a stolen TV or radio was a main "link" to information and the world. Churches may want to consider donating stolen items or providing funds to replace important stolen property. Some burglary victims feel they may not be able to adequately protect or defend themselves and their loved ones. These fears are reinforced by increased and graphic news media reports of burglaries and other violent crimes.

It is also very helpful to suggest devoting time to prayers of thanksgiving and Bible reading before bedtime. If individuals awaken during the night, they may find it helpful to again use prayer and Bible reading as a transition back into restful sleep. This does not mean that a faithful person should be fearless and not take normal precautions.

Helpful Things to Say and Do

- "Are you sleeping well?" "Does it take you long to go to sleep at night?"
- Offer to help them clean up, make a list of missing items, or contact their insurance agency.
- Helpful safety information can and should be shared at a time *after* the initial impact of the burglary during a later stage when the victim is searching or asking for ways to increase security and safety.

Hurtful Responses to Try to Avoid

- Do not tell a personal story to make it sound as if you know how the person feels, unless the victim asks you about your experience.
- Don't say: "You should have installed a burglary alarm system." "You shouldn't be living alone." "You should get yourself a watchdog." "You sure are lucky, it could have been worse." "You should have had insurance." "You should have had better locks." These comments only add to the victim's feelings of violation and self-blame.

If victims are supported, the help they receive can be an opportunity to counterbalance the hurt and violation they have experienced. Compassionate and appropriate assistance can also reaffirm the victims' confidence in others at a time when their trust has been compromised.

Related Scripture

Who will bring any charge against those whom God has chosen? It is God who justifies. Who is he that condemns? Christ Jesus, who died— more than that, who was raised to life—is at the right hand of God and is also interceding for us. Who shall separate us from the love of Christ? Shall trouble or hardship or persecution or famine or nakedness or danger or sword? As it is written: "For your sake we face death all day long; we are considered as sheep to be slaughtered." No, in all these things we are more than conquerors through him who loved us. For I am convinced that neither death nor life, neither angels nor demons, neither the present nor the future, nor any powers, neither height nor depth, nor anything else in all creation, will be able to separate us from the love of God that is in Christ Jesus our Lord. ROMANS 8:33-39, NIV

"Do not steal. EXODUS 20:15, NLT

"Do not murder. Do not commit adultery. Do not steal. Do not testify falsely. Honor your father and mother. Love your neighbor as yourself.'" MATTHEW 19:18, NLT

PRAYER

A prayer to share with your friend:

Dear God, I want to thank you that I did not have to walk through this burglary by myself, but that you were with me each moment. I want to thank you that you have placed people and other resources in my life to help me deal with this experience. I ask you to protect my family and our home from harm. I want to thank you, dear God, that each day the healing of my heart becomes more complete. Thank you, in Jesus' name. Amen

---

ADDITIONAL RESOURCES

The Crime Victim's Book by Morton Bard & Dawn Sangrey (Carol Publishing Group, 1986). A helpful book to understand the victimization experience.

Criminal Justice, Restitution, and Reconciliation by Burt Galaway and Joe Hudson (eds) (Willow Tree Press, Inc., 1990).

Counseling Victims of Violence by Sandra L. Brown (American Association for Counseling and Development, 1991).

BILL BARTON

Dr. Bill Barton is the senior pastor of Saint Andrews Presbyterian Church in Columbia, South Carolina.

HATE AND
BIAS CRIME

"I command you to love each other. When the world hates you,
remember it hated me before it hated you. The world would
love you if you belonged to it, but you don't.
I chose you to come out of the world, and so it hates you."

JOHN 15:17-19, NLT

On Super Bowl Sunday 1995, Friendship Missionary Baptist Church of Columbia, Tennessee, was fire-bombed. Three men tossed Molotov cocktails through the stained-glass windows of the modest country church. The bombs did not completely destroy the church building; however, pews and carpets were burned, and there was extensive smoke damage. The thing that caused the most damage was the message sent by the cross crudely nailed to the front door. To my mother, a member of this all-black church and someone who had grown up in rural Mississippi in the 1930s and 40s, the bombing was a cruel reminder of a time and an attitude she thought had long passed.
❑ *Author Rev. Lee A. Earl*

UNDERSTANDING THE CRISIS

The Federal Crimes Statistics Act of 1990 defines hate and bias crimes as crimes motivated by "hatred against a victim based on his or her race, religion, sexual orientation, ethnicity, or national origin."

In 1994 more than fifty-eight hundred hate-crime incidents were reported to the Federal Bureau of Investigation (FBI). Of those incidents, 60 percent were motivated by racial bias, 18 percent by religious bias, 12 percent by sexual-orientation bias, and 11 percent by ethnicity/national origin bias.[1]

EFFECTS OF THE CRISIS

When a bias crime is committed against a member of a minority community (whether a racial, ethnic, or other type of community grouping), the victim may be afraid to associate with other members of the group that has been targeted or, conversely, may respond by more strongly identifying with the group. In addition, the victim may refuse to seek needed services, especially if those services are primarily provided by the majority community.

My mother's first reaction to the crime was to personalize it. She thought that it might have something to do with her work of welcoming new members and counseling old members. Others in the church thought it was a conspiracy of some organized group sponsored by the entire white community. Some members were filled with fear and others with anger. Most in the white community were embarrassed, and some took too much responsibility to help repair the damage.

HOW YOU CAN HELP AND ENCOURAGE

In addition to individuals, communities also are significantly impacted by hate and bias crimes. When individuals are targets of hate because of their race, religion, sexual orientation, ethnicity, or national origin, their victimization can be projected to additional members of their community. Other members of the same group also will feel victimized and may be openly reactive. When places of worship are targeted for hate

[1] U.S. Department of Justice, Office for Victims of Crime, "National Victim Assistance Academy" manual, 21–1–2.

crime, the attacks on sacred and religious symbols may cause significant emotional and spiritual reactions and harm.[2]

Hate and bias crimes may have a more devastating effect than other crimes because they have a unique psychological impact on the victim(s). Here are some suggested ways you can respond to a hate and bias crime with an individual, a group, a congregation, and/or a community:[3]

1. Allow the victims to express their emotions, feelings, and even anger aroused by the hate crime.
2. Address the crisis of victimization as well as confront the wrongful act and the hate and prejudice exhibited by the crime.
3. If the case is prosecuted, provide support to the victims by accompanying them to court proceedings and by encouraging them to complete a victim impact statement if available in your jurisdiction. Your victim assistance advocate should be able to provide the information.
4. Be sure to provide referrals for cross-cultural assistance to the victims.
5. Serve as a healing influence in the community.

After the firebombing, the pastor of Friendship Baptist Church moved immediately to defuse the situation. Members of the local black community and even church members considered retaliation. When the pastor called for forgiveness and reconciliation, he received calls from across the country denouncing him and calling him an "Uncle Tom." But soon the situation and atmosphere changed. Members from local white churches worked side by side with the black members, pulling out burned carpet, repair-

---

[2] U.S. Dept. of Justice, Office for Victims of Crime, *National Bias Crimes Training for Law Enforcement and Victim Assistance Professionals: A Guide for Training Instructors,* published by the Education Development Center, Inc., and Massachusetts Criminal Justice Training Council. [3] U.S. Department of Justice, Office for Victims of Crime, "National Victim Assistance Academy" manual, 21–1–8, 9, 10.

ing damaged pews, and painting smoke-stained walls. By the following Sunday, the church was ready to hold worship services once again. But this time was different. Sitting in those repaired pews were as many white worshipers as black.

Note: If you are a pastor or leader in a church or community that has experienced hate and bias crime, you may have been a target yourself. Be aware that you too may need assistance and the support of others. You also may be the one to whom the rest of the community and congregation looks for guidance, as well as a model on how to respond.

HELPFUL THINGS TO SAY AND DO

- Express your concern for the person's immediate needs as a result of the crisis. Ask if he or she feels safe. If not, attempt to find a "place of safety" for the victim with his or her permission.
- Ask the victim whether he or she would like to discuss the victimization and its impact. Allow free expression of feelings without judgment.
- Let the victim know that you are sorry that the wrongful act has occurred.
- Ask the victim what could be done to help "repair" the damage—whether physical, emotional, or spiritual. If possible, take actions to accomplish the victim's suggestions.
- Offer to pray with and/or for the victims and for others who were impacted by the crime.
- Be aware of your own prejudices and biases as you address the needs of the victims and the community.
- Make certain that appropriate law enforcement is being made available to address the situation.

HURTFUL RESPONSES TO TRY TO AVOID

- Avoid platitudes that hold the victim responsible for the offender's crime.

- Be careful not to ask *why* questions, which tend to imply guilt and wrongdoing on the part of the victim.
- Be sure not to minimize the impact of the crime and trauma on the life of a victim and on a community.

Note: All the above (Helpful and Hurtful Responses) can be applied to groups of individuals victimized by hate crimes.

RELATED SCRIPTURE

Hatred stirs up dissension, but love covers over all wrongs.
PROVERBS 10:12, NIV

You have heard that it was said, "Love your neighbor and hate your enemy." But I tell you: Love your enemies and pray for those who persecute you, that you may be sons of your Father in heaven.
MATTHEW 5:43-45, NIV

Blessed are you when men hate you, when they exclude you and insult you and reject your name as evil, because of the Son of Man. Rejoice in that day and leap for joy, because great is your reward in heaven.
Luke 6:22-23, NIV

PRAYER

Dear Lord, truly you know what I/we have gone through. You know what it is like to be hated, hurt, wounded—just because of who you are. Lord, sometimes it is too much to bear—all this hatred and wrong. But you are a God of justice and righteousness. You, O Lord, are our defender and shield. Protect us and guide us to respond rightly to these acts of hate.

Lord, open our eyes to see your love. Open our heart to receive your comfort. And bring peace to our life and to this community once again. In your name we pray. Amen.

ADDITIONAL RESOURCES

A Legacy of Hatred by David A. Rausch (Moody Bible Institute, 1986). This book discusses the roots of the Jewish holocaust.

Counseling Victims of Violence by Sandra L. Brown (American Association for Counseling and Development, 1991).

Crime Victims: An Introduction to Victimology. 2nd ed. by Andrew Karen. pg. 261, 1990, Wadsworth, Inc. Belmont, CA.

LEE A. EARL

Reverend Lee A. Earl is chairman of the Neighbors Who Care National Board of Directors. Prior to moving to the D.C. area, Reverend Earl served as the senior minister of the Twelfth Street Baptist Church in Detroit, Michigan. As a pastor, he received national recognition as an activist and church builder.

VICTIMS AND THE JUVENILE JUSTICE SYSTEM

Do what is good and run from evil—that you may live!
Then the Lord God Almighty will truly be your helper, just
as you have claimed he is. Hate evil and love what is
good; remodel your courts into true halls of justice.
Perhaps even yet the Lord God Almighty will have
mercy on his people who remain.

AMOS 5:14-15, NLT

M ary, a secretary who had only a few years until retirement, had just gotten off work and was waiting at the curb for her bus. Suddenly, she felt a sharp blow and then a fierce pulling and tugging of her upper arm. Mary fell shoulder-first into the street below. Out of the corner of her eye, she saw a young boy running madly across the street with her purse tight under his arm.

"Just a purse snatching" left Mary in the intensive care unit for three weeks. She found out she was permanently disabled and could not return to work full-time. Mary later learned that a police officer had witnessed the crime, apprehended the youth within a few blocks, and made an arrest. During her convalescence at home a few weeks later, Mary called the juvenile court to find out the status of the case and what had happened to the boy. Mary was abruptly told that no information could be given out on the status of the case. The person on the other end of the line said, "It makes no difference that you claim to be the victim. The law prohibits me from giving out any information!"

UNDERSTANDING THE CRISIS

Crimes committed by juveniles can pose additional complications for victims compared to crimes committed by adults. One of the underlying reasons is that the juvenile justice system is designed to protect the confidentiality of the juvenile offender.

A "juvenile" is defined as a child or youth who has not yet attained the age of majority (the age at which full civil rights are accorded), usually eighteen years of age. Juvenile offenders are those who have violated a state or federal law or a county, municipal, or local ordinance. Although most states and the federal government use the age of eighteen to distinguish between juvenile and adult, some jurisdictions use lower ages. However, even when the offender is within the juvenile-age range, the offender may be tried in the adult system depending on the severity of the crime. It is important to know the age your jurisdiction uses to determine if the situation will be handled as a juvenile or adult matter.

EFFECTS OF THE CRISIS

There is little or no difference between the impact of a crime by juvenile offenders on a victim and the impact on a victim of a similar crime committed by adults. The victim experiences shock, disorientation, and trauma. If you are assisting a victim of a specific crime (e.g., rape or homicide, etc.), it will be helpful to refer to other appropriate sections of this book.

HOW YOU CAN HELP AND ENCOURAGE

In assisting someone confronting the juvenile court system, it is important for you or someone close to the family to gain an understanding of the juvenile process in your local jurisdiction. There is a good deal of variation among states, some are now providing victim assistance in the juvenile court system similar to those in the adult system. However, this is not the norm and you should be prepared to assist the victim in a court process that is established to protect the juvenile offender and provides limited or no access for the victim.

You may want to refer to the suggested publications listed at the end of this section that provide an introduction to the area of juvenile justice. Historically, there has been differential treatment of youth versus adults by the criminal justice system. Juvenile offenders have been viewed as "errant children" who should receive therapeutic treatment and rehabilitation. This may present victims with a heightened sense that the crimes committed against them are being minimized by the system. If this is the case, be sure to acknowledge and validate the impact of the crime on the life of the victim.

In addition, the juvenile justice system emphasizes alternatives to detention or incarceration for juvenile offenders, such as community service. Currently, there are major efforts to increase community-based placements for these children. Although this provides important opportunities for rehabilitation for the youthful offender, it can be very difficult for the victim, who may encounter the offender in the neighborhood. As you provide support, be sure to discuss and focus on safety issues concerning the victim. Many juvenile court systems are so overwhelmed with cases that sometimes even very violent cases are dismissed or delayed, with the youth not being detained (because there is a significant bias against detaining youth). The victim may be further victimized by seeing offenders essentially walk away from the system with little or no consequences for their actions.

There is a very high level of confidentiality granted to juvenile offenders. In keeping with the belief that the juvenile is in need of rehabilitation instead of sanctions, confidentiality is seen as essential to avoid problems with labeling and criminal records. Typically, the victim's first taste of this confidentiality is when he or she calls to find out about the status of the case. In many situations, the victim is informed that the court cannot acknowledge or confirm a matter involving the particular juvenile. As a rule, it does not get much better.

When assisting the victim of juvenile offenders, you may want to look for opportunities for the victim to participate in the system. Those juvenile court judges who have considerable control of their courtroom and its proceedings may have established their own policies regarding victim participation. There may be a statutory provision giving the victim the opportunity to make a victim impact statement, a written statement about the impact of the crime on his or her life. If possible, determine if a victim impact statement opportunity is available, and how the victim can participate.

In general, juvenile courts have not provided adequate resources to assist crime-victim needs. If allowed in your state, you may want to offer to attend the court proceedings with the victim or identify a friend, church member, or family member to attend. This is important since the court personnel may not be available or sensitive to the needs of the victim, and the court experience can be quite upsetting. Contact the prosecutor's officer or the juvenile probation officer to determine if there is a victim advocate assigned to the case. Ask how you can help.

However, in some communities there are innovative programs focused on juvenile crime that provide opportunities for potential healing and restoration of both victims and offenders. Some of these include juvenile restitution and victim-offender reconciliation programs, both of which have their roots in biblical principles. Restitution, or the compensation of the victim by the offender, is sometimes used as a sanction in the juvenile court. With its dual objective of holding the offender accountable and restoring the victim, restitution provides a potential opportunity for true victim healing while helping the offender understand the consequences of his or her behavior. Victim-offender reconciliation (or mediation) is an opportunity for a victim and an offender to meet on a voluntary basis to discuss the crime, its impact, and the consequences. Victim-offender reconciliation programs may be available in your area. Some churches provide victim-offender reconciliation programs as well. Check with the judge or the juvenile court to determine availability in your community.

HELPFUL THINGS TO SAY AND DO

- "It was not your fault. No one could have expected this from that child/youth." It is important to acknowledge and validate the victim's view that he could not have anticipated, nor did he contribute to the violence—if that is true.

- "We may not be able to monitor the progress of this case as well as you might like to, but we can help you work toward your recovery in several ways."

- "Perhaps we could help identify some support for you or help you find a support group of people who have had this happen to them."

- "If you choose to participate in a juvenile restitution or a victim-offender mediation program, could we provide some assistance to you?" Remember, a victim should never be forced or even subtly coerced into participating in these programs.

HURTFUL RESPONSES TO TRY TO AVOID

- "After all, he was only a child . . . this is to be expected." Never minimize the victimization and its aftermath by appearing to excuse the behavior of the "child."

- "You can't expect the system to punish this child as an adult." It is important to find a balance between raising the victim's expectations too high (particularly given what is known about the juvenile justice system), and putting the victim down for having certain hopes regarding appropriate justice.

RELATED SCRIPTURE

Every word of God proves true. He defends all who come to him for protection. PROVERBS 30:5, NLT

Speak up for those who cannot speak for themselves; ensure justice for those who are perishing. Yes, speak up for the poor and helpless, and see that they get justice. PROVERBS 31:8-9, NLT

PRAYER

A prayer to share with your friend:

Help me, O Lord, to know how to deal with this crime and hurt in my life. Help me when I become discouraged, and guide and sustain me today in all my thoughts, words, and deeds. Help me to have the right perspective toward those who have hurt me. Let me trust in you, God, to bring justice and righteousness in this situation. Let all my actions and thoughts remind me that you love me and are in control of my life. Amen.

ADDITIONAL RESOURCES

Juvenile Justice: A Guide to Theory and Practice by S. W. Cox and J. J. Conrad (Brown & Benchmark, 1996). This textbook provides a comprehensive overview of the historical roots and evolution of the juvenile court in America. The tension between juvenile rights and services versus victim rights and accommodations is apparent here.

Forgive and Forget by Louis Smedes (HarperSanFrancisco, 1984). A classic on forgiveness.

Desktop Guide to Good Juvenile Probation Practice by the National Center for Juvenile Justice (Office of Juvenile Justice and Delinquency Program, Washington D.C., 1993). This document is primarily a practitioner's manual. It contains a good historical account of juvenile justice issues, the current practices in probation, and some discussion of victim programs in juvenile probation practice.

Juvenile Offenders and Victims of Crime: A Focus on Violence by H.N. Snyder and M. Sickmund (Office of Juvenile Justice and Delinquency Prevention, Washington, D.C., 1995). This document contains a summary of current statistics regarding juvenile perpetrators and victims.

DR. MARIO GABOURY

Mario Thomas Gaboury, J.D., Ph.D., is associate professor of criminal justice at the University of New Haven where he also directs UNH's crime victim study center. He has worked in the area of crime victims' rights and services for almost two decades and is formerly deputy director of the U.S. Justice Department's Office for Victims of Crime and formerly legislative specialist at the National Organization for Victim Assistance.

IMPRISONMENT
OF A FAMILY MEMBER

But you, O Lord, are a shield around me, my glory,
and the one who lifts my head high. I cried out to the Lord,
and he answered me from his holy mountain. I lay down and slept.
I woke up in safety, for the Lord was watching over me.
I am not afraid of ten thousand enemies who surround me on every side.

PSALM 3:3-6, NIV

When Steve went to prison, his wife, Donna, was faced with a nearly impossible task. Not only did she now face having to parent a teenager on her own, but she was saddled with all kinds of tasks for which she was ill-prepared: managing the family finances, car and home maintenance, and dealing with the loss of the family's main source of income.

UNDERSTANDING THE CRISIS

When a family member goes to prison, the whole family system suffers. Since approximately 94 percent of the nation's prisoners are men, it is most often the wife and children who are left to fend for themselves when the husband and father goes.

But when a mother is incarcerated, there are even worse problems. As many as 80 to 85 percent of mothers, prior to imprisonment, had legal custody of children under age eighteen and were the primary source of financial and emotional support.

And for parents who see their children going to prison, there is a particularly devastating grief that accompanies the shame: the death of a dream and the particular frustration of being unable to help a son or daughter avoid further pain and hurt.

Although family members love and identify with the incarcerated, they often also feel anger and rejection toward the prisoner for having caused the situation. They experience disrepute and rejection in the community. Children cannot understand—no matter how frequent or honest the explanations—why their parent is no longer there for them. Older children often develop school performance problems. Symptoms, such as eating disorders, insomnia, or antisocial behavior often emerge.

Most marriages do not survive the prison experience. By some estimates, as many as 80 percent of marriages end in divorce when one partner goes to prison for a significant length of time. The odds against keeping the marriage together are staggering.

For the prisoner, who is in a controlled environment and isolated from his or her family, particular problems develop. Unrealistic expectations on the "outside spouse" bring pressure for constant communication, for financial support, or for more frequent visits. Prisoners often expect their free-world spouses to campaign for postconviction legal help or vindication. Cut off from regular, frequent communication, the imprisoned spouse often develops suspicions that erupt into unfounded accusations, which frequently lead to an end to their relationship.

Sexual frustrations build when a prisoner is separated from his or her spouse. Fear of unfaithfulness can lead to miscommunication between spouses, and this often leads to in-prison discipline problems.

Studies recently published by social scientists at the University of Michigan show that men and women, in adjusting to prison life, generally go through five predictable stages. Similar to the way terminally ill patients face death, prisoners experience denial, anger, bargaining, depression, and, finally, acceptance. Understanding this, and responding appropriately, may help family members deal with changing behavior on the part of prisoners.

Meanwhile, the spouse on the outside struggles with all kinds of problems. Regular income is often gone. New roles as disciplinarian and family manager become overwhelming. Sometimes the spouse develops resentment toward the prisoner, who basically has all needs cared for (food, clothing, shelter, recreation) and who carries no part of the load in daily family management.

How You Can Help and Encourage

How can families of the incarcerated best be supported? An important first step is to understand their feelings and the situation. Read relevant material. Spend time listening to ex-prisoners and the families of those currently and formerly incarcerated to learn specifics of what they face.

Recognize that spouses or "significant others" of incarcerated persons may also have unhealthy coping mechanisms of their own. Misuse of alcohol or drugs, abuse of credit cards, or other unhealthy habits often compound problems for struggling spouses or family members.

Understanding generic critical-incident stress-debriefing issues will help family members see that, subsequent to an incarceration, they may cycle through a normal range of emotions and symptoms that include anxiety, depression, guilt, feeling lost or abandoned, anger or irritability, difficulty in concentrating, poor attention span, and more.

The three areas in which family members of the incarcerated will need the greatest support and help are: (1) practical, physical help with finances or daily management; (2) nonjudgmental companionship that provides a listening ear and gentle advice when asked; and (3) a channel of spiritual strength and support to provide supernatural help to endure what seems to be insurmountable problems and obstacles.

Providing direct support such as child care, food, or help with housing may help in some cases. But often the best long-range assistance is to discover and link family members to existing social services or relief agencies that can provide help for the long term. This may include connecting them with a strong caring and sharing local church body.

Government, county, and Christian agencies often have counseling services available on a sliding fee scale. Finding dependable, low-cost car repair and maintenance help is a practical way to help. Offering to help with home repairs and seasonal maintenance routines (changing furnace filters, cleaning gutters, etc.) is a practical way to assist. Including the children of prisoners in outings and social activities (at no cost to the prisoner's family) can help them feel normal and accepted.

Often, spouses and the incarcerated can participate together in the in-prison Planted by Living Waters Marriage Seminars, as conducted by qualified volunteers through local Prison Fellowship area offices. Support groups for spouses of the incarcerated are frequently organized and conducted by local Prison Fellowship offices (for the nearest PF area office, contact Prison Fellowship Ministries at 703-478-0100).

Providing transportation for families to visit their incarcerated loved ones is another way to give tangible help.

Special needs arise as prisoners become "short," or near release. Now the issue becomes reorienting to a society in which the prisoners' every move is no longer controlled. Prisoners who have served even short sentences still report being nearly immobilized at the prospect of making choices in a grocery store or from a restaurant menu. A mentor, or helping friend, can help in transition. In finding employment, exiting prisoners may be helped by the Federal Bonding Program

(FBP)[1] or the Work Opportunity Tax Credit (WOTC)[2] the Targeted Job Tax Credit program, which provides a tax incentive to employers willing to hire ex-prisoners.

And ongoing spiritual and emotional support from extended family or a supportive church may make the difference in whether the ex-prisoner stays out or goes back, as nearly two-thirds do.

HELPFUL THINGS TO SAY AND DO

- Be sure the family's physical needs are met.
- Provide mentoring for children whose parent is incarcerated.
- Offer to assist with home repairs.
- Invite the children to participate in social activities.
- Holidays can be particularly upsetting and isolating. Prisoners' children may receive gifts for Christmas in the name of their incarcerated parents through Prison Fellowship's Angel Tree program.
- Assist in helping arrange visits to the prison or jail for the family.
- Assist in financial counseling or planning to help the family work through a plan to assure that they can make it through this situation. This may include offering financial support from the church as appropriate.

HURTFUL RESPONSES TO TRY TO AVOID

- Ignoring the families of prisoners or treating them in a demeaning or judgmental way inflicts greater shame and only magnifies the problems.
- Don't inquire about details of the crime or charges of the imprisoned. You can encourage the at-home parent to not engage in deception, particularly with children,

[1]For more information about the FBP, you may write to: Federal Bonding Program, 1725 DeSales Street, NW, Suite 900, Washington DC 20036. For immediate help, contact the local State Employment Service. [2]For more information about WOTC, contact your State Employment Service Office.

about where incarcerated parent is. Children will have a difficult enough time dealing with the absence. It is not helpful to say that the absent parent is dead, on a long trip, or other well-intentioned falsehoods. Offer to be present when the at-home parent explains the situation to the children.

- Assuming that prisoners "deserve what they get" and believing naive notions that prisoners enjoy "country-club living" in prison are also hurtful to families of the incarcerated. Find out the facts about daily prison life.

- While helping families, do not treat prisoners as non-entities. An occasional visit, letter, or telephone call to let them know how their families are doing, and that they are being cared for, can be a terrific "lift." Be aware, however, that in some cases there may be restraining orders or other legal constraints that must be obeyed. Providing something special for family birthdays or holidays—since the incarcerated member is unable to do so—will also support the whole family.

RELATED SCRIPTURE

I, the Lord, am your God, who brought you from the land of Egypt so you would no longer be slaves. I have lifted the yoke of slavery from your neck so you can walk free with your heads held high.
LEVITICUS 26:13, NLT

He has removed our rebellious acts as far away from us as the east is from the west. PSALM 103:12, NLT

Then Peter came to him and asked, "Lord, how often should I forgive someone who sins against me? Seven times?" "No!" Jesus replied, "seventy times seven!" MATTHEW 18:21-22, NLT

And forgive us our sins—just as we forgive those who have sinned against us. And don't let us yield to temptation. LUKE 11:4, NLT

Never pay back evil for evil to anyone. Do things in such a way that everyone can see you are honorable. ROMANS 12:17, NLT

Endure suffering along with me, as a good soldier of Christ Jesus. 2 TIMOTHY 2:3, NLT

PRAYER

Lord, thank you for loving not only the prisoners, but also the families they leave behind. Help us to deal with any hurt and shame we've experienced. Help us not to feel resentful or vindictive against those who don't understand, or who may shun us. You suffered as the result of the actions of others, and so do we. Help us to rise above that, to put our trust in you. Thank you for being there, even in the darkest hours. We love you and trust you to do what is best for us and for our loved ones in prison. In our difficulties, we want to glorify Christ. Show us how to do that, and give us the courage to follow you. In Jesus' name, Amen.

ADDITIONAL RESOURCES

Daddy, Why Are You Going to Jail? by Stephen P. Lawson (Harold Shaw Publishers, 1992).

Families of Adult Prisoners (December 1993). This research summary booklet from the Research and Development Department of Prison Fellowship Ministries is available by writing PFM at P.O. Box 17500, Washington, DC 20041-0500 or by calling (703) 478-0100. Contains a lengthy bibliography of selected books and articles.

Going to Prison? by Jimmy Tayoun (Biddle Publishing Co., 1997). Write P.O. Box 1305, #103, Brunswick, ME 04011, or telephone (207) 833-5016 for this booklet.

The Life Recovery Bible (Tyndale House Publishers, 1992). A Bible with helps for people in recovery.

TERRY WHITE

Terry White is Vice President of Communications for Prison Fellowship Ministries in Washington D.C. In addition to his experience as a journalist and journalism educator, he also spent 12 years on the pastoral staff of a large evangelical church in suburban Minneapolis prior to joining Prison Fellowship in 1992.

WHEN PEOPLE ARE VICTIMIZED

CHILD VICTIMIZATION

I weep for the hurt of my people. I am stunned and silent,
mute with grief. Is there no medicine in Gilead?
Is there no physician there? Why is there no healing
for the wounds of my people?

JEREMIAH 8:21-22, NLT

B illy and Mary had been brought to Sunday school by their elementary school friends. Their clothes were unkempt, and they had obviously not bathed for some time. When they wolfed down cookies, a handful at a time, their Sunday school teacher suspected that they might be more hungry than impolite. The next week she brought extra food and unobtrusively gave it to them. She then decided to try to visit their home to "let the parents know how pleased I was that the children were attending church." The small house appeared not to have been cleaned for weeks. A three-year-old sister was crying alone on a cot in the corner. No adults were in sight. Billy said that they didn't know where their father was. . . . And their mother? She was out with her new boyfriend. "She always is."[1]

---

[1] Reprinted with permission from *A Manual for Clergy and Congregations* by Rev. David and Anne Delaplane (self-published by The Spiritual Dimension).

UNDERSTANDING THE CRISIS

Child victimization is a crime that is punishable by law through-out the country. In most states, a child is considered anyone under the age of eighteen years. There are four areas of child abuse and neglect that will be considered in this section.

Child neglect is the failure of a caretaker to provide the ingre-dients essential for developing a child's physical, intellectual, and emotional capacities. This could take the form of with-holding or not providing adequate food, clothing, shelter, supervision, or medical care. Some potential indicators of neglect include apathy, chronic hunger, emaciation, and little sense of home and family.

Child physical abuse is nonaccidental physical injury inflicted by a person responsible for a child's welfare. Types of abuse include: excessive shaking, hitting, burning, tying up, immer-sion in scalding water, etc. Observable wounds and bruises are the generally accepted criteria in most states. Physical abuse of children rarely is a single incident but an action that is repeated over and over. Physical abuse can result in permanent damage, scarring, internal injuries, or even death of the child.

Some potential indicators and reactions of physical abuse include: cowering at sudden moves, excessive fear, deep-seated anger, fear of going home, and demonstrating overly aggressive behavior with peers.

Child sexual abuse is contact or interaction between a child and an adult or significantly older perpetrator for the purpose of control or sexual gratification of the perpetrator. It includes acts such as fondling, digital or penile penetration, exhibition-ism, and/or the involvement of the child in prostitution or the production of pornography. Some potential indicators and reac-tions include: physical complaints of pain or irritation in the genital area, depression, clinging, premature sexualized behav-ior or speech, sexual acting out, extreme reluctance to be around certain people, and suicidal gestures.

Child emotional abuse is a chronic pattern of behaviors in which the child is belittled, humiliated, or ridiculed. Child emotional neglect is the consistent failure of a parent or caretaker to provide a child with appropriate support, attention, and affection.[2] Child emotional abuse and neglect both include verbal and emotional assault, extreme forms of punishment and confinement, threatened harm, excessive blaming, and withholding love or affection to achieve a desired behavior.

Some potential indicators of emotional abuse and neglect include: low self-esteem, sense of worthlessness, eating disorders, sleeping disturbances, self-destructive behavior, chronic underachievement, and irrational and persistent fears.

HOW YOU CAN HELP AND ENCOURAGE

Because child victimization takes these many forms, helpful methods of support and encouragement will also take many forms. But one response that is both common and essential to meeting the needs of all child victims is that of giving highest priority to assuring their immediate safety and protection from further victimization. Just as Jesus gave this priority to the children when they were brought to him, stopping all adult discourse in favor of blessing them (Matthew 19:13-14), so, when it is found that any child is being victimized in any way, that child's welfare should take precedence over any other consideration.

As we become increasingly aware of the great extent of child victimization, we will become more alert to the likelihood of its occurrence in our community and congregations. When the indicators of possible abuse are observed, further investigation is required. The people of God have an obligation to be very vigilant to the needs of the child "for of such is the kingdom of God" (Mark 10:14, KJV).

There are certainly occasions when observation of reactions and indicators is confirmed by open disclosure. When the

[2] U.S. Department of Justice, Office for Victims of Crime, "National Victim Assistance Academy" manual, 15–18.

victimization becomes intolerable, the child, against all odds of intimidation, threat, and of simply being a child in an adult world, may find a way to let it be known to an adult that he or she is being abused. This may be by a hint, by saying it happened to a friend, by talking to a favorite stuffed toy in the presence of a caretaker, or by simply blurting out the problem, usually at an unexpected moment. It is important to remember that a child under such stress rarely lies. If there are unexpected repercussions, the child may recant merely because of them. Many children never disclose abuse and it is only through outside intervention and proper investigation that these cases become known.

By whatever manner the victimization is disclosed, the next step is the most vital. *Anyone* who suspects child abuse or neglect must report the abuse to the proper authorities. This means a call to the Child Protective Services of the state or county Department of Social or Human Services. All states require mandatory reporting of suspected cases of child abuse by anyone who is responsible for the care of the children. This can not only protect the child, but it also can prevent possible liability for failure to report. Inform anyone coming to you with information about possible abuse that you cannot hold the confidence of an issue that must be reported to the proper authorities.

The other is awareness of cases of false reporting and of some failures by social services to make appropriate responses. These concerns should not be the cause of avoiding reporting but rather a reason to become an advocate for the child to see that the protection system works as intended. It should be kept in mind that the child protection system is designed to discover the truth. Cooperation with this process is essential for the welfare of the child. A concerned and informed counselor or pastor will find a way to provide effective, immediate, and ongoing safety for the child, keeping in mind that this is the highest priority.

Give your assurance of assistance to the child and to the

supporting adult. Because there are often legal implications, the nonoffending spouse or caretaker will need assurance that he or she has done the right thing in bringing the abuse into the open. Often there are unpleasant family and congregational implications that will make all involved doubt the validity of the accusation or report. But, as in the lancing of a boil, the initial pain is the only way to effect long-term healing.

Be careful not to divide your assistance and support between the child and the alleged offender. This, of course, may be very difficult if both are in the same family, church, and/or known to you. The alleged offender may need assistance and encouragement to cooperate with the authorities. He or she also may need someone to walk with him/her through the process. If at all possible, enlist someone who is trusted and knowledgeable to work with the alleged offender in order to enable you to care and support the child without confusion.

HELPFUL THINGS TO SAY AND DO

- Be sure to know your state's reporting laws concerning child abuse and neglect. Realize that anyone reporting abuse and child victimization with honest intent to help is exempt from liability by the laws of every state. However, in some states there can be liability for failure to report and protect. Always report suspected abuse.
- Make every attempt to carefully listen to the child in the presence of someone trusted by the child but never in the presence of the alleged offender. Do not, however, attempt to conduct your own investigation. It may present severe problems later on.
- Assure the child that he or she is not to blame, and express appreciation for the disclosure.
- Let the child and the nonoffending caretakers know that you will walk with them through the entire process of protection and investigation.
- See that the child receives counseling from a qualified child-therapy specialist.

HURTFUL RESPONSES TO TRY TO AVOID

- Upon disclosure, do not overreact. This may intimidate the child and inhibit further disclosure.
- Do not take any indicator or disclosure statement lightly. Usually disclosure is very difficult for a child. Sometimes only small portions of the events will come out at a time and then only as the early limited statements are affirmed.
- Do not immediately take the alleged offender's word above that of the child victim if he or she denies the charge. Adults can be more convincing and may be active and well-known in the church. This does not mean they are innocent. Leave this to the investigative process. The safety of the child is the highest priority during initial disclosure.

RELATED SCRIPTURE

Even if my father and mother abandon me, the Lord will hold me close. PSALM 27:10, NLT

And anyone who welcomes a little child like this on my behalf is welcoming me. But if anyone causes one of these little ones who trusts in me to lose faith, it would be better for that person to be thrown into the sea with a large millstone tied around the neck.
MATTHEW 18:5-6, NLT

And now a word to you fathers. Don't make your children angry by the way you treat them. Rather, bring them up with the discipline and instruction approved by the Lord. EPHESIANS 6:4, NLT

PRAYER

With a child:

Dear Jesus, I feel sad about what has happened to me. I sometimes feel that I have been hurt because I have been bad. But I know that, even though I may sometimes have done things I should not have done, I should not have been hurt in this way. When you were here, Jesus, you were hurt by people when you did not deserve it. But you said that your heavenly Father was here to help you. And you have said that you will also be with me when I am hurt. Thank you for being with me, and for _____, who is here to help me. Amen.

For the caregiver:

O God, my loving Creator and Savior. I can never fully understand you, nor can I understand the pain and suffering of a child. I only desire to relieve that pain and suffering. I trust that in doing so I may more clearly understand your nature, that you are the Father of all mankind, and that even in the pain your compassion fails not. I pray for the safety and protection of this child. Please guide and grant strength as we do what is just and right in this situation. Through Jesus Christ our Lord, who loves each of us and who willingly suffered for us. Amen.

ADDITIONAL RESOURCES

Sexual Abuse in Christian Homes and Churches by Carolyn Holdread Heggen (Herald Press, 1993). An excellent perspective on the subject, with particular emphasis on its existence in the Christian community.

Cry Out by P. E. Quinn (Abingdon Press, 1988). The author, now the holder of a D.Min. degree, was severely physically abused as a child. He tells a compelling story of how the old hymn "Jesus Loves Me" had a powerful impact on his healing.

Unlocking the Secret World by Wayne and Diane Tesch (Tyndale House Publishers, 1995). The authors supply individual Christian and church staff members with detailed information on responding to child abuse they may see in their communities and churches.

DAVID W. AND ANNE DELAPLANE

Reverend David W. Delaplane is a pastor, educator, and advisor to clergy on crime victimization and the executive director of the Spiritual Dimension in Victim Services in Denver, Colorado. Anne, a criminal justice specialist, is associate director. They are recipients of the U.S. Presidential Award for Service to Victims of Crime.

ELDERLY
VICTIMIZATION

*"Show your fear of God by standing up in the presence of elderly people
and showing respect for the aged. I am the Lord."*

*We live our lives beneath your wrath. We end our lives with a groan.
Seventy years are given to us! Some may even reach eighty.
But even the best of these years are filled with pain and trouble;
soon they disappear, and we are gone. Teach us to make the most
of our time so that we may grow in wisdom.*

Eighty-two-year-old Henry believed that the Lord would have him help them. He had room in his once-filled but modest home. His wife of forty-three years had died just two years ago, and his three grown children lived in other states and other countries. Kindly, Henry took a needy mother and her twenty-year-old daughter in to live with him until they could get established on their own. It was pleasant enough company for him. But little did he realize that they had taken his credit card number and used it to buy over twelve thousand dollars' worth of clothes and gifts for themselves and other family members. When his phone bill came, over three thousand dollars' worth of long-distance calls were charged to his number.

UNDERSTANDING THE CRISIS

Elderly victimization is the committing of crimes against the elderly, individuals sixty-five and older, by strangers, relatives, or acquaintances. Crimes considered as *elder abuse* are committed predominantly by caretakers and family members and include such acts as sexual and physical violence, neglect, economic exploitation, and fraud.[1] Elderly victimization may leave individuals feeling frightened, angry, out-of-control, and especially vulnerable.

HOW YOU CAN HELP AND ENCOURAGE

Effectively assisting elderly persons after a trauma or crime entails both a special sensitivity and a specific understanding of the unique issues they face. These issues cluster around the latter stages of life: retirement or loss of employment, decline in health, loss of income, loss of mobility, and greater fear, as physical frailty sets in. Any significant setback, whether physical or financial, threatens loss of independence. Those who help need to understand the scope and presence of those losses and begin to weave an appropriate response to assisting elderly individuals in crisis.

Trauma and crisis can strike the elderly when they can be the most vulnerable. They are at a stage of endings, and any type of crisis or loss can have significant impact on their physical, emotional, and spiritual lives. Many older individuals identify easily with the words of the psalmist: "trouble and sorrow" (Psalm 90:10). When a crime or trauma happens, the elderly may perceive that their future is in jeopardy.

If an elderly individual has experienced a victimization by a caretaker or family member, this can cause a severe emotional crisis. It may produce shame and embarrassment that prevents disclosure, and obstacles to recovery, especially as this may be the primary support system. For the elderly, "home"

[1] U.S. Department of Justice, Office for Victims of Crime, "National Victim Assistance Academy" manual, 18–4. Also, see chapter on fraud, page 113.

may symbolize more than it does for the younger population, which will move four or five times and put down only temporary roots. Very often the house where older individuals reside is the same one where they raised their family. Inabilities and declining resources may prevent making needed and crime-preventative repairs to homes. Loss of property (especially sentimental items such as jewelry) because of a crime can significantly increase their trauma as the loss cuts the bonds that provide meaning and memory in their lives.

The sad fact for many elderly individuals is that living a long time results in the loss of their friends and loved ones. Often the elderly are left with little personal support. Those closest to them may have died or moved or may be ill and unable to offer support. In the wake of a crisis or trauma, a personal support system of friends, family, and fellow church members is key to the recovery and restoration of the elderly.

A crisis can strike the elderly in yet a different manner. Older individuals have the highest rates of hospitalization, chronic physical limitations, and per capita spending for physicians' services.[2] Vision, hearing and dental problems have become a way of life. A broken bone can be a major threat to health that may exacerbate other physical problems. Physiological changes as persons age render them less able to leave or escape potentially dangerous situations.[3]

Mental processes can mirror the physical. With the slowing of the cognitive functions, the ability of the elderly to deal with stress may decline as well. Some older individuals may be more easily confused and thus become increasingly vulnerable to fraud and larceny schemes.

These unique and significant issues impact an older person's response to trauma and crisis. It is important for those assisting the elderly to develop an understanding of these issues and appropriate crisis-response techniques. In that way,

[2] Network Information Bulletin, National Organization for Victim Assistance, Vol. 2, #2, 1985. [3] "National Victim Assistance Academy" manual, 18–5.

caring individuals and church leaders and members can more
effectively offer help and healing to older individuals in crisis.

VICTIMIZATION OF THE ELDERLY

Information gathered over the past decade indicates that the
elderly appear to be less victimized per capita than other age
groups.[4] They can, however, suffer greater impact from violent
crime because of their life situations. Violent crime attacks the
basic fabric of the later chapters of life and registers high,
numerous, and uncounted costs. Often the highest loss has
little to do with money. It is the broken spirit that can impact
the elderly most.

The elderly are more likely to be victims of fraud (see section on fraud).[5] The nature of the crime of larceny and fraud
impacts the elderly where they are most vulnerable. While sta-
tistically they may not have more money stolen per capita than
another age group, dollar for dollar they suffer greater damage. Their ability to replace lost income is significantly less
than that of other age groups.

The financial loss from crime for the elderly can also mean
a direct threat to their ability to provide for themselves and
loss of independence. It can impact their ability to provide for
food and medicine. It can prohibit payments necessary to
maintain utilities, insurance, their home, and health care.
Fraud schemes can deplete older individuals' savings, leaving
them bankrupt and possibly destitute.

The elderly also can have an increased fear of crime, which
impacts their trust of others as well as their interactions with
others. While the need for social interaction is central to their
mental and emotional stability, the fear of victimization may
prevent them from pursuing friendships and relationships
outside of their immediate circle. Although their actual risks
may be considerably less than their perceived fear, older individuals (as all people) operate on what they believe to be true.
For the elderly, their world shrinks.

[4] Elderly Victims, Bureau of Justice Statistics Special Report, 1987.   [5] Ibid.

Another area of victimization is elder abuse. It is estimated that over 800,000 older individuals became victims of various types of elder abuse in 1994. This may be generated by dependence upon family, caretakers, or institutional staff and may take the form of physical, emotional, and financial victimization or neglect. It is important for anyone who suspects elder abuse or neglect to report the abuse to the proper authorities. This means a call to the city or county department of social or human services, adult protective services, or to local councils on aging.

HELPFUL THINGS TO SAY AND DO

- Clearly communicate that "I am sorry that this crisis/crime happened to you," and let the elderly individual know that you are there to be a support and encouragement through the crisis.
- Offer to pray with and/or for the person.
- Assess the victim's perception of his or her safety and security. If safety is in question, immediately act to reestablish safety and security by repairing a broken door or window, changing a lock, or identifying a safe place for the person to stay.
- Assess the person's need for emergency services and/or financial assistance. In situations that involve theft or robbery of a victim's money, pension, or social security check, determine the need for emergency financial assistance to pay for food, medication, or utility bills. In cases of physical assault, the elderly victim's glasses or hearing aid may be damaged or destroyed. Check with your church or local agencies and emergency relief services to assist in providing finances to repair or replace essential items.
- Seek local resources that are prepared to address elderly victims' needs. These may include: victim assistance programs in local law enforcement or social service offices, family violence programs, adult protective services, councils on aging, etc.

HURTFUL RESPONSES TO TRY TO AVOID

- Be careful not to encourage overdependence on you as a caregiver. Keep in contact with the individual on a regular basis, but continue to encourage his or her own decision making and independence.
- Do not ask *why* questions, which can insinuate blame or guilt, especially in crime-related matters. Rather, allow the individual to talk freely about the crime or crisis and its impact on his or her life.
- Do not make suggestions as to how they should give up other aspects of their independence and move in with family or to a nursing facility.

RELATED SCRIPTURE

Today I have given you the choice between life and death, between blessings and curses. I call on heaven and earth to witness the choice you make. Oh, that you would choose life, that you and your descendants might live! Choose to love the Lord your God and to obey him and commit yourself to him, for he is your life. Then you will live long in the land the Lord swore to give your ancestors Abraham, Isaac, and Jacob. DEUTERONOMY 30:19-20, NLT

Be strong and courageous! Do not be afraid of them! The Lord your God will go ahead of you. He will neither fail you nor forsake you. DEUTERONOMY 31:6, NLT

We are pressed on every side by troubles, but we are not crushed and broken. We are perplexed, but we don't give up and quit. We are hunted down, but God never abandons us. We get knocked down, but we get up again and keep going. Through suffering, these bodies of ours constantly share in the death of Jesus so that the life of Jesus may also be seen in our bodies. Yes, we live under constant danger of death because we serve Jesus, so that the life of Jesus will be obvious in our dying bodies. 2 CORINTHIANS 4:8-11, NLT

PRAYER

A prayer to share with your friend:

Father, thank you for your love and care for us at each stage of our life. The crisis/crime we now face is difficult and painful, especially as we are older now. We ask for your comfort, your help, and your guidance at this time. We look to you to provide for our needs, to calm our fears, to heal our hurts, and to give us the strength to go on and to continue to trust in you. Help us to reach out when we need help, and give us the ability to comfort others with the same comfort you give to us. Amen.

ADDITIONAL RESOURCES

Elderly Victims. Bureau of Justice Statistics, U.S. Department of Justice. Updated periodically.

Crisis Intervention with the Elderly by Parham & Aubach Losee (C. C. Thomas Publisher, 1988).

ROBERT DENTON

Dr. Robert Denton is pastor and executive director of the Furnace Street Mission and its Victim Assistance Program in Akron, Ohio. He is adjunct professsor of sociology at the University of Akron.

DRUNK DRIVING CRASH VICTIMS

For he has not ignored the suffering of the needy.
He has not turned and walked away.
He has listened to their cries for help.

PSALM 22:24, NLT

The day began like any other but ended quite differently—and tragically. Patrick was driving to his apartment after an afternoon college class. He was proud to be able to attend this college—a significant distance from his home and family. His parents also were proud of their son for being accepted to the school and doing so well in classes. But sadly, that afternoon, Patrick's life was taken away by a drunk driver.

By that evening Jim and Nancy, Patrick's parents, knew the unbelievable and horrible news. Immediately a fog of pain, confusion, shock, rage, and bewilderment surrounded them.

Jim and Nancy found themselves engulfed by grief with no way to obtain a sense of justice or closure, for the drunk driver also was killed in the crash.

UNDERSTANDING THE CRISIS

Driving under the influence (DUI) is the unlawful operation of a vehicle while under the influence of drugs or alcohol.

DUI is the most frequently committed crime in the nation today. In 1994 over sixteen thousand people were killed and *one million* were injured in the United States in alcohol-related traffic crashes.[1]

EFFECTS OF THE CRISIS

Survivors of drunk-driving crashes (whether they were directly involved in a crash or had family members or friends involved) may experience all the "normal" reactions of a crisis, which include: shock, disbelief, anger, depression, physical injury, questioning of faith, and financial hardship. They also may experience frustrations with the criminal justice system or anxiety that the offender is "back on the road." Sadly, they may have lost a loved one or become permanently disabled themselves.

Survivors' grief and pain can be exacerbated by the fact that the death or injury was sudden and senseless. There was no warning or time to anticipate the loss of a loved one or prepare for the painful injuries. According to Janice Harris Lord, director of victim assistance for Mothers Against Drunk Driving (MADD), "Many additional feelings are involved in the grief of crash victims, and the grief will last longer. Rarely can victims work through it on their own without long and understanding support."[2]

HOW YOU CAN HELP AND ENCOURAGE

According to the National Highway Safety Traffic Association, every American has a one-in-five chance of being injured or killed by a drunk driver. Grieving families and friends as well as citizens concerned about drunk driving have initiated groups, such as MADD, which have continued to inspire legislative changes throughout the country.

It is important that these groups acknowledge the impact that the crash has had on the survivors. Drunk driving is

[1] Information supplied by MADD.   [2] Janice H. Lord, *"Your Grief: You're Not Going Crazy,"* (MADD, 1985).

considered a violent crime by the criminal justice system—*not an accident*. Drunk drivers are considered to be responsible for their choice to drink and drive.

Many individuals do not consider DUI a "violent" crime in the way they perceive other criminal offenses. This can be attributed to the perception that drunk driving lacks the usual criminal motives of taking property, harming another person, or trafficking in contraband. This unique perception creates additional hardship on the victims and surviving family members. Although laws have significantly changed and public attitude is less tolerant of the drunk driver, these crimes, unless unusually aggravated, are not given the same priority by the criminal justice system as other violent crimes.

Encourage the survivors to participate in the investigation and judicial process. Assist them in completing a victim impact statement and victim compensation forms if available in your state and jurisdiction, and/or participate in victim impact panels. (Check with your local victim assistance office for more information on each of these suggestions—see resources for information.)

Your (and your church's) care, concern, prayers, and assistance can be valuable to a family who has experienced a drunk-driving crash. Provide a shoulder to lean or cry on and opportunities for them to share their anguish and anger and talk about the crash or the loved ones lost. Offer to provide practical help by providing meals and transportation to doctors' offices or other locations. If the family must make funeral arrangements, offer to go with them or provide support at the funeral home.

In the aftermath of the crash, victims may wish to become involved in advocacy organizations, such as MADD or court watch groups that help insure that drunk drivers are held accountable for their actions. Many communities and jurisdictions have established victim impact panels, which provide a forum for victims to educate offenders about the impact of their decision to drink and drive.

HELPFUL THINGS TO SAY AND DO

- Validate the seriousness of the violent crime and explain the normalcy of the anger and rage that may be experienced as a result of the senselessness of the act.
- Listen without judgment. Some survivors will be angry with God, the offender, the judicial system, and anyone who is not experiencing the same pain and suffocating grief.
- Offer to pray with them or for them. As appropriate, you may also want to invite the survivors to join you in church or Bible study activities with other individuals who are sensitive to the survivors' situation and needs.
- Help them reestablish control—encourage them to pray, keep a journal, write poetry, participate in memorial services, erect a cross or memorial at the crash site, or volunteer with nonprofit agencies involved in drunk driving programs.
- Allow victims to tell the same story over and over again, and if a loved one was killed, be sure to use his or her name frequently.
- Remember holidays, birthdays, and even the crash "anniversary" with a call or a note.
- Be careful not to equate forgiveness with letting the offender "off the hook" or negating the offender's responsibility for the crash. In forgiveness, timing is everything. Allow the survivors to consider it in their own time and way. Encourage the survivors to consider the impact of unforgiveness on their lives. Some victims will never forgive. Others will begin the forgiveness process when they are ready to move beyond the crash and its control of their lives.

HURTFUL RESPONSES TO TRY TO AVOID

- "It was just an *accident.*" (The appropriate term to use for a drunk driving incident is *crash.*)

- "It must be God's will."
- "He/she didn't mean to kill _____. You should forgive him/her."
- "He/she is an alcoholic and didn't know what he/she was doing."

RELATED SCRIPTURE

Encourage victims to use personal pronouns when reading this Scripture:

This I declare of the LORD: He alone is my refuge, my place of safety; he is my God, and I am trusting him. For he will rescue you from every trap and protect you from the fatal plague. He will shield you with his wings. He will shelter you with his feathers. His faithful promises are your armor and protection. PSALM 91:2-4, NLT

Don't be afraid, for I am with you. Do not be dismayed, for I am your God. I will strengthen you. I will help you. I will uphold you with my victorious right hand. ISAIAH 41:10, NLT

All praise to the God and Father of our Lord Jesus Christ. He is the source of every mercy and the God who comforts us. He comforts us in all our troubles so that we can comfort others. When others are troubled, we will be able to give them the same comfort God has given us. You can be sure that the more we suffer for Christ, the more God will shower us with his comfort through Christ. So when we are weighed down with troubles, it is for your benefit and salvation! For when God comforts us, it is so that we, in turn, can be an encouragement to you. Then you can patiently endure the same things we suffer. We are confident that as you share in suffering, you will also share God's comfort. . . . We learned not to rely on ourselves, but on God who can raise the dead. And he did deliver us from mortal danger. And we are confident that he will continue to deliver us. He will rescue us because you are helping by praying for us. As a result, many will give thanks to God because so many people's prayers for our safety have been answered. 2 CORINTHIANS 1:3-7, 9-11, NLT

PRAYER

For a survivor:

O God, you see my trouble and grief. You consider it and take note of it. I commit myself to you for you are the helper of the helpless, of those who have experienced pain and loss. O Lord, hear my cry and give me comfort, peace, and justice. Encourage me and help me, Lord, to look to you. Help me to seek the support of others when I feel overwhelmed with grief. Let me grow beyond this tragedy and experience your love afresh. Amen (based on Psalm 10:14-18).

ADDITIONAL RESOURCES

No Time for Goodbyes by Janice Harris Lord (Pathfinders Pub., 1991). Coping with sorrow, anger, and injustice after a tragic death.

The following pamphlets may be ordered from your state office of MADD or call 1-800-GET-MADD:

- *Your Grief—You're Not Going Crazy*
- *Will It Always Feel This Way? For Parents Whose Child Has Been Killed by a Drunk Driver*
- *Helping Children Cope with Death in the Family*
- *We Hurt Too—A Guide for Adult Siblings*
- *Don't Call Me Lucky—For Those Injured in Drunk Driving Crashes*
- *How You Can Help*

LAURA SLADE HUDSON

Laura Slade Hudson is executive director of the South Carolina Victim Assistance Network and has served for twelve years as the state chair person and legislative liaison for South Carolina MADD.

SHIRLEY W. RUPLE

Shirley W. Ruple is the Violence Against Women's project coordinator for the South Carolina Department of Public Safety and has served as the state's victim assistance coordinator for MADD.

KIDNAPPING

Answer my prayers, O LORD,
for your unfailing love is wonderful.
Turn and take care of me,
for your mercy is so plentiful.
Don't hide from your servant;
Answer me quickly, for I am in deep trouble!
Come and rescue me;
Free me from all my enemies.

PSALM 69:16-18, NLT

Ten-year-old Carly was abducted by a 32-year-old man as she rode her bike home from a friend's house. Carly's bike was found in the woods near the road. Media interest in the case was intense and spread quickly from local news to state coverage. Several days after Carly's disappearance, a motel desk clerk, recognizing Carly as the young girl traveling with a man who registered the day before, called the police. Within hours the abductor was apprehended and Carly was recovered alive, but suffering from severe trauma. Her reunion with her parents and sisters took place in the driveway of her home as news cameras captured every move and word.

UNDERSTANDING THE CRISIS

Kidnapping is the act of unlawfully seizing or detaining another person whether adult, youth, or child. The motives for kidnapping by strangers or acquaintances can include: ransom, robbery, sexual assault, or the desire to permanently keep the victim. Kidnapping may also be committed by family members, typically a noncustodial parent. The U.S. Department of Justice estimates that approximately 350,000 parental kidnappings of children occur each year in the United States.[1] Most family kidnappings occur in the context of relationships that have a history of domestic violence. Child victims of parental kidnapping may have their names and appearances altered, experience medical or physical neglect, and be subjected to unstable schooling, homelessness, and frequent moves.

EFFECTS OF THE CRISIS

The person who is kidnapped is not the only victim; family members suffer tremendous agony waiting and hoping. The severity of the trauma to the victim and family is determined by the identity of the abductor, how long the victim has been gone, and what was inflicted on the victim. Trauma symptoms for victims and family members may last for up to four to five years after recovery. Families where the missing victim is found dead or is never recovered may experience the highest levels of emotional trauma.

Many kidnapping victims fear or believe they will never see their families again or that they will be killed. Victims will usually do whatever they believe they must do to survive. Later they may feel ashamed or guilty.

The majority of victims eventually come home, but the impact of the event doesn't end at that point. Upon return, victims may feel an initial euphoria that is usually followed by feelings of numbness. Victims may seem detached or distant from family or

[1]Finkelhor, Hotaling, and Sedlack. *National Incidence Studies on Missing, Abducted, Runaway and Throwaway Children in America*, U.S. Department of Justice, 1990.

friends and may seem apathetic and uninterested in activities they previously enjoyed. Victims may deny their feelings or avoid talking about the kidnapping. Victims also may suffer from severe stress and will need the help of a professional therapist or physician to assist them in dealing with severe and prolonged symptoms. Victims often live in constant fear of a reabduction.

For the family and close friends of a kidnapping victim, the world has been turned upside down. As a result, they may have difficulty mobilizing resources available to them. Individual family members have their own unique ways of coping with stress and loss. Some may throw themselves into helping with search activities but others may not. Some remain very optimistic while others feel the need to prepare for the worst. When differences are pronounced, family members may find it hard to understand and comfort each other. Some family members may feel guilty or may feel that they failed to protect their loved one.

HOW YOU CAN HELP AND ENCOURAGE

Kidnapping victims and their families will need emotional and spiritual support as well as practical help from the moment they discover what has happened until well after a victim is recovered alive or found dead.

Assist with immediate needs. Family members may be too distraught to deal with daily activities and will need help caring for children, grocery shopping, transportation, answering the phone. Find out what they need and offer to arrange to have it done by friends, church members, or other family members.

Help protect privacy. Kidnapping cases can be high-profile cases which attract a variety of people offering assistance. Some of these people are well-meaning and others may be seeking to exploit the tragedy. Family members may need assistance in dealing with intense media and public interest. It is best to help the family identify one trusted person who can serve as a liaison with the media and speak for the family when required.

Help with searching. In cases where the victim is missing for more than a few hours, families and police may need help searching for the victim or with printing and distributing posters. It is important to let the responsible law enforcement agency provide guidance in any volunteer search attempts.

Listen empathetically and nonjudgmentally. Being there is more important than particular words. Allow each family member to express feelings and emotions in his or her own way.

Make sure that children are not forgotten. Children, especially siblings of kidnapped children, may feel ignored or abandoned as parents focus on the investigation or are consumed by their own grief. Children should be given as much information as possible. Older children and teenagers may find it easier to express their feelings and fears with peers or with an adult other than a parent.

Be there for the long haul. When a kidnapping is prolonged or there is no resolution, it is even more important to maintain support and caring over time. After initial interest has died down, this period can be the loneliest time for families of victims. Remember to include them in church activities and other gatherings. Birthdays, missed graduations, and the anniversary of the kidnapping can be especially difficult times. If there is a criminal case, victims and family members will need help and support coping with court hearings, delays, the trial, and sentencing.

Pray and encourage victims and family members to seek spiritual support. Be faithful in prayer for the victim and family members. Offer to pray for and with them. You may want to hold a special prayer time or church service with friends and the church family as appropriate. Encourage church members to write notes of encouragement and support to the family.

Helpful Things to Say and Do

- "I can't begin to imagine how you must feel, but I will be here for you."
- "I believe that God gives each of us the strength to make it through each day and to face whatever happens."
- "Your feelings are understandable."
- Provide food or meals for the family. Assist with immediate needs.

Hurtful Responses to Try to Avoid

- "You need to accept what happened and get on with your life."
- "You still have other children."
- "You should have been more careful. I would never have allowed my child/spouse/teenager to . . ."
- "You shouldn't worry. God will make everything all right."

When something terrible happens to someone we know and love, it reminds us that we and our loved ones are vulnerable and mortal. Pointing out mistakes or what we would have done in the same circumstances is a way we deny that the same thing could happen to us.

Related Scripture

He heals the brokenhearted, binding up their wounds. He counts the stars and calls them all by name. PSALM 147:3-4, NLT

"For the mountains may depart and the hills disappear, but even then I will remain loyal to you. My covenant of blessing will never be broken," *says the Lord, who has mercy on you.* ISAIAH 54:10, NLT

Prayer

To pray for or with the family during the victimization:
Dear Lord, we come to you in the middle of our helplessness and pain. We don't know where our loved one is or how he/she is doing. We pray

now for your protection and comfort for _____. We pray that you will surround him/her with your power and love. We pray for your wisdom and discernment for those who are searching. May _____ be found and returned safely to us. We pray for your peace and hope as we wait and pray. God, grant us strength to trust in you. Amen.

ADDITIONAL RESOURCES

Children in the Crossfire: The Tragedy of Parental Kidnapping by Sally Abrams (Antheneum, 1993). Deals with children who are kidnapped by a parent.

Too Scared to Cry: Psychic Trauma in Childhood by Lenore C. Terr (Basic Books, 1990).

Recovery and Reunification of Missing Children: A Team Approach by Kathryn M. Turman (National Center for Missing and Exploited Children, 1995).

National Center for Missing and Exploited Children, 1-800-843-5678.

KATHRYN M. TURMAN

Kathryn M. Turman is chief of the Victim Witness Assistance Unit in the U.S. Attorney's Office in Washington, D.C. She was formerly director of the Missing and Exploited Children's Program in the U.S. Department of Justice.

Supporting Victims of Sexual Crimes

INCEST

And anyone who welcomes a little child like this
on my behalf is welcoming me. But if anyone
causes one of these little ones who trusts in me
to lose faith, it would be better for that person
to be thrown into the sea
with a large millstone tied around the neck.

MATTHEW 18:5-6, NLT

I t was just too hard to hear and much harder to believe. Theirs was a good family. A church family. An upstanding family in the small community. Kevin and Allison didn't want to believe it when their two young daughters revealed that their older fourteen-year-old brother had been sexually assaulting them. How could it happen? What could have gone wrong?

UNDERSTANDING THE CRISIS

Incest is a sin and a crime. It breaks the laws of God and man. Incest is the sexual abuse—from inappropriate touching or fondling to digital and penile penetration—of a child or adolescent by a blood relative, surrogate parent, or stepparent.[1] It is a terrible violation of the body and soul of a child because

[1] Ibid., 15–3.

the perpetrator is usually someone the child loves and respects very much.

An incestuous relationship is the hardest secret for a child to tell. There are usually underlying threats to keep the child quiet. Sometimes a reward of candy and even money is given to make sure the child does not talk. And many times, the child is told that if he or she tells, a loved one may be hurt or even killed. Perhaps the most overwhelming reason a child does not tell is that he or she does not think that anyone will believe it.

EFFECTS OF THE CRISIS

Once a disclosure is made, the child may retreat from family members and friends. He or she may consider suicide because of feelings of no self-worth—feeling soiled or defiled. At the opposite extreme, the child may experience intense rage and anger and physical and emotional acting out. The child may blame the nonoffending parent, in cases of interfamilial abuse, for failing to protect him or her. Older children may reenact the sexual abuse by engaging in inappropriate behavior, sexually abusing other children, becoming sexually active, and/or using vulgar language.[2]

In addition, younger children may become distrustful and overly fearful of strangers or family members. They may regress in development, i.e., quit talking, feeding, or dressing themselves.[3] They may experience eating and sleeping disorders and suffer from mental and emotional problems. In some extreme circumstances, children experiencing incest may even develop multiple personality disorders.

Incest may also impact a child's perception of God. These child victims often wonder why a God, who is supposed to be loving and kind, would allow such terrible things to happen.

[2] Ibid., 15–14. [3] See pages 181–183 of this book.

HOW YOU CAN HELP AND ENCOURAGE

If you are contacted by a child or a family member with a report or description of incest, allow that individual to express the situation in the way he or she is most comfortable. Listen without judgment to the story, and ask questions for clarification only at this point.

In supporting a child, allow the child to say and feel whatever he or she wants. Do not tell him or her to feel a certain way. More than anything, a child wants to be believed, trusted, and told that it was not his or her fault. Most incest victims feel that they were to blame—that they did something wrong that made the offender abuse them.

In most cases, children do not fabricate serious reports of incest to get family members in trouble or to bring attention to themselves. While most children don't create tales of incest, it must be noted that some have. If you are approached with information concerning an incestuous situation, do not allow the possibility of a false allegation or false memory to prevent you from listening, offering comfort, and gaining a thorough understanding of the victim's story before you take action.

Your first consideration should always be the safety and health of the child. Therefore, the abuse needs to be brought to the attention of the appropriate local official who is trained to investigate and to make protection recommendations.[4]

In all states and Washington D.C., professionals who work with children must report suspected physical and sexual abuse. Failure to comply can lead to criminal charges and civil liability. Individuals such as schoolteachers, guidance counselors, day-care workers, and pastors must report any suspected abuse to appropriate authorities. If you suspect abuse and are unsure if you must report, you can anonymously contact the national Child Abuse and Neglect Hotline at 1-800-252-2873 or your local law enforcement or social services agency, and they can advise you.

One of the most difficult situations is when a child must maintain contact with a perpetrator who is also a family member. Children expect parents and older adults to protect them and siblings to love them. In every case, all contact with the perpetrator needs to be suspended for a set period of time. Seek the guidance of a trained professional in helping the family make these kinds of decisions.

Be aware that family members may take sides with the offender. In these cases, victims need as much support, validation, and assistance as possible. To provide further support, you may want to encourage the appropriate parent or the child to seek professional help from a qualified Christian therapist who has experience in working with child sexual abuse victims. Incest also can be generational. It may be passed down from one generation to the next. To address this complex crisis, it is key to minister to the whole family. To help stop the cycle of incest it is important to understand how far back the incest goes.

It is important to continue to be available to the child and the family for support and encouragement throughout the crisis. If the case goes to court, you may want to offer to attend the court proceedings with the family as appropriate. If the offender is the family breadwinner, you may want to check on the family's need for financial assistance or the need to relocate and provide assistance through the church or other resources as available and appropriate.

HELPFUL THINGS TO SAY AND DO

- Always report suspected abuse to the proper authorities.
- Listen carefully to the child and allow him or her to talk openly about the abuse. Victims of incest may have put up barriers of self-defense in order to survive. Allow them the freedom to say whatever is on their minds without fear of being judged or condemned.
- Tell the child that you are sorry that this has happened. Affirm that the child has been wronged and that it was not his or her fault.

- Thank the child for his or her disclosure and let the child know that he or she has done the right thing in bringing this to your attention.
- Believe the child and give him or her the benefit of the doubt. A victim wants to know that someone he or she trusts understands and believes the story.
- Confirm God's love and your care and concern. Tell the child that he or she is loved by God and that you care about him or her.
- Pray with and/or for the child.
- Let the child know that you will continue to be there to offer support and help. Check with the child periodically to see how he or she is doing.
- Be sure to keep the information confidential beyond reporting the abuse to an appropriate official.

HURTFUL RESPONSES TO TRY TO AVOID

- Upon a child's disclosure, be careful not to overreact. This can intimidate the child and inhibit further disclosure.
- Do not push the victim to forgive right away. Forgiveness may come, but it will take a long time. And remember, forgiveness does not necessarily mean reconciliation.
- Do not ask the *why* questions: "Why didn't you stop him/her?" "Why didn't you tell someone sooner?" "Why didn't you just leave?" Asking *why* questions communicates blame and doubt. Instead, ask *"What* happened next?" etc. *What* questions are much less intimidating.
- Do not minimize the story or the abuse. Some may have the opinion that incest is just the expression of human curiosity. No person has the right to violate another's privacy.
- Do not react negatively to the story or outright question the report of the abuse and the identification of the abuser.
- Do not say, "How can you still love/like the person who did that to you?" Some children who experience abuse may continue to love their abusers and want them to love the child

in return. Do not make a child feel guilty or stupid for caring about the abuser.

RELATED SCRIPTURE

But you belong to God, my dear children. You have already won your fight with these false prophets, because the Spirit who lives in you is greater than the spirit who lives in the world. . . . But anyone who does not love does not know God—for God is love. 1 JOHN 4:4, NLT

Share each other's troubles and problems, and in this way obey the law of Christ. GALATIANS 6:2, NLT

For I can do everything with the help of Christ who gives me the strength I need. PHILIPPIANS 4:13, NLT

PRAYER

To pray with a child:
Dear heavenly Father, help me to deal with my hurt and pain. I know that you love me. Please help me to feel lovable. Lord, help me to trust again because someone I love very much has taken away my trust. I don't understand why this person did this to me. I feel so bad and dirty inside. Help me, Lord, to feel clean and pure again. Lord, please watch out for me. I don't want to feel this way ever again. I love you, Lord Jesus. Help me to know how much you love me, too. Amen.

A D D I T I O N A L   R E S O U R C E S

I Can't Talk about It: A Child's Book about Sexual Abuse by Doris Sanford (Questar Publishers, Inc., 1986).

A Safe Place: Beyond Sexual Abuse by Jan Morrison (Harold Shaw Publishers, 1990). This book, written from a Christian perspective, is geared especially to teens.

Released from Bondage by Dr. Neil T. Anderson (Thomas Nelson Publishers, 1993).

The Invisible Wound: A New Approach to Healing Childhood Sexual Trauma by Wayne Kritsberg (Bantam Books, Inc., 1993).

A Door of Hope: Recognizing and Resolving the Pains of Your Past by Jan Frank
Thomas Nelson, 1995). Written primarily for incest victims, this book includes an
explanation of abuse symptoms and tells how to establish a healthy self-image and a
right relationship with God and others. The author gives helpful advice on starting support groups and working through the issues with the help of a counselor.

STEVE AND LYNN EARGLE

Reverend Steve Eargle is a graduate of Southeastern Baptist Theological Seminary with
a Master of Divinity degree. He is presently pastor of Double Springs Baptist Church in
Anderson, South Carolina. Lynn Eargle is the past executive assistant of the S.C. Victim
Assistance Network. She is presently the director of a Christian preschool learning
center. Steve and Lynn have five children.

ADULT SURVIVORS OF SEXUAL ABUSE

*"Now, Jeremiah, say this to them: 'Night and day
my eyes overflow with tears. I cannot stop weeping,
for my virgin daughter—my precious people—
has been run through with a sword
and lies mortally wounded on the ground.'"*

JEREMIAH 14:17, NLT

J ulie's father, a religious man and respected community leader, began sexually abusing Julie at age nine. Her father had threatened her with his gun if she told. And she knew no one would believe her anyway. Julie felt powerless to protect herself.

During adolescence, she used drugs and alcohol to dull the pain. She even attempted suicide. During the next nine years, Julie became promiscuous, looking for love wherever and however she could find it.

Although twenty years have passed since Julie's sexual abuse stopped, she still suffers its devastating effects.

UNDERSTANDING THE CRISIS

Adult sexual abuse survivors are individuals who experienced sexual abuse as children and who may or may not have con-

217

fronted the impact of the past abuse. Child sexual abuse is the exploitation of a child or adolescent for the sexual and control gratification of another person. The young victims lack the emotional and intellectual development to enable them to resist the manipulation, authority, and power of the abuser. Therefore, the abuser alone is responsible for the abuse. Those who experience such abuse often do not disclose it as children, and the abuse may continue over and over, sometimes for many years. The abuse has a potentially harmful impact on the victim and his or her future life.[1]

The following factors can determine the extent of impact on the victims:

- age of the child/adolescent at the time of the abuse
- length and frequency of the abuse
- extent of the abuse (Was anal or vaginal penetration or oral sex involved?)
- threats on the victim or someone the victim loved
- intense fear of the abuse/abuser or the consequences of someone finding out
- pain, force, or violence surrounding the abuse
- relationship of the abuser to the victim (trusted adult? parent? sibling?)
- reaction to victim's attempt to share with a trusted adult, especially a parent (Victims are impacted most if a parent does not believe them.)

How You Can Help and Encourage

As adults, many child sexual abuse victims may be confronted with their painful past and may seek support and help through the church or with friends and family. It is essential that the church community reach out with understanding and compassion to those who have experienced past abuse and assist them on their road to recovery.

[1] U.S. Department of Justice, Office for Victims of Crime, "National Victim Assistance Academy" manual, 15–9.

To assist adult survivors in their restoration and recovery, the following seven areas are important for the caregiver and survivor to understand and address.

Areas that are important for the adult survivor to address include

1. *Rebuilding trust in others.* If the survivor was abused by a trusted adult (especially a parent), the trust factor in relationships with other adults also breaks down. To help rebuild trust, you will need to be consistent in your caregiving. You cannot and should not be everything to this person. You will need to set boundaries of what you can and cannot do with them. For instance, you might say, "I'd be happy to join you in a weekly Bible study if that would be helpful to you." But then be sure to follow through on what you say and commit to do.

2. *Restoring trust in the Christian community and God.* Because Julie's father was a religious man, she lost trust in Christians as well as God. Victims who have been involved in a church community may express anger toward the church and toward God as a result of the abuse. This flawed view of God sees only his judgment or apparent disinterest. Otherwise why would he allow this to happen? Why didn't he answer their prayers? They cannot see God as loving, powerful, gracious, and merciful.

    You will need to help victims feel safe in expressing these feelings and be careful not to judge or put them down. Instead of trying to offer a quick fix, show Christ's love to survivors through a consistent, caring, Christ-filled life. Victims may need to trust Christ in us before they can learn to trust God. Paul urges us to "share each other's troubles and problems" (Galatians 6:2). It takes time for victims to learn to trust again.

3. *Establishing a Christ-centered identity.* Sexual abuse damages survivors' self-identity. Shame permeates every part of their lives. They feel they can't be loved by others or even by God. Survivors may try to cover up shame in several ways:

   ■ perfectionism
   ■ people pleasing
   ■ compulsive behaviors
   ■ rationalism
   ■ secretiveness
   ■ rage

   Shame messages flood victims' minds. Julie saw herself as ugly, useless, good only for sex. Her mind told her, "Being a woman is bad," and "My body is dirty." Family and friends need to help survivors know the truth about the abuse, the abuser, and their identity in Christ.

   As survivors renew their minds (Romans 12:2) with the truth of God's Word, "the truth will set [them] free" (John 8:32) from a shame-identity to a Christ-centered identity. But first you can help them identify the shame (untrue) messages.

   For example, have survivors write down the shame messages they are hearing on the right side of a paper. Then help the victims find the true messages (from God's Word) to write down on the left side of the paper. You can encourage survivors to renew their minds daily by reading the truth messages in response to the shame messages.

4. *Addressing the guilt about behaviors stemming from the abuse.* Julie used drugs, alcohol, and sex to medicate the pain of the abuse and try to find love. These behaviors may

be understandable, but they are not healthy for the individual or right before God.

Be careful not to make judgmental statements about survivors' past behaviors. Survivors usually judge themselves harshly. They need to hear from a fellow Christian that God can and will forgive their sins and remember those sins no more (Hebrews 10:17). When doubts and fears plague victims, allow them to discuss them freely. As appropriate, you may want to offer to pray with them and remind them that "if we confess our sins to him, he is faithful and just to forgive us and to cleanse us from every wrong" (1 John 1:9, NLT).

5. *Exploring the issue of forgiving the abuser.* Sometimes we expect victims to forgive their abusers prematurely. Some victims may never be able to forgive. Before victims can forgive their abusers, they must take time to work through the pain of what the abusers did to them. Anger becomes a defense to protect themselves from being taken advantage of again.

   Survivors need to see that holding on to anger and bitterness only hurts themselves and gets in the way of their relationship with God and others. Forgiveness does not mean they have to trust the abuser again or put up with abuse. Forgiveness does not mean that what the abuser did was okay.

   As you assist victims, attempt to understand why it is difficult for them to forgive. Listen to them, try to put yourself in their shoes, and be patient with them. When they are ready to forgive from the heart—not just to please you—share Scriptures about forgiveness (Matthew 18:21-22; Luke 11:4).

6. *Building healthy relationships.* God planned for the sexual relationship to start in marriage, but sexual abuse dis-

torts God's truth about love, sexuality, and sex. When a young child such as Julie is sexually abused, love and sex become blurred. One message the child receives is "To be loved I need to be sexual." Other messages include: Sex is dirty, sex is bad, the body is ugly. Survivors seem to struggle with opposite behaviors and messages. Often they become promiscuous, dependent, or afraid of the opposite sex.

Take time to show survivors from God's Word that only God can meet their deep love needs. He is their ultimate source of love (1 John 4:8). Nothing can separate sexual abuse survivors from the love of God through Christ (Romans 8:39). As he fills them with his love, they can learn to build loving relationships with others.

Unconditional love of family, friends, and church members can support them as they work through these issues with a pastor or professional counselor. But only God can heal the wounds.

7. *Restoring hope.* Survivors need hope that God can redeem their shameful past. He can give them strength to face their pain and go on. A prayer partner who can meet regularly with them to claim God's promises for their recovery will be extremely helpful.

HELPFUL THINGS TO SAY AND DO

- "Thank you for sharing this with me. I'm very sorry this abuse happened to you."
- "It wasn't your fault. You were not responsible for that abuse."
- "It's okay to be upset, to cry, or to be angry."
- "You did the best you could at the time."
- "You can't change your past, but you may change the way it is impacting your life now."

HURTFUL RESPONSES TO TRY TO AVOID

- "Don't you think it's about time you got over this and moved on with your life?"
- "I know just how you feel."
- "It must have been God's will."
- "Time heals all wounds."
- Don't ask *why* questions, which could imply that the victim was partly to blame ("Why didn't you resist?" "Why didn't you tell anyone?").

RELATED SCRIPTURE

The Lord is close to the brokenhearted and saves those who are crushed in spirit.
PSALM 34:18, NIV

He heals the brokenhearted and binds up their wounds.
PSALM 147:3, NIV

"For I know the plans I have for you," declares the Lord, "plans to prosper you and not to harm you, plans to give you hope and a future."
JEREMIAH 29:11, NIV

PRAYER

A prayer to share with your friend:
Dear heavenly Father, I know that I am a child of God and that you love me with an everlasting love. Nothing will separate me from your love and care. I thank you that you have made me a unique person with special gifts and talents.

You know all about the sexual abuse, and you weep over what happened to me. It was not your plan. Yet I know you will work out these terrible things for my good and for your glory and honor.

Show me the truth about the sexual abuse, and give me strength to renounce the lies that come to my mind. Reveal the truth from your

Word that will help me find freedom. Then help me change my behaviors that displease you.

May you be my joy, my peace, my love. In Jesus' name I pray. Amen.

A D D I T I O N A L   R E S O U R C E S

A Door of Hope: Recognizing and Resolving the Pains of Your Past by Jan Frank (Thomas Nelson, 1995). This book includes an explanation of abuse symptoms and tells how to establish a healthy self-image and a right relationship with God and others.

The Wounded Heart: Hope for Adult Victims of Childhood Sexual Abuse by Dan B. Allender (NavPress, 1990). The purpose of this book is to show how sexual abuse damages the soul of its victims and to offer hope to those who are willing to face and work through the abuse of the past.

Helping Victims of Sexual Abuse by Jeanette Vought & Lynn Heitritter (Bethany House Publishers, 1989).

Child Sexual Abuse: A Hope for Healing by Maxine Hancock and Karen Burton Mains (Harold Shaw Publishers, 1987). This book offers help for adult victims and those who care about them in a Christian perspective.

Forgive and Forget by Lewis B. Smedes (HarperSanFrancisco, 1984).

The Courage to Heal: A Guide for Women Survivors of Child Sexual Abuse by Ellen Bass and Laura Davis (HarperCollins, 1989).

J E A N E T T E   V O U G H T

Dr. Jeanette Vought is founder and director of Christian Recovery Center in the Twin Cities area in Minnesota. The center specializes in sexual, domestic, and emotional abuse.

Rape and
Sexual Assault

"No, my brother!" she cried. "Don't be foolish! Don't do this to me! You know what a serious crime it is to do such a thing in Israel. Where could I go in my shame? And you would be called one of the greatest fools in Israel. Please, just speak to the king about it, and he will let you marry me." But Amnon wouldn't listen to her, and since he was stronger than she was, he raped her.

2 SAMUEL 13:12-14, NLT

Janna was working at a motel at night while going to school full time. One evening on her shift, two men came in under the pretense of getting a room. Instead, they kidnapped her at gunpoint, drove her miles down the interstate to a wooded area, where she was raped and left to find her way home.

Afterward, Janna made it back to the interstate and found herself flagging down anyone who would stop. A trucker finally pulled over and rolled his window down about two inches. He asked what had happened. In that instant, Janna had to decide whether she could actually tell this stranger about the horrible act. Could she say the word *rape*? She was embarrassed and ashamed. When she finally decided to tell him the truth, he flinched and rolled the window up. He did help her, but her immediate fears were realized. He was shocked and looked at her as if to imply something was wrong with *her.*

UNDERSTANDING THE CRISIS

Sexual assault or rape is an act of violence and is considered a crime by state and federal law. Sexual assault is when a person knowingly causes another person to engage in a sexual act or attempts to do so by using force, by threatening, or by placing that person in fear without the permission of that person. Sexual assault is not committed because the offender is sexually deprived. It is a crime of violence in which sex is the vehicle used to deliver pain, control, and humiliation. Rape is a heinous crime that can make the victim feel violated and even at fault as the wrongdoer.

EFFECTS OF THE CRISIS

Many rape victims exhibit a wide range of emotions, some of which may be surprising or even seem inappropriate: anger, withdrawal, bewilderment, laughter, rage. Those responding to a victim should not be judgmental about these emotions.

Sexual assault also leaves a woman feeling out of control. (Please note that men also may be victims of sexual assault. In cases where a man is raped, he may experience extreme embarrassment, shame, and guilt for not "adequately protecting or defending" himself. For the purposes of this chapter, the victim will be referred to as a woman.) In providing assistance, it is important to provide opportunities for her to gain back that control. Be careful not to make decisions for the victim. Rather, give the victim options. "Would you like some water or something else to eat or drink?" "Would you prefer to stay at your own home [if it is safe to do so] or with a friend or family member?"

Also, it is a typical response for sexual assault victims to feel ashamed and guilty. They blame themselves even after being reminded by counselors and others over and over that the rape was not their fault. Added to their own shame are the comments of friends, society, and sometimes family members who unwittingly say things that hurt. "Why did you go jogging by yourself in the park?" "Why did you have that outfit on anyway? You must have asked for it."

How You Can Help and Encourage

If you are asked to help a rape survivor, be aware that the needs of the victim are basic but oftentimes long term. Let the victim know that it was not her fault she was raped. The victim may feel that she used poor judgment by going somewhere or with someone she did not know well or that she did not see the "danger signs" in someone she did know. In that case, it is helpful to remind her that the offender had no right to rape her. No means no—in any setting, at any hour of the day or night.

For those survivors who question whether or not they did the right thing—said the right thing, acquiesced with only the threat of a knife, or other responses—they need to be reminded over and over that they are alive and whatever they did was the right thing to do.

Another need of sexual assault victims is the need to talk about the crime. Family, friends, and church members may sometimes react to crime like they do to cancer or death: Don't bring *it* up, then they will forget about it. Many times family members or friends are afraid to mention the sexual assault because they don't want to bring up a bad subject.

Sadly, the unspoken message conveyed is that the crime is too uncomfortable to discuss or that "we don't care about what happened to you." In many cases the victim often wants to discuss the crime and its aftermath in great detail with someone she trusts. The victim may interpret silence on the subject by others as disinterest or self-protection, which may establish barriers not only to relationships but also to the victim's recovery.

The key to helping a sexual assault victim is to approach the subject with care and concern. Allow the victim to take the lead by letting you know what she wants to discuss and when she wants to discuss it. Don't be afraid of the subject. The crime never leaves the memory of the victim. She needs to know that family, friends, and church members care about her and her recovery. Ask how she is doing. Allow her to talk about the crime and its impact on her life. Offer to pray for her or with her as she begins her recovery process.

The question "Why me, God?" is a common response of rape victims. They pose the question to God without ever feeling that a sensible answer comes. At this point, you can remind the victim of God's promise to strengthen and help (Isaiah 41:10) and to provide comfort for her in the midst of pain and suffering (2 Corinthians 1:3-4).

WHEN THE OFFENDER IS AN ACQUAINTANCE

According to statistics, a majority of rapes are committed by acquaintances of the victims. This, of course, includes date rape. These situations may be particularly difficult for victims as well as for family, friends, and church members, because they may know the offender as well. In such cases, the response of the community and the criminal justice system is sometimes not as supportive of victims as if the offenders were strangers. Not only do the victims feel the trauma of the crime, but they also may experience the hurt of being betrayed by someone they knew and perhaps trusted. Since victims are often not taken as seriously by the criminal justice system when sexually assaulted by an acquaintance, these victims are particularly vulnerable to self-blame and sometimes decide not to continue with criminal justice proceedings. These victims need a great deal of validation; they need to be reassured that rape by someone they know is still rape and that they are not to blame.

REPORTING THE CRIME

Some victims may not have reported the rape to the police or proper authorities. If that is the case, it is essential that you discuss reporting the crime with the victim. Attempt to determine the reasons that the victim has for not wanting to report, and sensitively but firmly encourage her to contact the authorities. Offer to go with her if possible.

MEDICAL EXAM

After a woman reports a sexual assault, she is required to have a medical examination to determine whether or not there is physical evidence of the assault. This exam usually takes place in the emergency room of a local hospital or clinic. Sometimes, the victim may find herself waiting for hours for the exam, which can be frustrating, discouraging, and humiliating.

In areas where rape crisis programs are available, a rape counselor may be called to stay with the victim during this procedure. If appropriate and timely, you may want to offer to accompany the victim to the hospital and/or offer to bring another set of clothes and drive her home. The victim may be in a state of shock after the exam and may need additional support or assistance after returning home.

WHEN THE CASE GOES TO TRIAL

If the case goes to trial, the needs of sexual assault victims are different from the needs of those whose cases are not prosecuted. There may be a variety of reasons that the case never gets to trial that are not reflective of the validity of the claims of the victims' sexual assault. Those victims who decide not to press charges may have been pressured not to do so because of the circumstances surrounding the incident and not because they weren't assaulted.

The victims whose cases go to trial usually have experienced thorough police investigation. Many victims relate their shock and ensuing trauma from the first visit to the police station, where they are interrogated and feel that *they* are treated like criminals.

The victim who makes it through the law enforcement investigation stage, the district attorney's questions and court preparation, the grand jury, and then the actual trial, needs a great deal of support, because every step can be difficult. The preliminary hearing and the trial are the two phases in which the victim may have to come face-to-face with the offender. Church friends and family are very important at this time. A show of support from friends, pastors, and family members in a courtroom can provide a great deal of strength to a rape survivor. Since everyone is different, it is important for friends and the church family to get permission to attend the preliminary hearing, the trial, or the sentencing from the victim herself, as well as from the appropriate court officials. In some cases the victim may be uncomfortable describing the details of the rape in front of friends or family, so it should be the victim's decision.

Church members and friends can be helpful to victims of sexual assault by praying for them, providing support, listening, being nonjudgmental, offering to attend the trial, and reminding them of the promises of God in the Scriptures. Caring friends can remind rape survivors that God doesn't leave them during their difficulties but rather, he carries them. "God is our refuge and strength, an ever-present help in trouble" (Psalm 46:1, NIV).

HELPFUL THINGS TO SAY AND DO

- "I am sorry this happened to you [or that you were raped]."
- "It wasn't your fault."
- "Whatever you did must have been right because you are alive and here with me now."
- "It is understandable to feel the way you do."
- "You are not going crazy, although at times you may feel disoriented and confused."
- "Things may never be the same, but they can get better, and you can get better."
- "It's OK to cry, to feel vengeful, or to be angry."

- "You did the best you could at the time."

HURTFUL RESPONSES TO TRY TO AVOID

- "I know how you feel" or "I understand."
- "It was God's will."
- "You'll get over it."
- "You need to get on with your life."
- "You shouldn't feel that way."
- "Time heals all wounds."

RELATED SCRIPTURE

God is our refuge and strength, always ready to help in times of trouble. So we will not fear, even if earthquakes come and the mountains crumble into the sea. PSALM 46:1-2, NLT

But when I am afraid, I put my trust in you. O God, I praise your word. I trust in God, so why should I be afraid? What can mere mortals do to me? PSALM 56:3-4, NLT

I will give you back your health and heal your wounds, says the Lord. JEREMIAH 30:17, NLT

I am leaving you with a gift—peace of mind and heart. And the peace I give isn't like the peace the world gives. So don't be troubled or afraid. JOHN 14:27, NLT

I have told you all this so that you may have peace in me. Here on earth you will have many trials and sorrows. But take heart, because I have overcome the world. JOHN 16:33, NLT

PRAYER

A prayer to share with your friend:
Lord, help me know your presence and feel your comfort and compassion in the midst of this pain. Break the grasp of fear, confusion, anger, despair, and isolation I'm experiencing. Help me reach out.

Please give me the grace to receive hope and help from those who love me and care for me. Amen.

ADDITIONAL RESOURCES

Quest for Respect: A Healing Guide for Survivors of Rape by Linda Braswell (Borgo Press, 1991).

Defending Ourselves: A Guide to Prevention, Self-Defense, and Recovery from Rape by Rosalind Wiseman (Farrar, Straus & Giroux, Inc., 1995).

Helping Victims of Sexual Abuse by Jeanette Vought and Lynn Heitritter (Bethany House Publishers, 1989).

ANITA ARMSTRONG DRUMMOND

Anita Armstrong Drummond is a licensed professional counselor who has been a crime victim advocate for nineteen years. Her work has included administration of a state agency for victims, management of a local victim service program, legislative efforts, cofounding victim service organizations, as well as providing direct service to victims.

WHEN A LOVED ONE DIES

DEATH OF
A LOVED ONE

God is our refuge and strength, always ready to help in
times of trouble. So we will not fear, even if earthquakes
come and the mountains crumble into the sea.

PSALM 46:1-2, NLT

R ight after my husband's death, I was so overwhelmed
by feelings of grief and abandonment that I was
very grateful to have caring people with me. And I
did sense God's comforting reassurance that my husband was
now in a more peaceful place."
❏ *A woman whose husband recently died*

EFFECTS OF THE CRISIS

The loss of a loved one brings grief, poignant sorrow, and
pain. (The effects of grief are more thoroughly covered in
"The Grief Process" on pages 17–22.)

HOW YOU CAN HELP AND ENCOURAGE

Many caring people who want to help the bereaved hesitate
because they are uncertain about the best ways to be helpful.
Whether the loss to death is that of a spouse, parent, grand-
parent, child, or friend, the bereaved need the gentle support
of their friends. In several places, Scripture commands
Christians to deliver help and hope: "Comfort all who mourn"

(Isaiah 61:2, NIV). Here are six ways to help someone through a time of grief as a result of the death of a loved one:

1. *Write a short note.* One of the most effective ways to comfort someone is through a written note. Unlike a condolence phone call, a letter can be saved to be read over and over again. When writing, share a personal memory of the deceased.

2. *Call and visit often.* In the weeks and months following a funeral, the bereaved person experiences a significant letdown as friends and family members resume their normal routines. The feeling of loneliness can be over-whelming. Consequently, a call or a visit from a caring friend can be a powerful antidote to those deep feelings of loneliness. In order to make your visits and calls truly effective, ask these types of questions:

   - Is there something I can do? (List a few specific things you could do to help)
   - Do you want to talk?
   - Would you like some company?
   - Do you need to get out of the house?
   - Would you like to take a walk?
   - Would you like to take a drive?
   - Would you like to see a movie?

3. *Recognize that recovery takes time.* Be patient with the griev-ing person and encourage him or her to be patient. There is great wisdom in Shakespeare's observation: "How poor are they that have not patience! What wound did ever heal but by degrees."[1] And the apostle Paul advises: "Encourage the timid, help the weak, be patient with everyone" (1 Thessalonians 5:14, NIV). There is no quick fix for the pain of grief. Generally, it

[1] From *Othello* by William Shakespeare, II, iii, 379.

takes the bereaved nearly three years before they begin to experience more good days than bad ones.

4. *Listen with the heart.* "The reason we have two ears and only one mouth is that we may listen the more and talk the less," noted Greek philosopher Zeno of Citium. The pain of grief is eased when the bereaved has a friend who will listen from the heart without making any judgments. That means making it as easy as possible for a bereaved person to speak whatever is on his or her mind and heart.

David, a young widower with two school-aged children, advises: "When you come to see us, be supportive and allow us to speak only about our feelings. Resist the urge to speak about your loss. We don't want to hear about it. This was our loss and we need to experience it in our own way. Be there to listen. Your willingness to listen is the most precious gift you can offer. The people I found most helpful made no attempt to distract me from my grief. They encouraged me to share my feelings over and over. It seemed that each time I told my story a layer of pain was peeled away, and the intensity of the bereavement was eased with each retelling."

5. *Resist any temptation to recite clichés.* One woman who experienced two miscarriages within a short period of time says, "I received all kinds of advice from friends, family, and coworkers. Most of it was useless." Her recommendation: "Suppress any temptation to say, 'It was for the best,' 'It wasn't meant to be,' 'At least you can get pregnant,' or 'You're young; you can try again.' And please don't say 'There was probably something wrong with the baby. This is nature's way.'" The problem with such clichés is that they minimize the sense of loss and further frustrate grievers. When respond-

ing to comments expressed by the bereaved, use short sentences to validate their feelings and convey your care. Here are some examples: "I'm sorry." "This must be very painful for you." "I feel very bad." "What can I do?" "I am concerned and want to help. Please call me at any time."

6. *Urge caution concerning hasty decisions.* Sometimes the bereaved are tempted to sell their house, move out of state, take a new job, or make a major investment shortly after a death. Unless absolutely necessary, all major decisions and changes should be postponed during the first year following a loss. The bereaved need time and distance from the loss in order to have a balanced perspective.

7. *Pray.* Finally, include the grieving in your prayers, asking God to give them daily strength and hope. Bereavement is a lonely journey, during which grievers experience a variety of confusing and conflicting emotions. Your gentle support is vital for the bereaved to experience peace in the place of pain, and healing in the place of hurting. With the help of kind friends, the grieving can gain a new direction for their lives.

HELPFUL THINGS TO SAY AND DO

- Send a short note or card.
- Express your sorrow by simply saying, "I'm so sorry about _____'s death."
- Provide meals for the family and inquire about other specific needs you may assist with, such as caring for pets or mowing the grass.
- Allow the family to talk about the loved one.
- Remember the family at holidays, birthdays, and at the anniversary of the death.

HURTFUL RESPONSES TO TRY TO AVOID

- Do not ignore those who have lost a loved one.
- Do not forget the children, siblings, and close friends of the deceased.

RELATED SCRIPTURE

This I declare of the Lord: He alone is my refuge, my place of safety; he is my God, and I am trusting him. . . . He will shield you with his wings. He will shelter you with his feathers. His faithful promises are your armor and protection. PSALM 91:2, 4, NLT

I cried out, "I'm slipping!" and your unfailing love, O Lord, supported me. When doubts filled my mind, your comfort gave me renewed hope and cheer. PSALM 94:18-19, NLT

The Lord is good. When trouble comes, he is a strong refuge. NAHUM 1:7, NLT

Come to me, all of you who are weary and carry heavy burdens, and I will give you rest. MATTHEW 11:28, NLT

Jesus told her, "I am the resurrection and the life. Those who believe in me, even though they die like everyone else, will live again." JOHN 11:25, NLT

All praise to the God and Father of our Lord Jesus Christ. He is the source of every mercy and the God who comforts us. He comforts us in all our troubles so that we can comfort others. When others are troubled, we will be able to give them the same comfort God has given us. 2 CORINTHIANS 1:3-4, NLT

PRAYER

Heavenly Father, we miss our loved one who has departed from us. Thank you for giving us the opportunity to have a relationship with _____. Comfort our hearts as we mourn _____'s passing, and give us peace and guidance as we face life on earth without this loved one. Amen.

A D D I T I O N A L   R E S O U R C E S

Grief Relief by Victor M. Parachin (Chalice Press, 1991). A basic primer on grief for those who are grieving and those who want to help.

What Helped Me When My Loved One Died, ed. Earl A. Grollman (Beacon Press, 1992). A collection of writings from people who have suffered loss and overcome grief.

The Lord Is My Shepherd: A Psalm for the Grieving by Victor M. Parachin (Liguori Publications, 1992). Healing meditations and insights for the bereaved.

What to Do When a Loved One Dies by Eva Shaw (Dickens Press, 1993). Practical information for best managing life after a loss.

When Will I Stop Hurting? Dealing with a Recent Death by June Kolf (Baker Book House, 1987).

How Can I Help? Reaching Out to Someone Who Is Grieving by June Kolf (Baker Book House, 1987).

V I C T O R   M .   P A R A C H I N

Reverend Victor M. Parachin is an ordained minister and counselor, having served churches in Washington, D.C., and Chicago. He is the writer of *Hope,* a monthly newsletter written for those who are grieving.

SUICIDE*

This I declare of the Lord: He alone is my refuge, my place of safety;
he is my God, and I am trusting him. . . .
He will shield you with his wings. He will shelter you with his feathers.
His faithful promises are your armor and protection.

PSALM 91:2, 4, NLT

W hen I first found out, all I could think was I want to die too. I was so angry at God. I yelled, 'God, you can't do this; he was mine!' Then I just cried for hours."

❑ *Woman whose fiancé committed suicide*

EFFECTS OF THE CRISIS

Although the aftermath of a suicide is similar in some ways to that of other sudden, violent deaths, it is different. Probably the most painful aspect of a suicide is acknowledging that it was the victim's choice. To a survivor, that realization leads to the question, *What did I do or not do that caused his or her life to be so unbearable that suicide was seen as the only way out?*

HOW YOU CAN HELP AND ENCOURAGE

Suicide can be so painful that family and friends may experience denial for some time, trying to believe the death was an

* This article was adapted from *Beyond Sympathy* by Janice Harris Lord (Ventura, CA: Pathfinders Publishing, 1988). Used with permission.

accident. If that is so, then honor it. Initially, it is best to approach the family as you would any grieving family, with no questions asked. Extend your sympathy with open arms, send flowers or other memorials, attend the funeral, and send a special note of remembrance of the deceased. Don't label the death a suicide until the family does.

Most important, don't blame the family for the deceased person's choice to end his or her life. Don't imply by question or comment that family or friends may have been responsible. They will suffer enough guilt on their own. Close family members will feel guilty for missing suicidal signals or not taking observed clues seriously. They will feel guilty for not being available if a final call for help was made. They will feel guilty if they allowed the suicidal instrument to be available.

If, as time passes, you believe the family is continuing to deny reality or feels too much responsibility, you can gently nudge them toward reality. The actual cause may have been physical or mental problems, an unwanted major life change, a highly self-critical personality, low self-esteem, the fantasy that death really isn't death, or combinations of the above. You can help family and friends understand that suicide is an extremely complex decision and that the victim was responsible for the suicide, not the family.

Those who were intimately involved with the suicide victim are often subject to numerous "secondary injuries." Insurance representatives, law enforcement officers, coroners, lawyers, and sometimes the media probe for information in such a way that survivors believe their integrity and moral character are being challenged. Regardless of the actions of outsiders, it is usually best for the family to cooperate with them and to understand that the professional role of these people is fact-finding, not emotional support. Not only will this frame of reference help family and friends feel some power in a powerless situation, but they may be able to obtain valuable information if they cooperate. Sometimes previously unconsidered rationales that can help explain the suicide may be uncovered. Autopsies can reveal bodies racked with pain, disease, or high blood concentrations of alcohol or other drugs. Investigations can reveal unknown pressures at work or other environmental circumstances. The more factual data obtained, the less blame one needs to put on oneself.

You may be curious to know why and how the suicide was committed. Questions like these are best unasked as you attempt to comfort the bereaved. While they may or may not know exactly how the suicide was committed, it is unrealistic to expect them to know all the details about it. Bits and pieces of evidence and speculation may be put together during the weeks and months following, but it is impossible to ever know the many intertwining variables that lead one to commit suicide.

Since survivors love to be reminded of the "good times" of their loved one, share these memories in a note sent after the funeral. Far more cherished than preprinted sympathy cards are handwritten notes that begin, "I'll never forget the time . . ." or, "Let me tell you why _____ meant so much to me." A handwritten note of special remembrances will be deeply appreciated, even from those who are not close enough to make a personal visit to the home.

On next year's calendar, mark the birth date and death date of the person who committed suicide so you can remember the family in a special way. Very few people remember the anniversary date of a death. For those dearest to the deceased, however, that date is indelibly imprinted on their minds. They will dread it. Many experience a resurgence of sadness and depression, not only on the death anniversary date but for weeks preceding it. To be remembered on these dates with a note, flowers, or other appropriate gift lets them know that they are not alone in their remembering.

Some communities have support groups and services for surviving family members of suicide. Check with your local mental health services or Christian counseling center.

HELPFUL THINGS TO SAY AND DO

- "Do you need help notifying people of _____'s death?"
- "I can't imagine the pain you are going through."
- Send notes often.
- Provide food for the family, assist with other essential tasks such as mowing the lawn or caring for children and pets.
- Keep in touch with the family in the following months.
- "It was not your fault. It was _____'s choice."
- Help prepare a press statement if the suicide is a high-profile case.

HURTFUL RESPONSES TO TRY TO AVOID

- "Did you notice any warning signals?"
- "Did you see it coming?"
- "Does suicide run in your family?"
- "How did _____ kill [him/herself]?"
- "Did _____ use alcohol or other drugs?"

RELATED SCRIPTURE

The Lord is my light and my salvation—so why should I be afraid? The LORD protects me from danger—so why should I tremble?
PSALM 27:1, NLT

God is our refuge and strength, always ready to help in times of trouble. So we will not fear, even if earthquakes come and the mountains crumble into the sea. PSALM 46:1-2 NLT

Because the Sovereign Lord helps me, I will not be dismayed. Therefore, I have set my face like a stone, determined to do his will. And I know that I will triumph. ISAIAH 50:7, NLT

Let not your heart be troubled. You are trusting God, now trust in me. There are many homes up there where my Father lives, and I am going to prepare them for your coming. When everything is ready, then I will

come and get you, so that you can always be with me where I am. If
this weren't so, I would tell you plainly. JOHN 14:1-3, TLB

That is why we have a great High Priest who has gone to heaven,
Jesus the Son of God. Let us cling to him and never stop trusting him.
This High Priest of ours understands our weaknesses, for he faced all
of the same temptations we do, yet he did not sin. So let us come boldly
to the throne of our gracious God. There we will receive his mercy, and
we will find grace to help us when we need it.
HEBREWS 4:14-16, NLT

PRAYER

Lord, we miss _____. As we walk through the dark shadows of this
tragedy, help us to lean on your promise that you will not forsake us.
Grant us courage and endurance to acknowledge the reality of what
has happened and the faith that your wisdom and love will sustain
us. Help us to feel your presence and rely on your promises till we
reach our journey's end. Amen.

ADDITIONAL RESOURCES

Silent Grief: Living in the Wake of Suicide by Christopher Lukas and Henry M. Seiden,
Ph.D. (Scribners, 1987). Written by a survivor and a psychologist, this book gives
understanding, support, and information to those whose loved one has committed
suicide.

My Son . . . My Son: A Guide to Healing after Death, Loss, or Suicide by Iris Bolton
(Bolton Press, 1983).

A Grief Observed by C. S. Lewis (HarperSanFrancisco, 1961). A classic on the subject
of grief.

If Only I Had Known . . . by Bill Grady, Anthony Grady, and JoAnne Grady
(A & S Publishers, 1992).

No Time for Goodbyes: Coping with Sorrow, Anger, and Injustice after a Tragic Death
by Janice Harris Lord (Pathfinder Pub., 1991). Coping with sorrow, anger, and injustice
after a tragic death.

J A N I C E   H A R R I S   L o r d

Janice Harris Lord is a licensed master social worker/licensed professional counselor who has served as national director of victim services at Mothers Against Drunk Driving for fourteen years. She is author of *No Time for Goodbyes: Coping with Sorrow, Anger, and Injustice after a Tragic Death* (Pathfinder Pub., 1987) and *Beyond Sympathy: What to Say and Do for Someone Suffering an Injury, Illness, or Loss* (Pathfinder Pub., 1989).

MISCARRIAGE

[Jesus said,] "Let the little children come to me; do not stop them; for it is to such as these that the kingdom of God belongs." And he took them up in his arms, laid his hands on them, and blessed them.

MARK 10:14, 16, NRSV

The doorbell rang. I had just come home from the hospital. The procedure had not taken long. What my body had begun, the doctor had to finish. I felt empty in more ways than one.

Mindlessly I went to the door and opened it. A woman from the church stood on the front porch. "I just had to come over the minute I heard. Don't doubt for an instant this was the Lord's will. God makes no mistakes. If this baby didn't get here, there must have been a reason. 'The Lord gives and the Lord takes away. . . .'"

The phone began to ring. When I answered it, a familiar voice said, "I am so sorry to hear about your miscarriage. I want you to know that I had one too, so I know the particular disappointment that you and your husband must be feeling. Please don't think that it was something you did, or that God is punishing you somehow. These things just happen, and they happen more often than you think. If the right conditions aren't present, the pregnancy can't thrive. I'll be praying that God will give you strength, both physically and spiritually."

A note came in the next day's mail. It said simply, "I can't presume to understand why this happened, but I do know several things. The first is that God loves you. Don't doubt this just because you are suffering. Second, God will give you strength to see you through this experience. Third, God can take this miscarriage and use it for a good purpose in your life or in the life of another person. It is a mystery why these things happen. But it is no mystery that we can count on God's presence and love."

UNDERSTANDING THE CRISIS

Pregnancy is an intensely *personal* experience for prospective mothers. While most men do not feel like fathers until they hold their infant for the first time, pregnant women often think of themselves as mothers-to-be as soon as their pregnancy test reads positive. As a result, a woman's attachment to her unborn child may be very deep. Others may not understand and may wonder how and why she can be so "wrapped up" in her pregnancy. In fact, carrying a baby consumes a pregnant woman's waking thoughts. The pregnancy often governs what she can and can't eat, drink, and take in the form of medicine. As one woman described it, "Pregnancy is when you are 'possessed.' You are no longer in control of your own body. Someone else has taken it over."

What makes miscarriage such a devastating crisis is that it is frequently a *private* loss. Many women miscarry before they have told friends or family of the pregnancy. Most miscarriages occur in the first trimester, before a woman begins to show. For these reasons, the significance of the loss may be ignored, or worse, denied. However, for the pregnant woman, the pain that accompanies the loss of a fetus is in essence the same grief that is felt when a loved one dies (see "The Grief Process" on pages 17–22).

EFFECTS OF THE CRISIS

Miscarriage is defined as a failure to carry a fetus to full term. Note the use of the word *failure*. Miscarriage feels like a personal failure. Not only has a woman's body let her down, but often she feels that somehow *she* also has let other people down and therefore is at fault. It is not hard to see why miscarriage can leave its mark physically, emotionally, and spiritually.

PHYSICAL

Physical changes in the body have physical consequences. When a miscarriage occurs naturally, there is a great deal of bleeding. Excessive blood loss leads to physical weakness as well as to fright from the experience. Many women report fearing their own death once the bleeding starts. Even when the miscarriage is completed at the hospital without massive blood loss, it still takes a number of days for the woman to regain her strength.

Hormones play a critical part in maintaining pregnancy, and hormonal changes will occur as the body adjusts to its loss. This temporary hormone imbalance can plunge the woman into postpartum depression. Consequently, it is important for the woman to stay in touch with her physician and to report any symptoms of depression that she experiences.

EMOTIONAL

Depression may arise from physical changes or from grief over the loss of the pregnancy. Miscarriage is emotionally devastating because it represents not only failure on the biological level but also dashed dreams and hopes for the future. These feelings are magnified if the pregnancy was difficult to achieve or was thought to be a couple's last chance to have a baby.

Many times the woman is alone in her grief, because those around her are not able to recognize the depth of her attachment to her unborn child. Without the understanding and support of a caring partner, family, and friends, the woman can begin to feel as if she is going crazy. In response, she may withdraw and become isolated, wondering why others don't feel the loss as acutely as she does.

It is not uncommon for women who have experienced miscarriage to feel jealous of women who have healthy children. For some it is especially difficult to be around those who have babies. Often the woman will remember and observe the day that would have been her baby's birthday.

Probably the most haunting question following a miscarriage is *why?* Women want to understand why the miscarriage happened, and many blame themselves either consciously or subconsciously. What did I do wrong? What could I have done differently? These questions are in the emotional forefront, but unfortunately there are not many answers. For reasons unknown, miscarriage occurs in one out of five pregnancies.

SPIRITUAL

Because miscarriage involves life and death, it has spiritual dimensions. The Bible describes God as Lord of life and death. Women who have miscarried may struggle with this, asking questions such as these: If God is Giver of life, then what does it mean when pregnancy ends in death? What part did God play? Is miscarriage a punishment from God? Is miscarriage a wake-up call to become more devout?

HOW YOU CAN HELP AND ENCOURAGE

Your response to the grieving couple should be one of comfort and compassion. Remember that what hurts is the *heart,* not the head. Accordingly, cerebral discussions and theological doctrines are not helpful (at least initially). The husband and wife need to know that people who care about them, whose strength can help get them through this crisis, surround them. Here are some concrete things that can start the grieving couple on their journey toward wholeness.

250

PHYSICAL

1. *Provide meals for the couple.* Sometimes there are groups in the church who have a food ministry. Call on them or solicit volunteers who will prepare meals for the first week.
2. *If there are other children at home, offer to take them out for a special treat.* Time alone to sleep, weep, or just relax is a luxury many cannot afford. This simple act can provide a fun time for the children as well as a healing time for the couple.
3. *Offer to run an errand or a car pool.* The woman is usually advised not to drive for a number of days.

EMOTIONAL

1. *Listen with your heart and forget what you hear.* What you are likely to hear is raw pain, anger at having been deprived of a healthy baby, and even some ranting about God's role in all of this misery. Your response should be to soothe the pain, *not* to judge or edit the content.
2. *Find someone who has experienced a miscarriage with whom the woman can talk.* Miscarriage is a particular kind of grief, and it really "takes one to know one." The best comfort comes from one who has been there and made it through.
3. *Keep in regular contact for at least the first month.* Miscarriage makes almost everyone uncomfortable. It is easy to make one contact and then put off making others. Calls, visits, and notes are all forms of contact. Some suggest that notes are best, since they can be kept and reread.
4. *Be aware that grief can cause marital problems.* Any crisis puts stress on a marriage. Because the wife is more personally involved in miscarriage than her husband, the disparity between their experiences of the same loss can cause tension. Counseling may be in order.

5. *Don't forget that healing has its own timetable.* It is unrealistic to set a date by which a couple should be through grieving. Especially if depression is involved, healing may take months and possibly years. Healing is accelerated by the love of God, of family, and of friends.

SPIRITUAL

1. *Anger at God is to be expected.* Remember that God can handle our honest feelings. The psalmists often cried out to God in pain, questioning why they suffered. What you can say with absolute certainty are these affirmations: (1) Despite your suffering and anguish, God still loves you. (2) God is with you even now, sharing your grief and willing your wholeness and healing. (3) God works through others to bring new strength. Right now there are people who are praying for your healing (don't say this unless it is so).

2. *The theology that heals is the theology of love.* As the opening story illustrates only too painfully, theology can help or hurt someone who is struggling with miscarriage. A "God is in absolute control" theology sends the message that this miscarriage represents the will of God. Certainly not to bless . . . must be to punish. The couple is left to wonder why God might do such a thing. The conclusion that miscarriage is a punishment from an angry God transforms a physical and emotional wound into a deep spiritual wound as well. Vastly more helpful is the biblical theology that asserts the love of God. God loves us in the midst of our pain and suffering, loves us even when we are angry and confused, loves us when we are tempted to turn away from divine love. Remind the couple that God continued to love Job in the midst of his grief over losing all ten of his children. And most impor-

tantly, God is a parent who suffered the loss of his only Son.

3. *Don't ask* why—*ask* how. The most frequently asked question is *why?* Usually there are no answers to this question. A better question to ask is *how? How* will God use this miscarriage for good? *How* can this tragic event be used to help others? *How* might this experience bring us closer to God, family, and others?

4. A *memorial service can often bring closure.* It is not necessary to have a body in order to have a memorial service. A brief service, which recognizes the loss of this life and calls on God's strength, is appropriate. Families may find it comforting to name the child, keep footprints, or register the death in church records.

HURTFUL RESPONSES TO TRY TO AVOID

- "You can have other children" or "At least you have other children."
- "At least you didn't get to know and love your baby."
- "It wasn't a real baby anyway."
- "You're not the only one this has ever happened to."
- "It was the Lord's will."
- "God doesn't make mistakes."
- "It was better for it to die if there was something wrong with it."
- "It probably would not have lived anyway."
- "God did this now to spare you later."
- "This is really a blessing, though you can't see it now."

RELATED SCRIPTURE

The Lord is merciful and gracious, slow to anger and abounding in steadfast love. He does not deal with us according to our sins, nor repay us according to our iniquities. As a father has compassion for

his children, so the Lord has compassion for those who fear him. For he knows how we were made; he remembers that we are dust.
PSALM 103:8, 10, 13-14, NRSV

Out of my distress I called on the Lord; the Lord answered me and set me in a broad place. With the Lord on my side I do not fear. What can mortals do to me? I was pushed hard, so that I was falling, but the Lord helped me. The Lord is my strength and my might; he has become my salvation. PSALM 118: 5-6, 13-14, NRSV

O Lord, you have searched me and known me. You know when I sit down and when I rise up; you discern my thoughts from far away. You search out my path and my lying down, and are acquainted with all my ways. Even before a word is on my tongue, O Lord, you know it completely. Where can I go from your spirit? Or where can I flee from your presence? If I ascend to heaven, you are there; if I make my bed in Sheol, you are there. If I take the wings of the morning and settle at the farthest limits of the sea, even there your hand shall lead me, and your right hand shall hold me fast. Search me, O God, and know my heart; test me and know my thoughts. See if there is any wicked way in me, and lead me in the way everlasting.
PSALM 139:1-4, 7-10, 23-24, NRSV

Come to me, all you that are weary and are carrying heavy burdens, and I will give you rest. Take my yoke upon you, and learn from me; for I am gentle and humble in heart, and you will find rest for your souls. MATTHEW 11:28-29, NRSV

PRAYER

You are an all-knowing and ever-loving God, who remembers even the sparrow when it falls. Although no one else may fully understand or feel our inward grief at this loss, you alone know and share all our hurts, our sorrows, and our broken dreams. You call us to cast all our burdens upon you and to find comfort and hope in you. Lord, we do not always understand the things that happen to us. We only know that where there was once fond expectation, now there is bitter disappointment; where there was once hope and excitement, now there is a sense of tragedy and loss. In our pain and confusion we look to you, for whom no life is without meaning, however small or brief. We pray that you will surround us with your everlasting arms. Draw us closer to you and to each other. Breathe into us your new life. Give us faith and courage, and enable us to feel your strong presence in unmistakable ways. Bring healing, hope, and health as only you can do, loving Father. Amen.

A D D I T I O N A L   R E S O U R C E S

M.E.N.D. (Mommies Enduring Neonatal Death), P.O. Box 1007, Coppell, Texas 75019. 1-888-695-MEND. www.mend.org

I'll Hold You in Heaven by Jack Hayford (Ventura, CA: Regal Books).

Empty Arms: Emotional Support for Those Who Have Suffered a Miscarriage, Stillbirth, or Tubal Pregnancy by Pam Vredevelt (Sisters, OR: Multnomah Press, 1984).

Miscarriage by Walter Williamson (New York: Walker and Co., 1988).

Miscarriage: A Shattered Dream by Sherokee Ilse and Linda Hammer Burns (Maple Plain, MN: Wintergreen Press, 1981).

Miscarriage: Women Sharing from the Heart by Marie Allen and Shelly Marks (New York: John Wiley & Sons, 1993).

When Pregnancy Fails: Families Coping with Miscarriage, Stillbirth, and Infant Death by Susan Borg and Judith Lasker (Bantam Press, 1989).

Following is a memorial service created by the chapter author that can be adapted as needed.

MEMORIAL SERVICE: A CHRISTIAN WITNESS TO THE RESURRECTION

Call to Worship
Jesus said, "Let the little children come unto me, and forbid them not; for of such is the kingdom of heaven." And he picked them up in his arms and he held them close, and he blessed them.

MARK 10:14, 16, paraphrased

255

We are here to worship God, to proclaim our belief in the resurrection to eternal life, and to declare that nothing in all creation has the power to separate us from the love of God, fully revealed in Christ Jesus. Here today we seek the comfort, the presence, and the strength of God.

Prayer
Eternal God, we are struggling with the pain of grief, and we come seeking your presence. Send your Holy Spirit to comfort and strengthen us, that we might have hope of life eternal and trust in your goodness and mercy. Open our ears to hear words of love, grace, and peace as we read Holy Scripture. For these things we ask in Jesus' name, amen.

Old Testament Lesson
The people of Old Testament times were people of the land. Life was hard for them. They knew what it was to lose children. Yet their faith in the goodness of God was undaunted. They acknowledged their pain and grief (like King David fasting in sackcloth and ashes after the death of his infant son; like Job questioning God after the deaths of all his sons and daughters). Yet every one of these people, despite their tremendous grief and loss, called on the presence of God for strength and comfort.

We, as Christians, don't have to deny our pain; but neither do we have to deny our faith in the goodness of God in circumstances such as this. God knows our grief, and God has promised that he will be with us always, even in the very midst of our suffering. Let's read these words of comfort and strength from Psalm 139. This psalm opens with an acknowledgment that we are intimately known and loved by our loving heavenly Father (verses 1-6). Then comes wording that sounds as if the baby is the one speaking (verses 13-16). The psalm concludes with a strong affirmation of God as the way to eternal life (verses 23-24).

New Testament Lesson
Read Luke 18:15-17 and Romans 8:28, 31-35, 37-39.

Remarks
We come to this time of prayer and worship seeking no easy answers—because there are none.

Life is a mystery . . . and likewise death is a mystery. Rather, we come asking God to mend these broken hearts of ours; asking God to fill us once more with hope; trusting in God's Word that he is always and forever at work for good; trusting that nothing, not even death, can separate us from God.

We claim God's promise that a place has been prepared for all the children of God. A place with our Lord, the one who declared, "Unless you enter the Kingdom of God like a little child, you'll not enter it at all" (Matthew 18:3, paraphrased).

Prayer
Loving and gracious God, you are our refuge and strength, a very present help in trouble. You have searched us and known us, created us and redeemed us, nourished us and sustained us. You know us better than we know ourselves. You alone know and share all our hurts and deepest sorrows. We thank you that you invite us to cast all our cares upon you.

We are especially distressed by this untimely death that brings not only the pain of grief and loss but also the pain of dreams dashed. Help us to accept what we cannot understand, and enable us to remain faithful to you, even in the midst of our suffering. Grant that we may trust in your love, which is eternal and steadfast. In the days ahead, Holy One, surround us with your everlasting arms. Draw us closer to you and to each other. Hold us, heal us, strengthen us, and bring us peace.

Hear our prayer this day, for we pray it in the name and for the sake of Jesus Christ, who taught us to pray, saying: "Our Father which art in heaven, Hallowed be thy name. Thy kingdom come. Thy will be done on earth, as it is in heaven. Give us this day our daily bread. And forgive us our debts, as we forgive our debtors. And lead us not into temptation, but deliver us from evil: For thine is the kingdom, and the power, and the glory, for ever. Amen" (Matthew 6:9-13, KJV).

Committal Prayer *(if this service is at the graveside)*

_____(parents' names), now we take _____'s (baby's name) body, and we return it to the ground. Earth to earth, ashes to ashes, dust to dust, in the certainty that God has already received his or her spirit into heaven and in the expectation that one day both of you will join him or her there.

Loving God, speak words of comfort and assurance to these parents and to all who mourn the passing of this one who was so loved. Take their sorrow and transform it into quiet acceptance; take their emptiness and replace it with a new awareness of their love for each other and for you; take their disappointment and turn it into new hope for the future. For you are the author of all peace, hope, love, and joy. Amen.

Benediction

And now may the peace of God, which truly passes all understanding, keep our hearts and minds in the knowledge and love of God, and of his Son, Jesus Christ our Lord; and may the blessings of God Almighty be with us now and forever. Amen.

Louise Upchurch Lawson

The Reverend Louise Upchurch Lawson is a wife, mother of two, and associate pastor of Germantown Presbyterian Church in Germantown, Tennessee. She has had three miscarriages, which has equipped her to reach out to others who have experienced the same loss.

DEATH
OF A CHILD*

The Lord is close to those whose hearts are breaking.

PSALM 34:18, TLB

I t's so wrong, so profoundly wrong, for a child to die
before his parents. It's hard to bury our parents, but that
we expect. Our parents belong to our past; our children
belong to our future. We do not visualize our future without
them. How can I bury my son, my future, my next in line?
He was meant to bury me!"

❑ *Father whose son died in a mountain-climbing accident*

EFFECTS OF THE CRISIS

Very deep grief follows the death of a child. Even mature
Christians have difficulty understanding that a loving God
sometimes allows an innocent child to die. This holds true for
the death of a child in the womb, a miscarriage, or even for an
adult child. Parents who lose children often quote from the
New Testament, "And a sword will pierce your very soul"
(Luke 2:35, NLT). These are the words of the prophet Simeon
to Mary, in anticipation of the death of her son.

It feels terribly "wrong" to be predeceased by one's child.

* This article was adapted from *Beyond Sympathy* by Janice Harris Lord (Ventura, CA:
Pathfinders Publishing, 1988). Used with permission.

How You Can Help and Encourage

What do the mourners need from you? First, they need your ear. Allow them to express their thoughts and feelings over time, and accept all the feelings they reveal.

Listening is crucial in comforting others. It is not helpful to talk trivia or keep the conversation light in the mistaken belief that they won't think about the pain in their life. Don't talk business or give advice when your friends are suffering from a breaking heart.

When someone has lost a child, the only real remedy is to restore the child. Unfortunately, you can't do that. But attempting to minimize the loss or suggesting alternatives for fulfillment won't work. Yearning to have one's child restored is absolutely normal. Since you can't make things the way they were before, you are of greatest service if you simply support the person's suffering, rather than trying to "make it better."

Once the loved one is ready, reminiscing about happier, healthy days and memories of the child as a fully functioning individual will help diminish the images of death. They also affirm the contributions the child made and help to balance the suffering of the child's last days.

Because of feelings that their child was cheated of life, it is important that the child be remembered in special ways. Mention his or her name often. Consider establishing a permanent memorial, such as a scholarship, or write a memorial poem about the child. Mention that support groups such as Compassionate Friends, Mothers Against Drunk Driving, and Parents of Murdered Children exist in most metropolitan communities to help parents cope with the death of a child.

Since survivors appreciate remembrances of the "good times" of their child, share these memories in a note sent after the funeral. Far more cherished than preprinted sympathy cards are handwritten notes that begin, "I'll never forget the time that . . ." or, "Let me tell you why _____ meant so much to me." For an infant, "_____ brought so much love into your family," or, "You gave so much of yourselves in order that _____'s brief time here was filled with love." A hand-written note of special remembrances will be deeply appreciated, even from those who are not close enough to make a personal visit to the home.

On next year's calendar, mark the birth date and death date so you can remember the family in a special way. Very few people remember the anniversary date of a death. For those dearest to the deceased, however, that date is indelibly imprinted on their minds. They will dread it. Many experience a resurgence of sadness and depression, not only on the death anniversary date but for weeks preceding it. To be remembered on these dates with a note, flowers, or other appropriate gift lets them know they are not alone in remembering.

HELPFUL THINGS TO SAY AND DO

- Provide meals for the family, and ask to help with other needs such as mowing the lawn or getting the car serviced, etc.
- Keep in touch with the family over the months.
- "I can't imagine how this must be for you."
- If possible, take siblings on outings.

HURTFUL RESPONSES TO TRY TO AVOID

- "You're lucky you have other children."
- "I know exactly how you feel."
- "I fully understand."
- "_____ is lucky not to have to suffer the difficulties of adult life."
- "You'll be able to have more children."

RELATED SCRIPTURE

The Lord is my shepherd; I have everything I need. He lets me rest in green meadows; he leads me beside peaceful streams. He renews my strength. He guides me along right paths, bringing honor to his name. Even when I walk through the dark valley of death, I will not be afraid, for you are close beside me. Your rod and your staff protect and comfort me. PSALM 23:1-4, NLT

Can anything ever separate us from Christ's love? Does it mean he no longer loves us if we have trouble or calamity, or are persecuted, or are hungry or cold or in danger or threatened with death? . . . No, despite all these things, overwhelming victory is ours through Christ, who loved us. ROMANS 8:35-37, NLT

From the depths of despair, O Lord, I call for your help. Hear my cry, O Lord. Pay attention to my prayer. . . . I am counting on the Lord; yes, I am counting on him. I have put my hope in his word. I long for the Lord more than sentries long for the dawn, yes, more than sentries long for the dawn. O Israel, hope in the Lord; for with the Lord there is unfailing love and an overflowing supply of salvation. He himself will free Israel from every kind of sin.
PSALM 130:1-2, 5-8, NLT

PRAYER

Dear Lord of life, your resurrection wrenched the iron doors of death off their rusted hinges. You gave a crushing blow to its dark and terrible reign. We thank you for your promise of our future resurrection, that we will be with you forever.

Yet, we miss this child we have loved and laid to rest. Absent is _____'s voice, _____'s smile, _____'s presence.

We may have to die, but you conquered death forever through your resurrection.

We thank you for that coming day when we shall be in heaven, and pain, illness, tears, loneliness, and despair will be no more.

Grant us eternal peace from the expanse of your love. Amen.[1]

---

[1] Prayer adapted from *Prayers for Every Occasion* by Gerrit D. Schut (Tyndale House Publishers, 1992), 64.

ADDITIONAL RESOURCES

When Good-bye Is Forever by John Bramblett (Ballantine Books, Inc., 1991). Learning to live again after the loss of a child.

Recovering from the Loss of a Child by Katherine Donnelly (Macmillan, 1982). A thoughtful and compassionate book for parents and siblings who have experienced the death of a child.

The Will of God by Leslie Weatherhead (Abingdon Press, 1944). Clear-minded thinking about God's part in personal loss and world disaster.

Lament for a Son by Nicholas Wolterstorff (Eerdmans, 1987). A Christian man articulates the pain and struggle he went through after his son's tragic death.

A Grief Observed by C. S. Lewis (HarperSanFrancisco, 1961). A classic on the subject of grief.

A Mother's Grief Observed by Rebecca Faber (Tyndale House Publishers, 1997). A personal account about how God brought hope and healing following the devastating loss of a son.

Empty Arms by Pam Vredevelt (Ingram, 1995). Offers emotional support for those who have suffered miscarriage or stillbirth.

JANICE HARRIS Lord

Janice Harris Lord is a licensed master social worker/licensed professional counselor who has served as national director of victim services at Mothers Against Drunk Driving for fourteen years. She is author of *No Time for Goodbyes: Coping with Sorrow, Anger, and Injustice after a Tragic Death* (Pathfinder Pub., 1987) and *Beyond Sympathy: What to Say and Do for Someone Suffering an Injury, Illness, or Loss* (Pathfinder Pub., 1989).

A
LOVED ONE
IS MURDERED

HOMICIDE

The Lord is my shepherd; I have everything I need. . . .
Even when I walk through the dark valley of death,
I will not be afraid, for you are close beside me. Your rod
and your staff protect and comfort me.

PSALM 23:1, 4, NLT

M y husband, Jerry, and I were in Ohio to present a Bible seminar at a large Christian music conference. On the morning of the seminar, the phone rang in our hotel room.

I glanced at Jerry as he answered and saw the blood drain from his face. His features literally collapsed. I watched his respiration deepen and accelerate. He dropped onto the side of the bed. I knew something terrible had happened.

He turned to me, drew me into the shelter of his arms, and said, "Steve was murdered last night. The police need to know who his dentist was for identification." Then he turned back to the phone.

I felt my heart shatter and break. I wrapped my arms around my rib cage to hold myself together. I couldn't breathe. The edges of my vision darkened, and my mind went numb. Aloud I whispered, "Oh God, oh God, oh God, oh God . . . Please no, no."

❏ *Author Mary A. White*

UNDERSTANDING THE CRISIS

Homicide includes all deaths caused by willful murder and nonnegligent manslaughter. The homicide victim is usually survived by family members, relatives, close friends, church members, neighbors, coworkers and community members—all who may feel deep loss and grief as a result of such a violent death.

EFFECTS OF THE CRISIS

Murder causes unimaginable complications. Loved ones face the paralyzing shock of the victim's untimely and often brutal death, endless consultations with the police, appalled reactions by friends, messages from the district attorney's office, newspaper interviews, television reports, court hearings—sorrow upon sorrow upon sorrow.

Murder not only destroys the loved one but continues to rip and tear and bruise the emotions and spirits of those left behind. Sometimes the wounds are never laid to rest, for the murderer goes uncaught and unpunished for the monstrous crime.

HOW YOU CAN HELP AND ENCOURAGE

IN THE FIRST HOURS, DAYS, AND WEEKS AFTER THE DEATH

Sudden death often immediately plunges family members into debilitating, terrible mourning, leaving them weak and stunned. At the same time they are required to make major decisions about which they have given no thought and for which they have had no preparation.

If you are in a pastoral role with family members who have lost a loved one through a homicide, you can assist by offering to help plan an appropriate funeral. Walk through the details with them, give guidance as asked, offer options, but be careful not to make decisions for them.

In some cases, the family will be asked to identify the body or will be given an opportunity to view the body. It will be a difficult decision. In your support role, you may want to offer to identify or view the body first to let the family know if it would be all right for them to go. You may also want to let them know that you are available to go with them for support and comfort.

An avalanche of kindness flowed toward our family from the moment friends, neighbors, colleagues, and even strangers, heard of Steve's murder. Some of our closest friends from around the country flew to Colorado Springs as soon as they could. Others who lived in town came over, called, or wrote us notes. With an unspoken awareness, they began to support and organize and help us plan for the days ahead.

Fred became our right hand as he listed all ideas, suggestions, and plans in the notebook that never seemed to leave his hand. Chris, Alice, and Lois worked tirelessly in the kitchen, preparing and serving an endless supply of food, which came from friends, neighbors, and church members. Stan answered the doorbell as it rang again and again for flower deliveries, visits, and the arrival of telegrams.

These unselfish efforts on our behalf freed us to grieve, to talk with those who came to offer sympathy, to rest, and to plan. Perhaps their greatest gift to us was their presence. They were willing to stand with us in our anguish, to remove whatever pressures they could, to help, listen, love, and cry.

Our family was blessed to have the love, presence, and support of so many people. Unfortunately, many families who lose a loved one to murder do not have that support and encouragement. You may want to make a point to reach out to families in your community that you may not know who have experienced a homicide.

When a murder occurs, family members of the victim need time and space to grieve. Grief is not abnormal but a healthy reaction to loss. Grief is a God-given process of letting go as it helps survivors cope with various reactions, such as shock, helplessness, fear, rage, and even murderous impulses. Grief allows family members and friends to begin to deal with the reality of the loss and to say an appropriate good-bye to the loved one.

It is important for caregivers to understand and be prepared for family members' intense and often frightening reactions. The number of friends who expressed deep anger over the senselessness of the murder amazed me. My shock and grief remained so overwhelming that I had no capacity for anger. But there was a sense of comfort that friends recognized the great injustice of Steve's death and were willing to state their rage. Their anger struck me as *righteous indignation,* a solid abhorrence for the act that deliberately destroyed an innocent human life.

Above all, pray for the family and friends of the victim. Pray for God's protection and comfort. My family will never know all of the effort, love, concern, help, and prayers that flowed our way through those days. We felt carried along on the love and prayers of friends as we functioned beyond our capacity during that terrible time.

IN THE MONTHS AND YEARS AFTER THE DEATH

No one can predict or prescribe healing for another. Each healing is as unique as the person going through it. Body, mind, and spirit—all are severely wounded through grief. All need healing. Each part of the human body and soul needs restoration and renewal. It takes time, a very long, painful time.

As a caregiver, allow the family and friends to grieve in their own way and at their own pace. Be careful not to set a time frame for another's healing and recovery. Some family members may want to seek professional counseling. If asked, you may want to offer to help them identify professional Christian counselors in your area who have experience working with crime victims.

HELPFUL THINGS TO SAY AND DO

- Allow the family and/or friends to talk about the victim. Let them tell you about his or her life as well as the details of the murder. Allow the survivors to talk about the good and the hard times.
- Allow survivors to express their anger—at the offender, the criminal justice system, the victim, you, and even God. Anger needs to be expressed to be addressed.
- Remember the family and friends at holiday times and on the anniversary date of the murder, as well as on the victim's birthday. Send a card or place a phone call to let the family know that you remember, too.
- Remember to continue to pray for the family and friends over the months and years after the murder. Although the pain and grief may ease, at some level the pain and grief still remain.
- Express your sorrow by simply saying, "I'm sorry this happened to _____ and your family, and it is horrible that someone you loved was killed."
- Encourage health. There is a tendency for people in great grief to put aside their physical health and well-being. Encourage family members and friends to guard their physical health with balanced nutrition, light exercise, and rest.
- Beware of the severe impact on siblings or friends of the victim. Allow them to fully express their grief and move through the healing process.

HURTFUL RESPONSES TO TRY TO AVOID

- Don't tell family members or friends that you know how they feel, even if you have experienced the homicide of someone you love. Continued expressions of love and support are vital. Say, "I care about you. I'm here for you."
- Don't tell family members or friends that the death "must be God's will." Rather, let them know that God is present

with them in their suffering—that he is the great Comforter and will provide them the comfort that he promises (2 Corinthians 1:3-4).

RELATED SCRIPTURE

Though you have made me see troubles, many and bitter, you will restore my life again . . . and comfort me once again.
PSALM 71:20-21, NIV

[God will] comfort all who mourn, and provide for those who grieve . . . to bestow on them a crown of beauty instead of ashes, the oil of gladness instead of mourning, and a garment of praise instead of a spirit of despair. ISAIAH 61:2-3, NIV

Praise be to the God and Father of our Lord Jesus Christ, the Father of compassion and the God of all comfort, who comforts us in all our troubles, so that we can comfort those in any trouble with the comfort we ourselves have received from God.
2 CORINTHIANS 1:3-4, NIV

PRAYER

A prayer to share with your friend:
Dear God, you alone are enough for me when I am suffering this deep sorrow. As I rest in the comfort of your love, I will find solace in my mourning. Please be with me and those I love as we grieve together. Thank you for your grace and strength and comfort. Amen.

ADDITIONAL RESOURCES

Harsh Grief, Gentle Hope by Mary A. White (NavPress, 1995). A painful yet tender story told by the mother of a homicide victim. This book testifies to the divine power and hope and offers genuine compassion to others experiencing severe loss.

It Hurts to Lose a Special Person by Amy Ross Mumford (Cook Communications, Chariot Books, 1982). This is an excellent booklet that can be used as a sympathy card.

No Time for Goodbyes: Coping with Sorrow, Anger, and Injustice after a Tragic Death by Janice Harris Lord (Pathfinder Pub., 1987). A practical book on dealing with sudden death.

MARY A. WHITE

Mary A. White holds a degree in English from the University of Colorado and has studied at Northwestern Bible College and the University of Washington. She and her husband, Jerry, who is the General Director of the Navigators, are involved in a discipling ministry, speak at seminars around the country, and minister in their local church. Mary is the author of *Harsh Grief, Gentle Hope,* a book about the death of the White's son, Stephen, who was murdered in 1990.

HOMICIDE
OF A CHILD

If my sadness could be weighed and my troubles be put on the
scales, they would be heavier than all the sands of the sea.

JOB 6:2-3, NLT

I n September of 1994, nine-year-old Michael was excited
to be starting fourth grade. For the first two weeks,
Michael's mother walked with him to school every day
before she went to work. After that, Michael had walked to
school with his older brother. One day Michael's brother
stayed home sick with a fever, and Michael walked to school
alone. He was abducted on the way and murdered. His body
was found two days later in a wooded lot near the school.
No suspect has been found.

UNDERSTANDING THE CRISIS

The intentional death of a child may occur in a variety of
ways: murder by a stranger, murder at the hands of a family
member or acquaintance, or vehicular homicide by someone
driving while impaired are among the most common. The circumstances of each homicide vary, as do the child's type of
injuries, but the ultimate result is the death of an innocent life
through violence.

EFFECTS OF THE CRISIS

The death of a child from any cause is one of life's most devastating losses. When that death is caused by intentional human brutality or recklessness, the sense of shock and horror is often compounded. Parents and other adult relatives, siblings, friends, or teachers are left to struggle with intensely painful immediate and long-term crisis reactions.

Commonly noted reactions of parents or close family members from the time of the murder through the first two years include:

- a feeling of shock, being stunned, numbness;
- a preoccupation with the loss of the child, like a part of the self was gone;
- a concern with the degree of brutality or suffering associated with the child's death and a need to know the details about the death;
- anger toward the suspect(s)/murderer(s);
- a decrease in appetite;
- dreams/nightmares about the child's death, and difficulty in falling asleep;
- the beginning use of sedatives/tranquilizers for sleep or nervousness; and
- a feeling of depression or hopelessness.

HOW YOU CAN HELP AND ENCOURAGE

Most parents expect that their children will outlive them, while siblings and friends have a hard time conceiving of the death of a person so close to their own age. There may be an overwhelming sense of unfairness that a young life was cut short—but even if the homicide victim is an adult, he or she may still be someone's "child," and the surviving parents of an adult victim can benefit from the same kind of support that may be offered to parents of a young victim.

Appropriate helping techniques are often simple and heartfelt. You can be a compassionate physical presence for the family. You don't have to do a lot of talking—just "being there" is often more comforting. Keeping in contact with the family (through calls, notes, visits) is also important, for after the immediate crisis is over, other supporters will stop contacting and family members may feel as though they have been forgotten.

When family members are ready to talk, listen nonjudgmentally. Focus on their perspective, and be careful not to "take over" their crisis by trying to calm them down. Their suffering—and our ability to tolerate it—is part of the healing process. Allow each person to express the pain and emotion in his or her own way.

As you listen, seek opportunities to let family members know that they have been heard. Let them know that in the face of such a senseless crime and such a precious loss, their reactions—whatever they are—are understandable. Don't be afraid to talk about the child who has died and to use his or her name frequently. Allow silences in the conversations, as survivors often need time to reflect. Remember to keep confidential what the survivors have told you.

PRAYER

Prayer can be a powerful form of expression and release. Let family members know you would be willing to pray with them, silently or aloud, if it would be comfortable. If the survivor cannot concentrate or is somewhat agitated, encourage the use of well-known prayers (such as the Lord's Prayer) or familiar Scripture passages (such as Psalm 23), which can be very calming and comforting.

CRIMINAL JUSTICE SYSTEM

Many survivors of a murdered child will become involved with the criminal justice system. At the very least, they will have contact with law enforcement officers and investigators. If a suspect is apprehended, the family will be facing meetings with prosecutors, victim service specialists, a judge, a jury, and perhaps even corrections personnel, including parole or probation officers.

Support the family during what may be a prolonged process. Ask family members whether they would like you or other friends or church members to accompany them to meet with the police or the prosecutor, or if you could go with the survivor to any hearings or to the trial. These events are often painful to experience alone, and most families consider that this is one of the last things they can do on behalf of their murdered child.

Let the family know that most prosecutors' offices have a victim-assistance program. Encourage the family to ask that a victim advocate be assigned to the case. The victim advocate can be an invaluable source of information about the criminal justice process, about victims' legal rights, and about communicating with the media. The advocate also has information about other kinds of assistance that may be available, such as crime victim compensation to help cover medical and counseling expenses, lost wages, and funeral costs. If there is no victim assistance program available, the family could call the National Crime Victim Information and Referral Hotline, operated by the National Organization for Victim Assistance, at (800) 879-6682, for referrals to the nearest victim assistance program.

SPECIAL ISSUES

In some cases family members may have had a troubled relationship with the child who was murdered. There may not have been an opportunity for the victim and certain family members to make amends or to say good-bye. Reassure those family members that everyone has difficult times in their relationships and that it does not mean they were not good parents, siblings, or friends. Encourage the survivors to find ways to resolve these feelings through prayer, counseling, or by writing a letter to the deceased child.

Survivors of a murdered child also will often feel intense anger, which may be directed at the assailant, at God, at themselves (for not protecting the child), and even at the victim (for being at the wrong place or doing something he or she should not have been doing). People often feel guilty about their inability to forgive—after all, Jesus forgave those who harmed and murdered him. Remind survivors that God did not tolerate injustice and that the Scriptures repeatedly condemn those who victimize their fellow human beings. Acknowledge that their forgiveness will not be a simple process in the face of such a horrendous tragedy.

Seek ways to remind the family that even in the darkest moments, God remains present and at work in the lives of his people. Nothing will better communicate God's love than your compassionate presence and nonjudgmental responses. Acknowledging the endless (but diminishing) pain can also give comfort.

HELPFUL THINGS TO SAY AND DO

- "I am truly sorry that your child has been murdered. Nothing in life can prepare any of us for such a painful loss."
- "Would you like to talk about what has happened?" (Or, ask more specific questions about when he or she first got the death notification, what he or she has done or felt since, etc.)
- "Sometimes the only thing you can do is take things one moment at a time."
- "Your [pain, anger, fear, etc.] is entirely understandable under the circumstances."
- "Even though no one understands why this tragedy has happened, I believe that God can and will help and comfort you in your grief and loss."

HURTFUL RESPONSES TO TRY TO AVOID

- "I understand how you feel." (Even if you've been through something similar, your feelings and reactions won't be exactly the same.)
- "Why was your child . . . ?" "Why did you allow your child

to . . . ?" (The word *why* connotes blame. Eliminate *why*, *should* and *ought* from your helping vocabulary.)

- "Your child's death was God's will." (This is not helpful as it is not comforting for the survivors to believe that God would have wanted their child to have been brutally murdered.)
- "You should rejoice because your child is in a better place." (Again, this is not helpful, since the survivor would prefer the child to still be with them.)
- "You need to get over this and move on with your life."

RELATED SCRIPTURE

Morning, noon, and night I plead aloud in my distress, and the Lord hears my voice. He rescues me and keeps me safe from the battle waged against me, even though many still oppose me.
PSALM 55:17-18, NLT

Give your burdens to the LORD, and he will take care of you. He will not permit the godly to slip and fall. PSALM 55:22, NLT

Three of Job's friends were Eliphaz the Temanite, Bildad the Shuhite, and Zophar the Naamathite. When they heard of the tragedy he had suffered, they got together and traveled from their homes to comfort and console him. JOB 2:11, NLT

PRAYER

A prayer to share with your friend:
Dear God, my heart aches with sorrow and despair. Our child has been taken from us by violence. We struggle to understand why this has happened and to find meaning and value in this pain. O God, we have no answers. But we know that you, whose own Son was murdered, are not blind to human evil and that the darkness of evil does not conceal your presence. Grant us the strength and courage to live through this pain with unwavering hope and faith, and help us to see your goodness through our tears. Provide your comfort to us,

and help us to reach out to receive the help we need. We ask this through Christ, our Lord. Amen.

ADDITIONAL RESOURCES

Life after Loss: The Lessons of Grief by Vamik D. Volkan, M.D., and Elizabeth Zintl (Macmillan Publishing Company, 1993). Simple and eloquent, focusing on mourning and healing.

Remembering with Love: Messages of Hope for the First Year of Grieving and Beyond by Elizabeth Levang, Ph.D., and Sherokee Ilse (Fairview Press, 1991). Daily messages of encouragement and hope from survivors who have made the journey.

The Shadow of Evil: Where Is God in a Violent World? by Jeffrey M. Davis (Kendall Hunt Publishing Co., 1996).

When a Bad Thing Happens to Faith-Ful People: Crime Victims and God by A. Robert Denton, Ph.D. (Write or call the Victim Assistance Program, P.O. Box 444, Akron, OH 44309-0444; telephone (330) 376-0040.) This booklet helps people to cope with a loss and not lose faith.

CHERYL GUIDRY TYISKA

Cheryl Guidry Tyiska is a survivor of violent crime and has worked in the field of victim's rights and assistance for ten years. She is the director of victim services for the National Organization for Victim Assistance in Washington, D.C.

LINE-OF-DUTY DEATH

God blesses those who work for peace,
for they will be called the children of God.
MATTHEW 5:9, NLT

You love what is right and hate what is wrong. Therefore
God, your God, has anointed you, pouring out the oil of
joy on you more than on anyone else.
PSALM 45:7, NLT

I first met Spencer when we were working together developing new policies for his agency. Spencer was the deputy chief and had paid his dues on the street. He was now "riding the desk" (holding down an office position) most of his shift. He had stopped working swing shifts so he could attend important family events, such as ball practice and school plays. Spencer was no longer in the line of fire. He was enjoying his family and career. He was even waiting for the day when he might be asked to be chief.

But Spencer never had that opportunity. While making a routine traffic stop in his hometown, Spencer was shot as he approached the car. He was killed doing his job. In 1994, the year Spencer died, seventy-six other officers across the United States lost their lives in the line of duty."

UNDERSTANDING THE CRISIS

Line-of-duty death is any action, felonious or accidental, that claims the life of a law enforcement officer or other emergency service personnel who are performing work-related functions, either on or off duty. These officers and personnel include: police, sheriff and sheriff's deputies, firefighters, prison guards, FBI agents, Secret Service agents, military personnel, and others.

From moments until months after learning about the death, many survivors (family members, close friends, and colleagues) will experience the often devastating shock and disruption resulting from the event. Although some family members may have understood (or have feared) that the person was in the kind of job that put him or her in life-and-death circumstances, the survivors often experience disbelief and denial that "this can't be happening to me." This early denial is predictable and is one of the most common defense mechanisms used to deal with high levels of anxiety.

The family, friends, and colleagues of the victim may experience sleeplessness, restlessness, and even nightmares. In addition, some may complain of physical difficulties. This is also a time when the family will ask, "Why me?" "Why my cop?" "What did we do wrong?" "I wish [the offender] was dead too!" This is a critical time for support. This is a time when the family and friends need to talk and have someone listen nonjudgmentally.

The emotional and spiritual impact of the death will continue as the family attempts to return to normal activity, socialize with friends, and interact with their church and community. Family members may not wish to discuss the trauma with friends or relatives. Some survivors may want to talk about it frequently. Allow the victims to talk about their loved one's life and death as little or as much as they would like.

How You Can Help and Encourage

DEATH NOTIFICATION

If you are asked to make (or participate in) the death notification, remember the shock of what you are about to say. Death notification should be in person, in time, in pairs, in plain language, and *with compassion*. Death notification should always be made in person, not by telephone. Notification should not be delayed. Too many survivors are devastated by learning of the death of a loved one or a colleague through the media. If at all possible, notification needs to be made by individuals the survivors can trust. Law enforcement chaplains or family pastors are especially helpful in this area. Be aware that support may be needed for the notifiers as well.

Inform the survivors by speaking slowly, carefully giving any details that are available. Then calmly, honestly answer any questions the survivors may ask. Avoid ambiguous statements such as "He was lost." Use the victim's name and state the fact: "He died." Remember that your presence and compassion are critical resources—not necessarily your words. Accept the survivors' expressions of emotion. Many survivors report that statements such as "It was God's will" or "She had a full life" or "I know how you feel" appear less than honest. Your role at this phase is to be helpful and provide support and encouragement to those who are experiencing great grief and loss.

FUNERAL

Offer to assist the family in making funeral arrangements, as appropriate. Even if asked, be careful not to make decisions for the family on your own. Rather, do "the homework" and provide options to help the family make important decisions. Also, at this time provide support for the family by being present and/or participating in the funeral if asked.

FINANCIAL CONSIDERATIONS

After the funeral, help the family meet with the appropriate agency personnel to discuss insurance and benefits from the death. If the person who died was the primary breadwinner in the family, you may want to ask the surviving family members if they would like to discuss financial matters with a professional financial planner. If so, provide suggestions of reputable financial consultants for the family to select. As appropriate, your church may want to consider giving a "love offering" to the family to help cover immediate expenses.

COMMUNITY AND MEDIA REACTIONS

Many survivors perceive that they are treated differently by their friends, fellow church members, and the community. In some cases, the media's attention and publicity of the death causes survivors increased trauma and suffering. Most survivors have never interacted with the media prior to this event and are unfamiliar with their interviewing and reporting processes. You may be able to provide important assistance by offering to help the family in responding to the media. Help them think through and decide if they want to be interviewed and, if so, what they want to say. Also, inform family members that they have a right to say no to any media interview.

Although in most cases public opinion is on the side of the officer and his or her family, public opinion may be mixed—for or against the agency or the officer. In certain situations, charges may be filed against the agency as a result of the event. In small communities, the children of the officer and the alleged offender may attend the same school. Whether such extenuating circumstances exist or not, the family needs the presence and support of the church, friends, and community.

SPIRITUAL IMPACT

At this time family members may question their faith, exhibit anger toward the church or toward God, develop an interest in faith issues, or rely on their faith in greater ways. Whatever the reaction and response may be, encourage the survivors to ask questions, express their anger, and/or seek solace in prayer and in worship—as appropriate.

HELPFUL THINGS TO SAY AND DO

- Express your own sorrow over the loss by simply saying, "I'm sorry this happened to _____ and your family. It is horrible that someone you love was killed."
- Affirm the trauma and difficulty of the death and their reaction to it: "You are having a normal reaction to an abnormal event."
- Help survivors anticipate the cognitive, emotional, physiological, and spiritual reactions that they may experience in the weeks, months, and even years after the event.
- Help predict what survivors may experience from the media and others in the community. Offer to assist the family in making statements to the media.
- As appropriate, offer to help organize a special prayer or church service or other ceremony in which a plaque could be presented in memory of the officer. You may want to coordinate this with the agency and/or the family's church congregation.

HURTFUL RESPONSES TO TRY TO AVOID

- Avoid ambiguous statements such as "It was God's will" or "She had a full life" or "I know how you feel" or "It was his destiny."
- Do not set time limitations on when the family or colleagues should recover from the death.
- Do not try to make decisions or fix problems for the family. Allow the family members to continue to take responsibility and to make decisions as they can. If you are asked to help in making decisions, offer options and suggestions.

RELATED SCRIPTURE

The salvation of the righteous comes from the Lord; he is their strong-
hold in time of trouble. The Lord helps them and delivers them;
he delivers them from the wicked and saves them, because they take
refuge in him. PSALM 37:39-40, NIV

But you, O Lord, are a compassionate and gracious God, slow to
anger, abounding in love and faithfulness. Turn to me and have
mercy on me; grant your strength to your servant. . . . Give me a sign
of your goodness, that my enemies may see it and be put to shame, for
you, O Lord, have helped me and comforted me.
PSALM 86:15-17, NIV

PRAYER

Dear Father, we pray for all those who live and work for justice, free-
dom, safety, and peace in our communities. Almighty God, in whose
hand are the living and the dead, we give you thanks for all the ser-
vants who have laid down their lives for the safety of others. Grant to
us who love and miss them your tender mercy and the light of your
presence. Please give us faith and courage that we may meet the days
to come with patience, hope, and strength. Help us to remember your
great goodness and love, and let us live in joyful expectation of eternal
life with you. This we ask in the name of Jesus Christ, our Savior.
Amen.

A D D I T I O N A L   R E S O U R C E S

Keeping It Simple, Sorting Out What Really Matters in Your Life by G. S. Aumiller
(Adams Publishing, 1995). Gary Aumiller offers a step-by-step plan that anyone can
use for getting their priorities straight and simplifying their lives. This self-help book
includes spirituality as part of mental health.

Traumatic Stress: The Effects of Overwhelming Experience on Mind, Body, and Society
by B. A. Van der Kolk, A. C. McFarlane, and L. Weisaeth (The Guilford Press, 1996).
This book is an excellent resource for those who desire a more in-depth understanding
of traumatic stress.

Support Services to Surviving Families of Line-of-Duty Death by S. F. Sawyer (Concerns of Police Survivors, Inc., 1994). This is one of many publications available from the nationwide support agency for survivors of police death.

ANDREW H. RYAN JR.

Andrew H. Ryan Jr., Ph.D. is a father of two, a husband, and a licensed psychologist. He consults with local, state, and federal law enforcement agencies. He currently serves on the South Carolina Governor's Juvenile Justice Advisory Council, is the president of the Council of Police Psychological Services, and the president of the South Carolina Victim Assistance Standards & Certification Board.

Study Guide

TABLE OF CONTENTS

Study Guide Introduction 295
Crisis Intervention 300
The Grief Process 303
The Tool of Forgiveness 305
Divorce 308
Domestic Violence 310
Community Tragedy Caused by Crime 313
Substance Abuse 316
Employment Crisis 318
Child with Special Needs 320
Life-Threatening Illness 323
Burglary and Theft 325
Child Victimization 327
Elderly Victimization 330
Adult Survivors of Sexual Abuse 332
Rape and Sexual Assault 334
Death of a Loved One 336
Suicide 338
Homicide 340

STUDY GUIDE
INTRODUCTION

NEIGHBORS WHO CARE

If you have read Chuck Colson's foreword to this book, you know that Neighbors Who Care (NWC) is a Christian ministry assisting churches to serve victims of crime in their congregations and communities. Types of service to victims include spiritual, emotional, and practical support. NWC specifically assists churches by providing advisory consultation, resource materials, and training. Affiliated with Prison Fellowship Ministries (founded by Chuck Colson in 1976), NWC is a vital part of a "full circle" approach to understanding and responding to those involved in and affected by crime.

PURPOSE OF THE STUDY

The purpose of this study is to help you and/or the members of your group or church to better understand and respond to people in crisis—whether that crisis is crime-related or not. The study guide has been designed to provide a basic introduction to helping family, friends, and neighbors who are experiencing certain types of crises. While there are thirty-four crises covered in the book, this study guide focuses on eighteen of the most commonly experienced ones. The study guide has been designed to be adapted to your study group. Depending on the number of weeks you have set aside for studying *Helping a Neighbor in Crisis,* you can select the study guide chapter and topics that best fit the interests and needs of your group. By studying and discussing the matters raised in each chapter, you will deepen your understanding of the topic and how you can offer help and support to those in crisis.

STUDY OBJECTIVES

- To examine different types of crises and develop a deeper understanding of their impact and effect in individual lives
- To develop practical skills and gain knowledge in responding to crisis to provide help and support to family, friends, and neighbors in need
- To identify ways that you as an individual, your group, and your church can respond faithfully and concretely to victims of crime

SCOPE AND FORMAT OF THE STUDY

This study guide is intended for use by an individual or in a small group, whether a Sunday school class, an evening study group, or part of a college or seminary course. Using the study, the reader, group, or class will examine the impact of different crises and how to offer help and support in each one.

Each study is designed around the following sections:

Objectives	Significant points to be learned through the lesson
Reviewing	Summary of main ideas in the chapter
Discussion Starters	Questions to help you begin thinking about the topic and its impact
Understanding the Crisis	Questions and discussion points to help you examine the issues raised in the chapter
How to Help	Questions and discussion points to help you apply what you have learned

SUGGESTIONS FOR INDIVIDUAL STUDY

- It is not necessary to go straight through the book. You may want to pick the topics that interest you the most and study those chapters.
- Use a notebook to write down your thoughts, questions, and responses as you read the chapter; then think about the questions in the study at the end of each chapter.

SUGGESTIONS FOR GROUP STUDY

Here are a number of suggestions for structuring your group study. As you get to know your group, you can adapt the studies to fit your group's style and needs.

- Determine the number of weeks you and your group will study *Helping a Neighbor in Crisis*. Then select the chapters and study-guide lessons that best fit the interests and needs of your group.
- To get the most out of the book and the discussion times, group members should read the assigned chapter prior to each meeting.
- With the flexible format of the study guide for assistance (adapted as you see fit), the group can meet weekly, biweekly, or even monthly to discuss the chapter that has been read.
- At the beginning of the meeting, you may want to review the Objectives and Reviewing sections as a group. The Reviewing section can be particularly helpful if a person is new to the group, or if a member of the group was unable to read the chapter prior to the meeting.
- Then the leader guides the group through discussion. You may use one or all of the questions and discussion points in the Discussion Starters, Understanding the Crisis, and How to Help sections of the lesson. Or you may want to raise questions and issues more directly related to your group's situation. Some weeks this may involve hav-

ing a member of the group read aloud a Scripture passage or a small section of the chapter as background.
- The amount of time you have for each meeting depends on your situation. Here are two possible ways to structure your time—one for a longer meeting and one for a shorter one. You may, of course, adapt the time and structure to suit your group.

TOTAL TIME	75 MINUTES	45 MINUTES
Prayer and introduction	15	10
Discussion	45	30
"Housekeeping" details and closing prayer	15	5

WHAT YOU NEED FOR THE STUDY

- A copy of *Helping a Neighbor in Crisis*
- A Bible
- Paper and pen
- Open minds and hearts
- A commitment to preparation, attendance, and participation

LEADING SMALL GROUPS

A small group can be a dynamic experience of people growing in knowledge and in spirit, with the whole being greater than the parts. It can also be a positive experience of forging relationships. Indeed, it could be argued that the best experiences of growth in knowledge and spirit are most likely to occur in the context of growing relationships. What things can you, as leader, do to foster such experiences? The following ideas may help you in preparing for and leading the group study and discussion. Your role as leader is to assist group members in taking on the intellectual and spiritual challenges of this subject matter. This is a vital and valuable role. Enjoy it!

Leadership Role

You do not need to be an expert in theology, criminology, or victimology. Your primary role as leader is to facilitate and coordinate the study and discussion of the group to help the meeting run smoothly and purposefully.

Through your role as facilitator, you can blend direction to ensure the study's logistics and maintain its focus with the freedom and flexibility to allow members to participate creatively. The goal is to maximize individual involvement—allowing for personal style—in the study and in the group meetings. The following points about group dynamics and logistics may help your group achieve that goal.

Group Dynamics

Often each participant has a different reason for undertaking a study, which may affect that individual's participation—for example, what questions or issues have importance; what emotions the study touches; or what a person hopes to accomplish through the group study.

Additionally, members of the study will have different styles of participation. As you begin to recognize their different styles, you can seek balance among those differences through comments, direction, and questions.

Be prepared for the possibility that the subject matter may be emotional for some members of the group. A person may have experienced or be experiencing a certain type of crisis or been close to someone who was. Allow for emotions to be part of the group process. In addition, group members may share information that they wish to be kept confidential. Discuss the issue of confidentiality with the group before starting the study.

Facilitating Group Discussion

The group discussion can often be the most significant and meaningful part of the study for the participants. At the same time, for the leader it can be the most intimidating. Here are some ideas that may assist you in facilitating discussion.

- Encourage all members to take part in the discussion. You may, with discretion, ask direct questions of participants. Sometimes you may need to carefully direct the discussion away from some group members.
- Do not be afraid of moments of silence. Silence can be a powerful motivator for people to initiate discussion; sometimes people need to digest ideas before speaking.
- Encourage sensitivity toward each type of crisis. Discourage judgmental thoughts toward crises that seem remote or "not likely to happen here." Remind members that any crisis can happen in any place, at any time, to anyone.
- Try to keep the discussion focused on the subject; people in groups have a tendency to stray from the subject and find it difficult to return to it on their own. At the same time, leave room for the Holy Spirit to guide the direction of the discussion. If the group seems on a tangent, but people are interested and engaged, you may want to stay with that line of discussion for a while.
- Welcome new ideas, questions, and perspectives.

CRISIS INTERVENTION

Who shall separate us from the love of Christ? Shall trouble or hardship or persecution or famine or nakedness or danger or sword? For I am convinced that neither death nor life, neither angels nor demons, neither the present nor the future, nor any powers, neither height nor depth, nor anything else in all creation, will be able to separate us from the love of God that is in Christ Jesus our Lord.
ROMANS 8:35, 38-39, NIV

OBJECTIVES

Through this study your group will:

- Examine the "anatomy" of a crisis
- Identify the three stages of crisis
- Identify eight survival strategies for moving from victim to survivor
- Begin to identify opportunities for ministry during each stage of crisis

REVIEWING

When we hear the word *crisis,* many of us remember times when we found ourselves in a situation out of our control. Events outside our normal experience can throw us into a mode of coping—trying to make sense of the events and emotions we are experiencing and to "handle" our world.

What makes an event a crisis is that our normal coping mechanisms are not capable of handling the event we have just experienced. The death of a loved one, the robbery of our house, the failure of a marriage or business—all of these situations are out of the realm of our normal everyday lives. As a result, our usual methods of establishing control and dealing with things do not work for this new problem; thus we find ourselves in the midst of crisis.

Marion Bard and Dawn Sangrey, authors of *The Crime Victim's Book,* identify three stages of crisis: the impact, recoil, and reorganization stages. During impact the safety and security of the victim are vital. Recoil provides space for the victim to tell and retell what has happened to him or her. During reorganization a victim begins to anticipate and prepare for the future.

Crisis intervention is a process for assisting someone in crisis to develop the resources to effectively cope with and heal from a situation in the long term. Crisis intervention is not long-term counseling; it is a short-term, immediate support that provides help and assistance in the aftermath of a crisis. But, as Bard and Sangrey point out, "minutes of skillful support by any sensitive person immediately after the crime (or other crisis) can be worth more than hours of professional counseling later."[1]

This chapter identifies the basics of crisis intervention—what it is, what it is not, and how you can help a "neighbor in crisis."

DISCUSSION STARTERS

- What makes a situation a crisis? Why do some events result in a crisis while others do not?
- Describe some physical, emotional, psychological, and spiritual reactions a person in crisis might experience.
- List the types of events that can result in crisis. Ask members of your group to share about times in their lives when they experienced crisis. What emotions did they feel? What questions did they have? What help did they receive? What was helpful to them? What was not helpful?

UNDERSTANDING CRISIS INTERVENTION

- Discuss the impact stage of crisis. List some feelings associated with this stage. What needs does a person in crisis have during this stage?
- Discuss the recoil stage of crisis. What is the purpose of "boiling down the problem" or "ventilating"? How do the following provide assistance to the person experiencing crisis: (1) asking them to describe their memory of the crisis; (2) asking them to tell their story; (3) assisting them to determine if the crisis reaction is interfering with normal life activities.
- Discuss the reorganization stage. Why does crisis often cause people to reassess or reaffirm their lives, values, and beliefs? How do you help someone to anticipate and prepare for the future after a crisis?

[1]Morton Bard and Dawn Sangrey, *The Crime Victim's Book* (New York: Brunner/Mazel, Inc., 1986).

HOW TO HELP

- What does it mean to cause "secondary victimization" or "secondary trauma"? How can you prevent a secondary victimization?
- Review the eight survival strategies on page 15. As a group, brainstorm specific actions that you could take to assist a person walking through each of those steps.
- Ask those in your group who know someone in crisis to share about the situation (as appropriate); then discuss ways the individual or the group can assist this person.

THE GRIEF PROCESS

But you, O God, do see trouble and grief; you consider it to take it in hand. The victim commits himself to you; you are the helper of the fatherless. PSALM 10:14, NIV

OBJECTIVES

Through this study your group will:

- Develop an understanding of the symptoms of grief and the grieving process
- Identify ways to offer comfort and support during grief
- Explore ways in which grief can affect our spiritual life and how we think about and relate to God

REVIEWING

Simply defined, grief is emotional suffering caused by loss. That loss can include the death of a loved one, the loss of an important relationship, the death of a dream, the loss of one's job or property, or an emotional or physical violation that results in loss. All of these types of loss lead us to grieve. Grieving is part of a normal, healthy process. However, knowing that doesn't make it any easier to go through the grief process.

Those who are experiencing grief often experience certain symptoms such as shock, denial, loneliness, crying, pain,

303

anger, anxiety, guilt, depression, hope, and readjustment. Some who grieve experience all of these symptoms, while others experience only certain ones. One of the difficult things about grief, both for the griever and the helper, is that grief does not progress in any order or format. Each person grieves his or her own way and on his or her own timetable. Many people move in and out of the different stages of grief in no particular order and can experience each stage multiple times.

Grief often involves a spiritual crisis in addition to an emotional crisis. Grieving persons struggle with questions about who God is and why this happened to them. Many of the emotions they feel during the grief process may feel "ungodly," and they may struggle with how to relate to God in the midst of their great anger, pain, and anxiety.

Through this chapter you and your group can begin to understand the different components of grief and how to offer practical, emotional, and spiritual support to those who are grieving.

DISCUSSION STARTERS

- Ask members of your group to share their experiences that caused them grief. What did their grief process look like? What surprised them about their grief? What comforted them?
- Why do we grieve? What is the purpose of grief?
- Grief can be defined as emotional suffering caused by loss. Brainstorm with your group about the types of loss that can cause grief.

UNDERSTANDING GRIEF

- Discuss the process of grief. What does a person experience during the process?
- What spiritual issues and/or questions can be raised by grief?

- How can our grief draw us to God or away from him?
- The author describes grief as a "healthy, human response." How is grief healthy?

HOW TO HELP

- The process of grief often does not progress in any certain order. How will understanding grief prepare you to assist a loved one who is grieving?
- Review the process of grief again. How can you, your group, or your church provide comfort and support during these different stages? Discuss practical ways that could help meet the needs of a grieving person.
- What things could hinder a person's grief process? For those trying to help, what should they avoid saying or doing?
- Those experiencing grief often need to tell and retell what they have experienced and are currently experiencing. Why is this important? How can you offer support?

THE TOOL OF FORGIVENESS

Once when Jesus had been out praying, one of his disciples came to him as he finished and said, "Lord, teach us to pray, just as John taught his disciples." He said, "This is how you should pray: 'Father, may your name be honored. May your Kingdom come soon. Give us our food day by day. And forgive us our sins—just as we forgive those who have sinned against us. And don't let us yield to temptation.'"
LUKE 11:1-4, NLT

OBJECTIVES

Through this study your group will:

- Develop a deeper understanding of God's purpose and plan for forgiveness
- Begin to identify concrete ways to incorporate practices of forgiveness into everyday life

- Identify the questions and issues that individuals face when struggling to forgive
- Identify concrete ways to offer help and support to those struggling with forgiveness

REVIEWING

Forgiveness can be a complex, confusing, difficult, and painful process. But it is also a freeing, life-giving restoration of broken or damaged relationships for both the offended and the offender.

Forgiveness can free the offender from the bondage of guilt and fear of retribution by providing an opportunity for repentance and reconciliation. Forgiveness doesn't excuse or forget actions or words that have caused great harm and wrong; but forgiveness frees the offended from the bondage of rage, hate, and a desire for revenge through the "giving up" of one's right to retribution, and the extension of grace and mercy to the offended.

But what is forgiveness? How does a heart riddled with betrayal, anger, and hate change to a heart willing to share hurt with the offender and offer an opportunity for repentance and restoration? Why should the offended bear the burden of struggling to forgive? Are some offenses unforgivable? Should forgiveness be offered when there is no repentance? What is the responsibility of the offender in the forgiveness process?

These are just a few of the challenging questions that each of us faces whenever we determine that we are going to walk the path toward forgiveness. The good news is that the way has been prepared and the path, though not always clearly marked, has been scouted for us. Christ walked the path of forgiveness, absolving those of us who trust in him of our deserved punishment and taking on the guilt of our sins that we might live each day in the freedom and joy of forgiveness and grace.

This chapter is an exploration of forgiveness. You may come

away with unanswered questions, but hopefully you will also come away with a deeper and fuller understanding of the power and freedom Christ has made available to us through the tool of forgiveness.

DISCUSSION STARTERS

- What are some possible definitions of forgiveness?
- Why is forgiveness so difficult? What are some of the emotions involved?
- Why can both offering and receiving forgiveness be difficult processes?
- Ask the group to share times when they struggled to forgive someone or when they were forgiven.

UNDERSTANDING FORGIVENESS

- What is forgiveness? Read page 25, the paragraph under the heading A Costly Tool and discuss with your group.
- Why would God ask someone who has already suffered great pain to sacrifice even more by offering forgiveness?
- Review the section How the Tool Works: Stages of Forgiveness on pages 25–27. Why is each stage important? What are the emotions/challenges the victim faces during each stage?
- Read and discuss the following Scriptures on forgiveness: Matthew 6:9-15; 18:21-35; Luke 17:3-4; 23:33-34; Colossians 3:13.
- What is the responsibility of the *offended* during each stage? What is the responsibility of the *offender* during each stage? Is forgiveness dependent on the repentance of the offender?
- What is the difference between forgiveness and reconciliation? How do they complement one another?

HOW TO HELP

- Review the section entitled Offering the Tool on page 27. Discuss each of the four characteristics with your group.
- Why is the idea of forgiving and forgetting so threatening? How does the process of forgiveness actually hold the offender responsible rather than excuse the offense?
- From the perspective of the person who has been offended, brainstorm tangible ideas of what remorse, repentance, restitution, and regeneration would entail. What is the victim's role in each of these steps? When the offender is not repentant, how can the Church assist in the healing process?
- How can the church body assist in the process of forgiveness?

DIVORCE

Peace has been stripped away, and I have forgotten what prosperity is. I cry out, "My splendor is gone! Everything I had hoped for from the Lord is lost!" The thought of my suffering and homelessness is bitter beyond words. I will never forget this awful time, as I grieve over my loss. Yet I still dare to hope when I remember this: The unfailing love of the Lord never ends! By his mercies we have been kept from complete destruction. Great is his faithfulness; his mercies begin afresh each day.
LAMENTATIONS 3:17-23, NLT

OBJECTIVES

Through this study, your group will:

- Identify the process of grief and recovery divorced people often experience
- Develop an understanding of the types of loss involved in divorce
- Identify ways you, your group, or your church body can help those in your congregation who have been through or are going through divorce

REVIEWING

Almost all of us know someone, maybe ourselves, who has been impacted by divorce. Divorce can be complicated and very painful. Knowing how to balance biblical truth with compassionate support for those who are divorced is truly a learned skill.

Divorce is not God's plan for marriage, yet unfortunately many marriages do not last. This chapter seeks to avoid the often sticky, emotionally charged debate about the morality of divorce. Instead, it focuses our attention on the fact that everyone in a divorce ends up wounded and everyone needs help and support.

As you go through this lesson, be careful to address the sensitivity of the issue. Many people who are divorced or going through a divorce are experiencing guilt, rejection, failure, loss, shame, and hopelessness. They must be handled with care! They need long-term care to heal from the brokenness and to move forward in hope.

It has been said that divorce is much like death—only it can be even more traumatic. Losing a loved one to death involves a clean break. And there usually isn't guilt, remorse, blaming, etc. However, divorce is usually highly charged emotionally and does not involve a clean break—often the spouses move in and out of each other's lives for many years.

When loved ones or the Church are silent or do not provide concrete help, most divorced people feel rejected again. This chapter will provide you, your group, or your church with helpful information on the issues surrounding divorce and practical suggestions for ministering to those experiencing the crisis of divorce.

DISCUSSION STARTERS

- Many in your group probably know someone who is divorced, have divorced parents, or are themselves divorced. As appropriate, ask your group to share their experiences. What were their needs? What were their hopes and fears?

- Why does the Church often struggle with reaching out to those who have been or are going through a divorce?
- How has your church responded to those in your congregation who are divorced?

UNDERSTANDING DIVORCE

- Why is divorce sometimes as difficult or even more difficult than the death of a loved one?
- What types of loss are experienced during divorce?
- What are some of the emotions experienced during and after a divorce?
- The typical recovery time from a divorce is between two and five years. With your group discuss the elements of divorce that cause the healing to be a lengthy process.

HOW TO HELP

- Discuss the stages of grief and recovery that divorced people often experience.
- How can you support divorced people when they place the blame elsewhere and then as they move through self-blame?
- Discuss why the Church is sometimes slow or void in efforts to reach out and minister to those who have experienced divorce.
- List concrete ways you, your group, or church body can reach out to those in your congregation who are divorced or are going through a divorce. Review the stages of recovery again as you think about ways to help.

DOMESTIC VIOLENCE

It is not an enemy who taunts me—I could bear that. It is not my foes who so arrogantly insult me—I could have hidden from them.

Instead, it is you—my equal, my companion and close friend. What good fellowship we enjoyed as we walked together to the house of God.
PSALM 55:12-14, NLT

OBJECTIVES
Through this study your group will:

- Be able to define what constitutes domestic violence
- Develop an understanding of the effects of domestic violence on the victim(s)
- Identify ways to help a friend or neighbor who is caught in or recovering from an abusive relationship

REVIEWING
Domestic violence refers primarily to the sexual assault, rape, aggravated assault, or simple assault by a spouse, relative, or other person well known to the victim. Both women and men may be domestic-violence victims but most are women.

Domestic violence can be a short-term or long-term abusive situation with significant physical and emotional injuries. In some situations, the abuse is not only life threatening but can even end in the death of a victim as well as other family members.

The most effective helpers for domestic-violence victims are those who encourage the victim to make choices to protect herself and any children who may be involved.

Domestic violence both within and without the Church poses a significant threat to families today. Historically, fearful of disrupting the family, churches have remained silent on the issue of domestic violence. Today, however, the Church is beginning to see domestic violence as a serious violation of God's design for family life and is speaking out and reaching out to those in need of help.

This chapter will provide you and your group with a deeper understanding of the issues involved in domestic violence and with practical suggestions for how you and your church can reach out to victims of domestic violence.

DISCUSSION STARTERS

- Ask your group to share experiences (as appropriate) of others who have experienced domestic violence. If one of your group members has experienced an abusive relationship and is willing to share, allow time for that.
- Ask your group members to put themselves in the place of Ginny in the story at the beginning of the chapter. Have the group brainstorm both emotions they would experience as well as fears and other considerations.

UNDERSTANDING DOMESTIC VIOLENCE

- From the perpetrator's perspective, one of the primary purposes of domestic violence is to control the spouse or other person. Review the effects of domestic violence on page 50. How do the effects of abuse work to limit the victim's ability to make independent decisions and choices?
- Discuss with your group why the Church sometimes finds it difficult to get "in the middle" of domestic-violence situations.
- Do you think the Church has contributed to the problem of domestic violence? Biblically, how is the Church called to respond to victims of domestic violence?

HOW TO HELP

- "The most effective helpers are those who encourage the abused woman to make choices that protect her and her children and hold the abuser accountable." How can you, your group, or your church support and assist in this process? What emotional, spiritual, and practical help can you, your church, or your group provide to victims of domestic violence? How can you practically enter into the victim's pain with her or him?

- Victims of domestic violence may struggle with significant spiritual crises during and after the abuse. How can you and your church offer support during this time?
- What should you or your church avoid doing or saying that could negatively impact the victim as she or he deals with the physical, emotional, and spiritual crisis of domestic violence?

COMMUNITY TRAGEDY CAUSED BY CRIME

God is our refuge and strength, always ready to help in times of trouble. So we will not fear, even if earthquakes come and the mountains crumble into the sea. Let the oceans roar and foam. Let the mountains tremble as the waters surge! PSALM 46:1-3, NLT

OBJECTIVES
Through this study your group will:

- Explore the dynamics of crime that affect an entire community
- Identify concrete ways you and your church can minister to your community in the wake of a community-wide crisis
- Examine the need to prepare for responding to a community tragedy and ways in which your church can plan its response ahead of time

REVIEWING
In the past few years, our country has dealt with some significant community tragedies resulting from crime: the Oklahoma City bombing; the bombing of the World Trade Center in New York; school shootings like the ones in Paducah, Kentucky, Jonesboro, Arkansas, and Littleton, Colorado; the bombing of the Centennial Olympic Park in Atlanta; and the church burnings throughout the South, just to name a few.

These tragedies have focused our attention on crimes that affect not just one or a few individuals but on crimes that traumatize an entire community and, at times, the entire country. As a result, clergy, social-service providers, and community members have seen the need to develop support systems within communities to assist them in dealing with the effects of a community tragedy and in helping the people heal.

A community crisis often results in shared loss and destruction as well as in questioning individual faith and community values. In responding to a community crisis, the primary goal is to provide safety, support, and assistance to those most directly impacted by the crisis. The Church can play a key role in responding to a community tragedy by caring for physical, emotional, and spiritual needs.

This chapter explores the dynamics of crime that affect an entire community. It examines the needs of a community after such a crime and provides specific suggestions for how you and your church can help reach out and bring restoration to a community impacted by crime.

DISCUSSION STARTERS

- Has your community (your church community or the larger community in which you live) experienced a crime or other tragedy resulting in significant upheaval and loss? How did the tragedy affect the community? What needs did the community have in the aftermath of the crime? How did the Church and the community respond to people's needs?
- If your community has not experienced a major crisis, have your group discuss how it might have felt to be in Oklahoma City when the bombing took place or in Littleton, Colorado, when students were shot and the school bombed.
- Discuss with your group how your church would respond if faced with a community tragedy caused by crime. Is the

church prepared? Would your church be aware of the needs in the community and know how to meet them?

UNDERSTANDING COMMUNITY TRAGEDY

- In a disaster a community experiences *shared* loss, damage, destruction, etc. How does this element of shared experiences impact the community? What community-wide needs does it bring to the surface?
- Discuss the difference between direct and indirect victims of a community disaster. Both direct and indirect victims have needs. What are these needs? How can the local church help to address and heal these wounds?
- Communities as well as individuals can undergo spiritual crisis in the aftermath of trauma and tragedy. How have you seen spiritual crisis in a community manifested (either in your own community or through observing other communities through the media)? How can the Church witness to a community struggling with emotionally charged spiritual questions in the aftermath of a disaster?

HOW TO HELP

- On page 66 several suggestions are listed for how you and your church can help in recovery after a community tragedy. Discuss the suggestions with your group. Which of the suggestions are most appropriate for your community and your church? Are there other ways in which your church can help?
- Crisis is always unexpected. In order to minister effectively to your community after a crisis, you and your church will need to prepare. Identify and discuss what steps your church or group would take if a crisis happened in your community. (You may want to develop a crisis scenario to help develop your response.)
- Do you or your group want to commit to preparing to

respond to a community or church crisis? What concrete actions will you, your group, or church commit to do in order to prepare?

SUBSTANCE ABUSE

Save me, O God, for the floodwaters are up to my neck. Deeper and deeper I sink into the mire; I can't find a foothold to stand on. I am in deep water, and the floods overwhelm me. I am suffering and in pain. Rescue me, O God, by your saving power. PSALM 69:1-2, 29, NLT

OBJECTIVES
Through this study your group will:

- Examine the effects of substance abuse both on the abuser and on those close to him or her
- Better understand the nature and role of the abused substance in the lives of those who are addicted to drugs or alcohol
- Identify specific ways you and your church can help those impacted by substance abuse

REVIEWING
In his recent book *Body Count,* author Bill Bennett indicates that an estimated 10.5 million Americans are alcoholics and 73 million have been directly affected by alcoholism in some form. In addition, in 1994 over 12 million Americans were using some type of illicit drug on a monthly basis.[2]

Anyone who has struggled with substance abuse or lived with someone struggling with an addiction knows the insidious battle that must be faced by the abuser and by his or her loved ones. Many people actively abusing drugs or alcohol deny that there is a problem. However, the impact of the abuse is often apparent to those closest to the abuser.

While extremely harmful in itself, substance abuse often

[2] William J. Bennett, John J. DiIulio, and John P. Walters, *Body Count* (New York: Simon & Schuster, 1996), 66, 150.

leads to other problems, compounding already painful and difficult issues. Substance abuse can lead to marital problems; employment problems; broken relationships; emotional, physical, and sexual abuse; and involvement in other criminal activity.

This chapter is written to help you better understand the issues involved in substance abuse and how you and your church can support an individual who is an abuser as well as those who may be living with and affected by the substance abuse.

DISCUSSION STARTERS

- If you or someone in your group has dealt with substance abuse personally or with family or friends and are comfortable sharing, ask them to tell their "story." What were the effects of substance abuse? What was hardest about it? How did they or the other person address it? What type of help and support did they receive?
- The statistics above reveal the appeal of alcohol and drugs in our culture. As a group, discuss why our culture is so drawn to drugs and alcohol. Discuss the social, moral, economic, and spiritual aspects of our culture that help to make illicit substances so appealing.

UNDERSTANDING SUBSTANCE ABUSE

- Page 74 describes abused substances as the abuser's "best friend." How does an abused substance play the role of best friend in an abuser's life? What are the implications of this for an abuser who is struggling to overcome his or her addiction, for those close to the abuser, and for those trying to help?
- Discuss the definition of substance abuse on page 74. Must a person be *addicted* to an illicit substance to be *abusing* it? What observable warning signals indicate that a person may be abusing an illicit substance?
- Discuss the effects of substance abuse. Make two lists: one

for the effects in the abuser's life and one for the effects the abuse has on the abuser's family and close friends.

HOW TO HELP

- As a group, develop a definition for "tough love" in relation to someone dealing with substance abuse.
- Tough love is a delicate tool that must be used with great discernment. How can tough love be misused to harm rather than heal? How does practicing tough love help the substance abuser and those impacted by the abuse?
- Look over the two lists of effects developed by the group. Brainstorm ways you and your church can help those impacted by substance abuse. What needs arise from the effects of substance abuse? How can you, your group, or your church meet those needs?
- Review Hurtful Responses to Try to Avoid on page 76. How could you or your group respond to a friend or a family member of a substance abuser who believes that "keeping quiet is the best approach" or that he or she has "failed as a spouse, parent, child, or friend"?

EMPLOYMENT CRISIS

"I know the plans I have for you," declares the Lord, "plans to prosper you and not to harm you, plans to give you hope and a future. Then you will call upon me and come and pray to me, and I will listen to you. You will seek me and find me when you seek me with all your heart. JEREMIAH 29:11-13, NIV

OBJECTIVES
Through this study your group will:

- Develop a better understanding of the crisis of unemployment or underemployment

- Examine attitudes toward those who are facing an employment-related crisis
- Identify ways in which you and your church can assist those in need as a result of unemployment or under-employment

REVIEWING

Downsizing. Reorganization. Layoffs. Career change. These terms are familiar to all of us. We no longer live in a time when we can expect to keep the same job for most of our career. In today's economy, organizations are constantly changing and reengineering themselves in an effort to stay competitive. Job changes and shifts in career are an expected part of life as we have adjusted to the economic reality of our world.

Unfortunately, job and career changes can be extremely stressful, particularly when they are not planned for or chosen. Losing a job suddenly can cause extreme financial, emotional, relational, and/or spiritual crisis. It is a crisis that can impact a person's identity and touch almost every area of life.

Employment crisis is very common. Most of us know someone who has experienced the loss of a job through events beyond his or her control. This chapter examines the nature of employment crisis and helps equip you and your church to reach out to those in need.

DISCUSSION STARTERS

- If someone in your group has dealt with an employment crisis and is comfortable talking about it, ask them to share the experience. What struggles did they face? How did they feel? What support and help did they receive from the church? How did it affect their marriage, their kids, and their friendships?
- As a group, discuss what employment provides to each of us as individuals (i.e., economic means, purpose, identity).

UNDERSTANDING EMPLOYMENT CRISIS

- Many people struggle with an employment-related crisis in a vacuum, keeping it hidden from family and friends. Why is employment crisis embarrassing? Why do we hesitate to tell those close to us and ask them for help and support?
- Our jobs can have different meanings for us as men and women. How does an employment crisis affect men and women differently? Why?
- How does an employment-related crisis impact the individual and his or her family? What needs do those struggling with unemployment or underemployment experience?

HOW TO HELP

- Before reaching out to someone in an employment crisis it is essential to first examine your own attitude. Why? How can unexamined prejudices get in the way of offering help and support?
- What kinds of "hints" might a person give that he or she is in an employment crisis? How can you respond sensitively to these hints?
- The author suggests that helpers should "allow the person to grieve the loss of a job." How would you do that in a sensitive way?
- Does your church have a support effort to assist church and community members facing an employment crisis? If so, is it effective? How can it be more effective in meeting needs? If your church doesn't have an effort, how could you or your group help start one?

CHILD WITH SPECIAL NEEDS

All praise to the God and Father of our Lord Jesus Christ. He is the source of every mercy and the God who comforts us. He comforts us in all our troubles so that we can comfort others. When others are troubled, we will be able to give them the same comfort God has given us. You can be sure that the more we suffer for Christ, the more God will shower us with his comfort through Christ. 2 CORINTHIANS 1:3-5, NLT

OBJECTIVES

Through this study your group will:

- Be able to define a developmental disability
- Better understand the needs of families with a child who has a disability
- Identify ways you, your group, or your church can minister to families dealing with a special needs child

REVIEWING

"When parents learn that their child has a disability, it becomes a moment frozen in time. All parents can tell you how they felt when they heard news of their child's disability. From that day their lives are changed." These opening words from the chapter on children with special needs give us a great deal of insight into the challenge of parenting a child with a disability.

Families with a special needs child face a unique type of crisis. There is the initial crisis of discovering that your child has a disability and of trying to grasp the implications for every area of your family's life. There also are the long-term challenges—life will never be the same. The future you have envisioned has been permanently altered and is being replaced with a new future, which may not be clear for quite a while. In addition, parents with a special needs child face other crises throughout raising that child. Health or emotional problems may develop in the special needs child along the way, causing the family to face additional crises as they learn to deal with new issues.

Families with a special needs child can use a great deal of ongoing support and help. It is important for those who desire to help to put aside fears and awkwardness in order to come alongside the family in prayer, support, and love. This chapter will assist you, your group, or your church to better understand the needs of families with a special needs child and to learn how you can provide help and hope.

DISCUSSION STARTERS

- If an individual in your group has a child or a sibling with special needs or knows a family with a special needs child (and is comfortable talking about it), ask them to share with the group. What was their reaction when they discovered the disability? How did it change their life? What help and support did they receive? What help and support did they need and did not receive?
- Ask your group to share why they chose this chapter of the book to study. Is there a specific family in the church or community that you are hoping to help? What do you hope to learn from the study? What would you or your group like to be able to offer to families who have a special needs child?

UNDERSTANDING CHILDREN WITH SPECIAL NEEDS

- Review the definition of *developmental disability* on page 130. What can we learn from the definition about the challenges facing a family with a disabled child? What does the definition tell us about the nature of the crisis?
- Why are we sometimes hesitant to reach out to parents and families who have a special needs child? What is the first step helpers should take toward acceptance? (See page 130, Understanding the Crisis.) How does this open the door to begin offering help and support?
- Discuss the long-term nature of dealing with a child with special needs. What does it mean for the family? What does it mean for those who want to offer help and sup-

port? What does it mean for the Church in ministering to families with a special needs child?

HOW TO HELP

- People tend to say, "Let me know if you need anything," but a better question that will lead to giving real help is "What do you need right now?" Why is this a better question?
- Using pages 130–131 as a starting point, brainstorm with your group about meaningful ways to help families with a special needs child. For each idea that you list, indicate who is best positioned to offer the support—an individual, a small group, or the Church. You may also want to discuss those things that can cause more pain or indirectly hurt a family with a special needs child that you, your group, or your church can avoid doing.
- What can your church do to make its worship, fellowship, and educational activities more accessible to families with a special needs child?

LIFE-THREATENING ILLNESS

For God hath not given us the spirit of fear; but of power, and of love, and of a sound mind. 2 TIMOTHY 1:7, KJV

OBJECTIVES

Through this study your group will:

- Understand the difficult crisis of facing a life-threatening illness for the individual or his or her loved ones
- Identify the physical, emotional, and spiritual needs a person with a life-threatening illness may have
- Determine practical ways you, your group, or your church can minister to those facing a life-threatening illness

REVIEWING

The reality of facing death due to a life-threatening illness can cause anger, hopelessness, isolation, and despair. All of these have their roots in fear: fear of dying, fear of the illness, fear of pain, fear of what the remainder of one's life could be like after the illness.

The lens through which a person who has a life-threatening illness views life and death has changed forever.

For the family and friends of a person facing a life-threatening illness, it can be difficult to know how to help. The person is facing the crisis at several different levels—a physical crisis as his or her body fights the illness, an emotional crisis with the possibility of dying, and a spiritual crisis as he or she seeks to make sense of who God is in the midst of the suffering.

Through this chapter, your small group and your church can better understand the crisis a person with a life-threatening illness often experiences and how you can reach out to them and their loved ones and offer help and comfort.

DISCUSSION STARTERS

- If you or someone in your group is facing or has faced a life-threatening illness and they are comfortable, ask them to share the experience. What was their reaction when they found out? How did they feel? What kind of help and support did they need the most?
- Discuss how facing the possibility of death would affect how you view the present and the future. What questions or emotions would it raise?

UNDERSTANDING LIFE-THREATENING ILLNESS

- Facing a life-threatening illness brings a host of emotions—anger, hopelessness, frustration, confusion, despair. All of these have their roots in fear. Why does life-threatening illness result in great fear? How does fear cause these other emotions? Discuss the relationship between feeling helpless in the face of the illness and fear.

- Discuss the possible physical effects (p. 136) a life-threatening illness can have on an individual. Do the same for the emotional effects (p. 137) and the spiritual effects (p. 138). Discuss the effects on both the person suffering from the illness and the caretakers, family, and close friends.

HOW TO HELP

- Thinking about the physical, emotional, and spiritual needs resulting from a life-threatening illness, brainstorm ways you, your group, and your church can offer help in each area. Use pages 136–139 in the book as a starting point.
- Review the section Hurtful Responses to Try to Avoid. Has anyone in your group heard these statements in regard to a life-threatening illness? Why are these things hurtful? What possible effect would saying or doing these things have on the suffering person?
- Discuss or find out how your church responds to members who are facing a life-threatening illness. Do you think that the response adequately meets the needs? If so, let your pastor know. If not, discuss ways that you and your group can help prepare the church to respond.

BURGLARY AND THEFT

Unless the Lord builds a house, the work of the builders is useless. Unless the Lord protects a city, guarding it with sentries will do no good. It is useless for you to work so hard from early morning until late at night, anxiously working for food to eat; for God gives rest to his loved ones. PSALM 127:1-2, NLT

OBJECTIVES
Through this study your group will:

- Understand what constitutes burglary and theft
- Identify ways in which burglary and theft negatively impact a victim's sense of security
- Determine ways you, your group, or your church can help victims of burglary and theft

REVIEWING
People often think of their home as their castle. It is their private domain—the place where they come after work to be with their loved ones, to relax and feel safe and secure from the stresses of the world.

Burglary is unlawful entry into a business or dwelling that usually involves theft. Victims of burglary often feel victimized on two different levels. There is the threat to their possessions—valuable things may have been stolen; items of significance to the person may be permanently lost. Then there is the threat to their emotional safety and security—knowing that someone has entered their "castle" and gone through their things leaves many victims feeling violated and frightened.

Victims of burglary need both practical help and emotional support in the aftermath of the crime. This chapter will provide practical ways that you, your group, or your church can help those who have been victims of burglary and theft.

DISCUSSION STARTERS

- Discuss ways you or your group members protect your homes, offices, schools, etc., against burglary (i.e., alarm systems, watchdogs).
- Imagine you've been burglarized. How would you feel? What would you do?
- If someone in your group has been burglarized and is comfortable talking about it, ask them to share the experience.

What happened? How did they feel afterward? What helped them to regain a sense of security? Do they still feel the impact of the burglary?

UNDERSTANDING BURGLARY AND THEFT

- Develop a definition of *burglary* and *theft* using pages 151–152 as a starting point. Why do you think most burglaries occur in warmer weather and between midnight and 6 A.M.?
- Why do burglary and theft feel like such a violation of space and person to the victim? Why do some people dismiss a burglary as a minor crime—"It was only some things"?
- Discuss the short-term and long-term impact of burglary on victims. How does a victim's age or life situation influence the burglary's impact on his or her life?

HOW TO HELP

- What immediate and long-term help can you, your group, or your church offer to victims of burglary and theft?
- What practical things can you do to increase a victim's sense of security after the crime?
- Victims of burglary often need to tell and retell what's happened to them. Why is this important? How can you offer support to a victim in this process?
- Why is it important not to say things like "Did you lock your doors?" or "You should have installed an alarm system"? How can comments like these revictimize the victim?

CHILD VICTIMIZATION

Anyone who welcomes a little child like this on my behalf is welcoming me. But if anyone causes one of these little ones who trusts in me to lose faith, it would be better for that person to be thrown into the sea with a large millstone tied around the neck. MATTHEW 18:5-6, NLT

OBJECTIVES

Through this study your group will:

- Develop definitions for *child neglect, child physical abuse, child sexual abuse,* and *child emotional abuse*
- Learn to detect signs that child victimization is taking place
- Determine how you can offer help and support when child victimization is discovered

REVIEWING

Every day in America, children are victimized. They are beaten, sexually abused, murdered, and neglected by family members. Children who are not targets for physical acts of victimization are often victimized by emotional neglect or abuse, or by witnessing the murder, rape, or robbery of family members and friends. They are forced to deal with emotions, fears, and losses that adults often find hard to face.[3]

Child victimization can be categorized in four main areas: child neglect, child physical abuse, child sexual abuse, and child emotional abuse. Because child victimization takes many forms, helpful support and assistance will also take many forms. For those wanting to help, it's important to understand the impact of child victimization on the victim as well as the legal ramifications for reporting abuse and walking with the victim and their family through the criminal-justice process.

This chapter provides an overview for how to detect signs that child victimization has taken place, what is involved in reporting the abuse, and practical ways you, your group, or your church can help children who have been victimized and their families.

DISCUSSION STARTERS

- Using Matthew 18:5-6 as a starting point, discuss Jesus' attitude toward children throughout Scripture. What direction does Scripture provide about how to treat children?

[3]National Victim Assistance Academy, Office of Victims of Crime, U.S. Department of Justice.

- Discuss possible reasons for the prevalence of child victimization in our culture today. What factors contribute to child victimization? What role can the Church play in preventing and addressing child victimization?

UNDERSTANDING CHILD VICTIMIZATION

- Reviewing pages 180–181 in the book, discuss with your group the definitions of *child neglect, child physical abuse, child sexual abuse,* and *child emotional abuse.*
- What are the differences among the four terms?
- What are the indicators for each type of abuse?
- What signs and signals might a child send that indicate he or she is being abused?

HOW TO HELP

- Discuss the immediate needs of children who have been abused, once the abuse has been discovered (page 181).
- Using the list of Helpful Things to Say and Do (page 183) as a starting point, discuss ways to offer help and support once child victimization has been discovered. Discuss this for the child, the supporting adult, and the offending party.
- "All states require mandatory reporting of suspected cases of child abuse by anyone who is responsible for the care of the children." How could this information impact your local church and those responsible for overseeing the children?
- What if a child in your neighborhood or church indicated that he or she was being abused? Discuss what you as an individual would do in response.
- Discuss what your church can/should do to prepare a response plan to implement upon learning that a child has been abused.

ELDERLY VICTIMIZATION

Show your fear of God by standing up in the presence of elderly people and showing respect for the aged. I am the Lord.
LEVITICUS 19:32, NLT

OBJECTIVES
Through this study your group will:

- Understand the issues involved in elderly victimization
- Identify ways in which you, your group, or your church can help elderly victims of crime
- Determine how to help the elderly prevent becoming victims of crime

REVIEWING
Elderly victimization is the committing of crime against the elderly by strangers, relatives, or acquaintances. In 1997, adults aged 50 or older made up 30 percent of the general population, 12 percent of all murder victims, and 7 percent of all serious violent crime victims. Nationally, nearly 70 percent of Adult Protective Service agencies' annual caseloads involve elder abuse.[4]

Elderly adults who are victimized need special sensitivity and understanding regarding the unique challenges to their situations. Any physical, financial, or emotional violation can threaten their independence and control as they deal with issues such as retirement, decline in health, loss of income, and loss of mobility. In addition, for the elderly, "home" may be even more significant than for the younger generation. Many elderly individuals have lived in the same place for many years and raised their families within those same walls. A violation of the home, violation of self, or loss of independence will be even more grievous for the elderly.

This chapter will help you, your group, or your church

---

[4] U.S. Department of Justice, Bureau of Justice Statistics (September 1997).

develop a better understanding of the needs of elderly victims and of how you can practically meet those needs and offer help and support.

DISCUSSION STARTERS

- With your group discuss ways in which the elderly are more vulnerable than other population groups to victimization. What factors make them seem like easy targets?
- Discuss why your group chose to study this chapter. Do you have specific people in mind whom you are hoping to minister to as a result of this study?

UNDERSTANDING ELDERLY VICTIMIZATION

- Describe the difference between elderly victimization and elder abuse.
- What unique issues do the elderly face that can cause victimization to have a significant negative impact on their lives?
- How does elderly abuse at the hands of a family member impact the victim?
- How do awareness of one's vulnerability and fear of crime affect the elderly?
- What does Scripture say about how we should treat our elders?

HOW TO HELP

- Brainstorm the needs elderly victims have in the aftermath of a burglary, purse theft, physical assault, or fraud. What can be done to assist in each situation? Looking back to the fourth question under Understanding Elderly Victimization, what needs do elders who are living in fear of crime have?
- Why are the elderly more likely to become victims of fraud? How can your church help prepare your older

members to recognize fraud and protect themselves against it?

- Discuss specific, practical ways that you, your group, and your church can reach out to the elderly members of your community to inform and protect them against crime.
- Review the section Hurtful Responses to Try to Avoid on page 192. Why are these responses hurtful? What negative impact could they have on an elderly victim?

ADULT SURVIVORS OF SEXUAL ABUSE

Now, Jeremiah, say this to them: "Night and day my eyes overflow with tears. I cannot stop weeping, for my virgin daughter—my precious people—has been run through with a sword and lies mortally wounded on the ground." JEREMIAH 14:17, NLT

OBJECTIVES
Through this study your group will:

- Be able to define what constitutes childhood sexual abuse
- Identify the factors that determine the extent of the abuse's impact on the victims
- Determine ways you, your group, and your church can help adult survivors of sexual abuse in their recovery

REVIEWING
Most adult survivors of sexual abuse experienced the abuse as children and may or may not have confronted the impact of the past abuse. Child sexual abuse is the exploitation of a child or adolescent for the sexual and control gratification of another person. Many different factors determine the extent of the impact on a victim: their age at the time of the abuse, the extent of the abuse, the relationship with the abuser, etc.

Some of us may know individuals who have been victims of childhood sexual abuse. The scars left by the abuse and its impact over a lifetime can be daunting to face and address.

Confronting past abuse and dealing with the impact can be a complex and difficult process. Adults who have been sexually abused as children and who are confronting their past abuse need a great deal of support and assistance, often over a long period of time.

This chapter will help you, your group, or your church to better understand the needs of adult survivors of childhood sexual abuse and to learn how you can offer practical emotional and spiritual support to someone dealing with these issues.

DISCUSSION STARTERS

- If someone in your group has experienced childhood sexual abuse himself or herself or in their family and is willing to share, let them tell their experience. How did the abuse affect them? their family? their life?
- Why does childhood sexual abuse often remain unconfronted by the victim?

UNDERSTANDING SEXUAL ABUSE

- Using page 218 as a reference, discuss the definition of *childhood sexual abuse* with your group.
- Why do children who are experiencing sexual abuse rarely tell an adult about it? What factors make a child feel helpless and powerless in the face of sexual abuse?
- Discuss the factors that determine the extent of the abuse's impact on the victims. Which of the factors would seem to have the greatest long-term impact on the victims?
- Discuss the issues that could inhibit healing and restoration of a victim who confronts his or her childhood sexual abuse.

HOW TO HELP

- Pages 218–222 list seven important areas that adult survivors of sexual abuse who are confronting their past need to address. Spend some time reviewing each of these as a group. What does each of these areas reveal about the needs of adult survivors of sexual abuse?

- Choose two or three of the areas and for each area discuss how you, your group, and your church can support victims of sexual abuse who are dealing with their painful past. How can you walk with them through the process and provide help and support?
- Where and to whom in your church would someone go if he or she was confronting childhood sexual abuse? Do you believe your church has a support system ready to help them? If not, how can you and your group be a catalyst for establishing that support system?

RAPE AND SEXUAL ASSAULT

"No, my brother!" she cried. "Don't be foolish! Don't do this to me! You know what a serious crime it is to do such a thing in Israel. Where could I go in my shame? And you would be called one of the greatest fools in Israel. Please, just speak to the king about it, and he will let you marry me." But Amnon wouldn't listen to her, and since he was stronger than she was, he raped her. 2 SAMUEL 13:12-14, NLT

OBJECTIVES
Through this study your group will:

- Be able to define what constitutes rape and sexual assault
- Determine the impact of rape and sexual assault on the victim
- Identify ways you, your group, or your church can assist those who have been victims of rape or sexual assault

REVIEWING
According to the Federal Bureau of Investigation's Uniform Crime Reports, in 1997 there were 96,122 reported rapes in the United States.[5] One out of every six women and one out of every thirty-three men in the United States have experienced

an attempted or completed rape as a child and/or as an adult.[6]

Sexual assault or rape is an act of violence and a severe violation of a person. Victims of sexual assault or rape may experience a range of emotions from anger to shock to even laughter. Victims of sexual assault or rape must face both what has happened to them and, if they decide to report the crime, the trauma of dealing with the criminal-justice process. These victims need much help and support in the aftermath of the crime.

This chapter will provide you, your group, or your church with a deeper understanding of the issues these victims face and specific ways you can reach out to assist them in their time of need.

DISCUSSION STARTERS

- Read 2 Samuel 13:1-21, concerning the rape of Tamar, David's daughter. Discuss how she responded. Discuss how her offender responded to her. Discuss what David did as the king and as her father.
- Discuss why rape and sexual assault are considered crimes of violence rather than crimes of passion.

UNDERSTANDING RAPE AND SEXUAL ASSAULT

- Review the definition of *rape* and *sexual assault* on page 226 of the book.
- Sexual assault leaves the victim feeling completely out of control. Why? How can you help that person regain a sense of control immediately after the victimization?
- Why do victims of sexual assault or rape often blame

[5]Federal Bureau of Investigation. Crime in the United States 1997, Uniform Crime Reports, Washington, D.C.: U.S. Department of Justice, 26.   [6]P. Tjaden and N. Thoennes, "Prevalence, Incidence, and Consequences of Violence Against Women Survey," Research in Brief. Washington, D.C.: National Institute of Justice, U.S. Department of Justice, November 1998, 2, 5.

themselves for what has happened? What things should you avoid saying that can make the victim feel they are to blame?

HOW TO HELP

- Using pages 227–228 as a starting point, list ways you, your group, or your church can provide help and assistance to a victim of rape or sexual assault. What are their needs after the victimization?
- A majority of rapes are committed by an acquaintance of the victim. How can this complicate the process of providing help to the victim? How can you, your group, or your church best provide support and help in this situation?
- What are the needs of a victim of rape or sexual assault during the medical exam and afterward if the case goes to trial? How can you, your group, or your church help during these stages?
- Date rape is growing among our high school and college youth. How can your church's youth program sensitively and effectively address this issue?

DEATH OF A LOVED ONE

When Mary reached the place where Jesus was and saw him, she fell at his feet and said, "Lord, if you had been here, my brother would not have died." When Jesus saw her weeping, and the Jews who had come along with her also weeping, he was deeply moved in spirit and troubled. "Where have you laid him?" he asked. "Come and see, Lord," they replied. Jesus wept. Then the Jews said, "See how he loved him!"
JOHN 11:32-36, NIV

Objectives
Through this study your group will:

- Develop a deeper understanding of the process of grieving a loved one's death

- Identify the needs of those who have recently lost a loved one to death
- Determine ways you, your group, or your church can help those who have recently lost a loved one to death

REVIEWING

The death of a loved one brings significant pain, sorrow, and grief. Grief is a normal, healthy human response to any type of significant loss. Grief is a process involving many different emotions from anger to loneliness to despair to hope.

The death of a loved one alters the future. The bereaved must adapt to a new and different future and learn to live without this person in their life. Scripture has a great deal to say to us about how we comfort those who mourn—in fact, Scripture tells us to offer hope and help to those who are grieving: "Comfort all who mourn" (Isaiah 61:2, NIV). We are to walk in the bereaved one's shoes with them and help carry their load of grief.

This chapter will provide several practical ideas for how you, your group, or your church can offer comfort and hope to those who mourn the loss of a loved one. You will also develop a deeper understanding of the nature of grief and the process of grieving significant loss.

DISCUSSION STARTERS

- If someone in your group has lost a loved one to death and is comfortable sharing about it, ask them to tell their story. How did they feel? What did they need? What help and support did they receive from family, friends, and the church?
- Read John 11:1-37, the story of Lazarus's death. Discuss Jesus' reaction to losing a beloved friend to death and to seeing those around him grieve. How is this a comfort to us?

UNDERSTANDING THE DEATH OF A LOVED ONE

- Review and discuss the grief process on pages 17–22 of the book. What will a grieving person feel? What will he or she need during the grief process?
- Discuss the different types of loss that a person grieving the death of a loved one may be dealing with (i.e., loss of companionship, loss of financial security, loss of stable future). For those in your group who may have lost a loved one, if they are comfortable, ask them to share the types of loss they experienced as a result of the loved one's death.
- Often, caring people are hesitant to reach out and help when a close friend loses a loved one. Why? What do potential caregivers fear that could inhibit them from offering help and comfort?

HOW TO HELP

- Review the seven ways to help that are listed on pages 236–238 of the book.
- Thinking back on the different types of losses involved in losing a loved one to death, brainstorm how you, your group, or your church can offer practical assistance that will address the losses.
- What does your group or church currently do to comfort those who are mourning?
- Are there additional things that your group or church can implement to support those grieving the death of a loved one?

SUICIDE

That is why we have a great High Priest who has gone to heaven, Jesus the Son of God. Let us cling to him and never stop trusting him. This High Priest of ours understands our weaknesses, for he faced all of the same temptations we do, yet he did not sin. So let us come boldly to the throne of our gracious God. There we will receive his mercy, and we will find grace to help us when we need it. HEBREWS 4:14-16, NLT

OBJECTIVES

Through this study your group will:

- Develop an understanding of the impact of suicide
- Identify the needs of the surviving friends and family
- Determine practical ways you, your group, or your church can assist those impacted by suicide

REVIEWING

While suicide is similar in many ways to other sudden or violent deaths, it is different in one very significant aspect—the person chose to take his or her own life. This aspect of the victim's death makes it particularly difficult for the grieving family and friends. It raises many questions: Did I cause this? What could I have done to prevent it? What shouldn't I have done? Why didn't I see how unhappy he or she was?

Suicide may be so painful for the victim's family and friends that they are in denial for a time, trying to believe that the death was an accident. Those trying to help can support the family and friends by allowing them to come to terms with the suicide in their own time frame. They may be in shock and denial as they try to absorb what has happened.

Family members and friends need a lot of support during the immediate aftermath of the suicide. Walking through the legal, police, funeral, and insurance processes can be overwhelming and bring intense and recurring pain.

This chapter will provide you, your group, or your church with a deeper understanding of the needs of surviving family members and how you can minister to them during the crisis of a suicide.

DISCUSSION STARTERS

- If someone in your group knows a friend or family member who committed suicide and is comfortable talking about it, let them share their experience.
- Discuss the "stigmas" around the act of suicide.

UNDERSTANDING SUICIDE

- Discuss how suicide differs from other sudden or violent deaths.
- What impact does suicide have on the surviving family members and close friends?
- Family members and friends often deal with a lot of guilt after a suicide. What might they feel guilty about? How can you help them relieve the guilt?

HOW TO HELP

- Brainstorm a list of emotional, practical, and spiritual needs that close friends and family members of a suicide victim may have. How can you, your group, or your church reach out to meet these needs?
- Surviving family members and friends often have to walk through several painful processes as they deal with police, lawyers, coroners, insurance agents, etc. Often these different players in the process unknowingly revictimize the victim's family and friends. How do they do that? What can you do to assist family and friends as they deal with these processes?
- Review the Hurtful Responses to Try to Avoid on page 244 of the book. How could comments like these be harmful or damaging to the family and friends of a suicide victim?
- When a young person commits suicide, it can be particularly difficult for an entire school, church group, or community. What tangible ways can the church provide to these groups to help them through the grieving process?

HOMICIDE

The Lord is my shepherd; I have everything I need. Even when I walk through the dark valley of death, I will not be afraid, for you are close beside me. Your rod and your staff protect and comfort me.
PSALM 23:1, 4, NLT

OBJECTIVES
Through this study your group will:

- Better understand the impact of the sudden death of homicide on surviving friends and family members
- Identify the needs of family and friends of the homicide victim
- Determine practical ways you, your group, or your church can reach out to family and friends of a homicide victim

REVIEWING

In 1997, the estimated number of persons murdered in the United States was 18,209. Of those murdered, over 48 percent knew their assailants. Thirteen percent were related to their assailants, and 35 percent were acquainted.[6]

Murder causes overwhelming grief and sorrow. Because of the sudden and often brutal nature of murder, surviving family and friends deal with complex emotions and processes. Without warning, family members are plunged into confusion, shock, pain, and sorrow. At the same time, they must deal with police investigators and possibly media—all requiring that they make major decisions that they are not prepared for and have never contemplated.

Family and friends of homicide victims often require a long time to heal. There is no prescribed process or timeline—each person must move through the grief process at his or her own pace. It is important that surviving family and friends receive love and support during the immediate aftermath of the murder and in the long months and years to come.

This chapter will provide you, your group, or your church with practical suggestions for ministering to family and friends of homicide victims.

[6]Federal Bureau of Investigation. Crime in the United States 1997, Uniform Crime Reports, Washington, D.C.: U.S. Department of Justice, 16–17.

DISCUSSION STARTERS

- If someone in your group has lost a friend or family member to homicide and would like to share the experience, provide time to do so. Or you might discuss a recent homicide in your community or on the news and how the family might be reacting and responding in the aftermath.

- In many communities (especially urban areas) homicides occur almost daily. Discuss why Americans may be immune to the tragedy of homicide unless it strikes too close to home.

UNDERSTANDING HOMICIDE

- Review the definition of *homicide* at the top of page 268 in the book. How does the sudden and often brutal loss of a loved one to homicide complicate the crisis and grief?

- Immediately after learning of the homicide, family and close friends are plunged into making difficult decisions they have not prepared for. What types of decisions would a family member have to make in the aftermath of a murder? As the family walks through the process of dealing with police investigators and media, what kinds of support might they need?

HOW TO HELP

- Using pages 268–270 as a starting point, brainstorm the different ways you, your group, or your church could help in the immediate aftermath of a homicide and over the long-term healing process. Which areas of care are best provided by a pastor, an individual, or the church body?

- What can you, your group, or your church practically do to provide a safe environment for surviving friends and fami-

lies of homicide victims to grieve and process the va.
emotions they will feel?

- How can you, your group, and your church walk with the
  grieving families over the long period of healing? Are there
  support groups in your community that incorporate spiritual
  support for family and friends of homicide victims? If not,
  would your church be interested in establishing such a group?[7]

[7] Contact Neighbors Who Care for more information on support groups at
Neighbors Who Care, P.O. Box 16079, Washington, D.C. 20041.

...o Care was organized to mobilize and
...rches to reach out to crime victims. As part
...mission, Neighbors Who Care has resources
...s that will help you and your church serve local
...crime.

...ghbors Who Care has also established structured victim-
...stance programs in different U.S. cities. With Neighbors
Who Care's assistance, churches of various denominations
have joined forces with local law-enforcement agencies, victim-
assistance experts, and community business leaders to furnish
support and resources for victims of crime. In such communities, Neighbors Who Care provides extensive training as well
as a planning and organizational process to help churches
address victims' needs with compassion, sensitivity, and practical help.

If your church is interested in finding out more about
Neighbors Who Care, starting a local Neighbors Who Care
program, receiving victim-assistance information, and/or
receiving the Neighbors Who Care newsletter, please contact
us at the address below.

If your church is already working with victims of crime,
please let us know. Neighbors Who Care is developing a
national data bank.

P.O. Box 16079
Washington, DC 20041
(703) 904-7311